THE POLITICS OF ETHNICITY AND FEDERALISM IN PAKISTAN

Local, National, and Comparative Perspectives

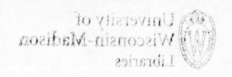
THE POLITICS OF ETHNICITY AND FEDERALISM IN PAKISTAN

Local, National, and Comparative Perspectives

Edited by
Ryan Brasher

OXFORD
UNIVERSITY PRESS

OXFORD
UNIVERSITY PRESS

Oxford University Press is a department of the University of Oxford.
It furthers the University's objective of excellence in research, scholarship,
and education by publishing worldwide. Oxford is a registered trade mark of
Oxford University Press in the UK and in certain other countries

Published in Pakistan by
Oxford University Press
No. 38, Sector 15, Korangi Industrial Area,
PO Box 8214, Karachi-74900, Pakistan

ISBN 978-0-19-070045-4

Typeset in Adobe Garamond Pro
Printed on 55gsm Book Paper

Printed by Mas Printers, Karachi

Contents

Introduction

Ryan Brasher

When we organized a conference on ethno-federalism at Forman Christian College in April 2015, it was clear that two distinct yet interconnected issues stood at the forefront of the conversation: centre–periphery relations and ethnic identity. To begin, there has been a recurring debate about the formal structure of federalism in Pakistan, specifically the proper distribution of power between the centre and the periphery. Secondly, scholars and policymakers have asked about the extent to which ethnolinguistic and religious identity should serve as the basis of provincial territorial boundaries. This question also connects with a large body of literature on ethnic identity and its politicization. To date, very little research has sought to pursue both of these issues at the same time, and most of these have only done so from a top-down perspective, with little time given to the details of particular regional cases. This volume thus presents a novel endeavour to include both the national perspective as well as grassroots voices from the local level.

Furthermore, in contrast to much of the scholarship on the politics of ethnicity in Pakistan, an attempt has been made to ground the contributions to this volume in comparative social science theory beyond Pakistan, both here in the introduction and in subsequent chapters. The goal of this volume, therefore, is not simply to add a local perspective, but to join the broader conversation and to be useful to those studying centre–periphery relations in other countries and regions. Above all else, all of the authors are fundamentally committed to a strong, united, unified, and democratic Pakistan, even if they might disagree over the particular means to achieve this. The authors of this volume essentially seek to understand how Pakistan's ethno-federal setup works, both formally and informally, and how it has interacted with, encouraged, or hindered ethnolinguistic mobilization in various provinces and sub-provincial units.

Interesting sub-questions emerge from this overriding theme: how did Pakistan's ethno-federal system emerge and develop over time? Why are only some ethnolinguistic identities recognized, and not others? Would it be useful to subdivide current provinces on the basis of smaller ethnic identifications? And what about entities like Gilgit-Baltistan (GB) and Azad Jammu and Kashmir (AJK): why do they not enjoy official provincial recognition? Would it be better if they were made into full-fledged provinces, integrated into pre-existing ones, or linked to the centre as formally recognized autonomous but not fully independent territories? All of these questions are addressed by this volume's contributors, with some more and some less definitive answers. In the following pages, I briefly introduce each of the chapters, while weaving them into a broader discussion of centre–periphery relations, the relative merits of ethno-federalism, and the problematics of ethnic identity.

Federalism, Sham-federalism, and Centre–periphery Relations

At its most basic level, federalism concerns the territorial distribution of state authority. On one hand, unitary states centralize all power in the centre, whereas on the other hand, power in federal systems is shared between at least two layers of government. But beyond this simple distinction, a variety of models to devolve power from the centre to the periphery exist, as described in 'Comparing Federal Systems in the 1990s'.[1] In contrast to unitary states, unions recognize their constituent member-units but, like centralized unitary states, do not provide separate regional institutions for representation. Regional representation occurs only through state organs located in the centre. In full-fledged federations, power is shared between the centre and its constituent units, which in turn can be subdivided into smaller, localized units. Additionally, some federations are organized symmetrically, where all constituent units share the same relationship with the centre. In asymmetric federations, one or more constituent units have unique rights vis-à-vis the central government not shared by others. Confederations generally form when previously independent units decide to join together to form a common government that remains dependent on its constituent units. Furthermore, both unitary and decentralized states can have unique arrangements, referred to as federacies, with small peripheral units, in which the smaller unit enjoys considerable autonomy, except for defence and foreign affairs, while having little to no role in central governance. Federacies can only be dissolved through mutual agreement, while, according to Watts, similarly structured 'associated states' can dissolve their status unilaterally.

It is precisely these federacies, or 'partially independent territories', which David Rezvani focuses on in his chapter in this volume. Contrary to the widely held belief that federacies and associated territories are in an ambiguous institutional stage that will either lead to full inclusion in the federation or secession, Rezvani argues that partially independent territories provide an ideal balance between the desires of self-governance for regional units with the concern for unity and stability of the national centre. Furthermore, partial independence tends to benefit both actors economically to a far greater degree than if there was greater centralization or full independence. This argument clearly has great relevance to Pakistan, given the fact that territories like Gilgit-Baltistan and Azad Jammu and Kashmir have not been fully incorporated into the federation. It could even be an option for other units, which have been pushing for greater autonomy. Rather than seeking to change the status quo, Rezvani argues that these territories can harness the ambiguity of their status for their, and Pakistan's, greater benefit if self-rule is formally institutionalized to a greater degree and protected from meddling by the central government. Of course, partial independence generally works best when units are territorially and demographically insignificant relative to the nation-state. Whether this is the case in Pakistan is a different question.

The formal centralized or decentralized organization of the state, of course, does not necessarily correspond to the political realities on the ground. McGarry and O'Leary argue that communist Czechoslovakia, Yugoslavia, and the USSR constituted 'sham' or pseudo-federations, as decentralized constitutional powers were often ignored by the central government.[2] They also lacked authentic representation at the subnational level, since none of these countries held free and fair elections. In addition to sham federations, Rezvani discusses sham federacies in this volume as well. These are separately governed territories with formal autonomy that are, however, effectively governed as colonies, without a true voice or input in their relationship with the centre. Examples include the Bantustans of South Africa during apartheid or France's attempt to retain their colony in Southeast Asia through an autonomy arrangement with Indochina. In the context of Pakistan, Julie Flowerday and Rashid Ahmad Khan examine the relationship of Gilgit-Baltistan and FATA, respectively, with the centre.

While both Gilgit-Baltistan and Azad Jammu and Kashmir are within the historical 'greater' Kashmir, which was ruled by a Hindu monarch up until Partition (1947), these territories are internationally recognized, with the exception of India, as part of Pakistan due to their location west of the Line of Control (LoC). People in Gilgit-Baltistan generally argue that they are ethnolinguistically, culturally, and historically distinct from Kashmir, and should not be drawn into this seemingly intractable dispute. Elsewhere, the extensive archival research in *A Princely Affair: The Accession and Integration of the Princely States of Pakistan, 1947–1955*[3] supports this claim by showing that the rulers of the northern princely states of Hunza and Nagar had previously been opposed to their inclusion into Kashmir, and were in favour of the accession of their territories to Pakistan. A military coup in Gilgit in 1947 against Kashmir—to which it had never fully belonged—and for accession to Pakistan, with full local support, further cements the case for Gilgit-Baltistan's separateness.

The Pakistani government itself, however, in order to not jeopardize its claims on Indian-held Kashmir, has not formally incorporated either Gilgit-Baltistan or AJK into its federation as constituent provinces, despite full local political identification with Pakistan. Historical Chinese claims of suzerainty over the region, as well as Pakistan's geopolitical tilt toward China, further explain Islamabad's hesitancy in this regard. It is this ambiguous status of the northern areas, a result of indirect rule and unresolved territorial claims between the British Raj and China, which Julie Flowerday's chapter in this volume focuses on. According to her, the people in the region are caught between two conflicting ideas of sovereignty. On one hand, Pakistan is operating according to the now dominant Western conception of territorial control and sacrosanct borders, even though Gilgit-Baltistan is not directly referenced in Pakistan's Constitution and its boundaries have not been officially recognized by either China or India. China, on the other hand, sees itself at the centre of a concentric system of tributary alliances that serves to expand its economic influence through open borders. Given China's increasing role in the region, and thus presumably its claim on it, Flowerday does not foresee a resolution to Gilgit-Baltistan's unresolved status in Pakistan's federation anytime soon.

Like Gilgit-Baltistan ad Azad Jammu and Kashmir, the Federally Administered Tribal Areas were not fully incorporated into Pakistan's federal system until significant constitutional changes in 2018. Until then, the seven agencies that make up FATA were historically governed through political agents accountable to Islamabad. Other differences emerge, however, in Rashid Ahmad Khan's chapter on FATA and Pashtun political identity in this volume. Just like the people of GB and AJK, residents of FATA have always been considered full Pakistani citizens. But, while local representative institutions, albeit without real decision-making power, exist in the former, FATA did not have any representative local assembly, as the federal government continued the British colonial policy of local autonomy through the traditional jirga mechanism. FATA has had reserved seats in the national assembly but, due to the Frontier Crimes Regulation (FCR), national or provincial legislation did not apply to its residents. The FCR have governed the region since British colonial times and are meant to convey the traditional autonomy given to its tribally organized people from laws and responsibilities regulating the rest of the country. Given the FCR's emphasis on collective identity, self-egulation, and punishment, it has also meant that residents of FATA did not enjoy the same civil liberties and recourse to due process as afforded to Pakistanis elsewhere.

According to Rashid Ahmad Khan, an even more complex picture emerges when taking into account the historically fluctuating map of provincially administered tribal areas (PATA) in both Balochistan as well as Khyber Pakhtunkhwa (KP). While nominally under provincial jurisdiction, these areas have also largely been governed by the executive from the centre. Efforts to extend the reach of the state into FATA and PATA by fully incorporating them have been made, according to him, since before Pakistan's independence. This has included proposals to merge FATA with KP, to make it into a province itself, or to maintain its autonomy and unique social institutions by creating a status similar to partial independence. In February 2017, the Pakistan Muslim League-Nawaz (PML-N) government approved a plan to merge FATA with KP over a period of time, ending the controversial Frontier Crimes Regulation and its principle of collective punishment, finally extending the jurisdiction of Pakistan's courts to local residents and allowing direct elections to KP's provincial assembly in Peshawar.

Given the relatively lengthy process of publishing an edited volume, Rashid Ahmad Khan's account understandably does not include most recent developments in the region. In May 2018, the 25th

Constitutional Amendment was passed by the National Assembly and Senate in Islamabad, as well as the Provincial Assembly of KP, making the merger official. The implementation of the merger, sooner than some had recommended, has carried with it some initial difficulties. While traditionally autonomous tribal governance is being replaced, KP provincial police institutions, as well as local courts, have not been set up quickly enough to fill the resulting vacuum. It remains to be seen how these changes will effect local residents, heretofore used to quick and cost-effective decisions by local tribal jirgas. Also, for the first time ever, the tribal districts participated in a special election to the KP provincial assembly in July 2019, having been allocated 21 (16 elected members and 5 reserved seats for women and minorities) out of a total of 145 seats. While saddled with relatively low turnout and intermittent campaign restrictions in certain districts, the elections are an important step in the integration of FATA into KP.[4]

In their chapter in this volume, Younis and Shafaat trace the development of federalism from before Partition to today by examining Pakistan's constitutional development from the national perspective. They argue that even before 1947, the Muslim League consistently advocated for a federal structure that would ensure the rights of religious minorities in an independent India. However, in order to construct a sense of Muslim unity, Pakistan movement leaders did not emphasize ethnolinguistic identity, but were still committed to federal decentralization. After Independence, the weakness of political leaders and the constitutional powers of the Governor General, combined with the swift ascent of Punjab-centric civilian and military bureaucracy, led to the establishment of a de facto unitary state. Despite constitutional provisions providing for a decentralized federal form, leaders under both civilian and military rule ensured that the centre remained dominant, able to override provincial legislatures at will if conflicting with central demands. This spirit of centralization led to Bengali separatism and the secession of East Pakistan in 1971, as well as post-1971 unrest in Sindh and

Balochistan. According to Younis and Shafaat, even the relatively pro-federal Constitution of 1973 allowed the central government to veto initiatives from the periphery that were perceived to fall within the purview of the national government. The Eighteenth Amendment to the Constitution, passed in 2010, has devolved significant powers to the provinces, perhaps creating a true federal spirit in Pakistan for the first time in its history. However, Younis and Shafaat feel that the newly empowered provincial governments in turn, have centralized control in the provinces and reversed Musharraf era attempts to strengthen local governance.

Mussarat Jabeen argues in her chapter that it is precisely the gap between Pakistan's formal federalism and informal unitary tendencies that has led to repeated unrest in Balochistan since 1947. She starts from a primordial premise in grounding Baloch national identity and cultural unity in centuries of common historical experience. According to her, specific political grievances against the centralizing state began with the advent of the British, who used the region that comprises today's Balochistan primarily as a supply route and staging ground for troops, but did little to enhance economic development. Instead, autonomy on internal issues was given to local traditional authorities, including the Khan of Kalat. After Partition, the region, which was roughly put together from three separate political entities, was not fully incorporated into Pakistan's federation as a constituent province until 1970. While Baloch political leaders had initially been divided on the issue of accession to Pakistan vis-à-vis outright independence in 1947, it was primarily the central government's subsequent unwillingness to give full provincial autonomy to the region that ignited recurring resistance to the state. Socioeconomic grievances were added because the state did not make an effort to invest in infrastructural and socioeconomic development beyond a heavy-handed, coercive footprint. And fuel was added to the fire when large repositories of natural resources were discovered, particularly natural gas in 1952, and these were regularly supplying Pakistan's major cities by the 1960s, but not Quetta or other regions within Balochistan until the 1980s. In essence, according to Jabeen, the underdeveloped province of Balochistan has been subsidizing the rest of the country. Jabeen argues that the Eighteenth Amendment passed in 2010 has gone a long way in addressing some of the concerns of the people of Balochistan, such as increased revenue-sharing and withdrawal of military cantonments, but many of these are yet to be implemented. In summary, Jabeen argues that political and socioeconomic grievances have been needlessly stoked in a region whose inhabitants' demands for more autonomy and revenue-sharing could have been easily met decades ago.

Ethno-federalism and Ethnic Identity

The above contributors to this volume discuss the extent to which the centre has shared and continues to share power, formally and informally, with its subnational constituent units. Additionally, one can distinguish between simple territorial federalism—where provincial and local boundaries are not meant to coincide with cultural boundaries—and ethno-federalism. Although scholars generally agree that in ethno-federal systems constituent units are designated as homelands of particular ethnic groups, there has been some disagreement as to the precise definition. Hale, in *Divided We Stand*, argues that only one subnational unit with an ethnic designation is necessary to qualify as an ethno-federation,[5] whereas Bunce and Watts[6] as well as Roeder[7] argue that a large number, if not all, subnational units need to be demarcated on an ethnic basis. According to Liam Anderson, there are three subcategories of ethno-federalism.[8] Ethno-federal states are full ethno-federations where all provinces reflect an ethnonational homeland. In partial ethno-federations, only some, or even just one, do so. Lastly, in ethnic federacies, otherwise unitary states give autonomy to ethnically defined regions, as reflected in the relationship of Northern Ireland, Scotland, and Wales with the UK.

With the renaming of the NWFP to KP in 2010, one can say that Pakistan qualifies as a full ethno-federation, as all of its constituent units bear an ethnolinguistic marker, even though there are many ethnic groups without official representation.

A lively debate on the relative merits and disadvantages of ethno-federalism currently exists in the literature. Many scholars, with the recent inclusion of Bunce and Watts[9] as well as Roeder,[10] deriving their arguments from the breakup of former socialist states of Yugoslavia, Czechoslovakia, and the USSR, oppose the ethno-federalist setup for ethnically heterogenous societies. They argue that ethno-federalism helps encourage, or outright create, feelings of ethnic nationalism and togetherness, that would have been weaker or non-existent in a unitary or non-ethnic federal arrangement. In ethno-federal systems, ethnic entrepreneurs possess the institutional arrangements and bureaucratic powers necessary to struggle for independence from the centre, thus making ethno-federalism uniquely vulnerable to state collapse and secession. Accordingly, over 70 per cent of ethno-federal systems have failed by either disintegrating, losing regions to secession, or centralizing their constitutions. Hale modifies this argument by contending that it is specifically ethno-federal states with large ethnic cores—ethnic groups with an outright majority or large plurality, concentrated within a single provincial boundary—which are inherently unstable.[11] In these states, the core province tends to ignore the concerns of other provinces and thus may exacerbate grievances and create conditions for secessionist movements and state breakup. Without an ethnic core region, ethno-federalism is likely to prove a useful way to govern ethnically diverse societies like India, for instance.

McGarry and O'Leary concede that ethno-federalism can make it easier for ethnically defined territories to secede.[12] However, they argue that the existence of a dominant *Staatsvolk*, a national people equivalent to Hale's 'ethnic core', actually ensures the survival of ethno-federal states. These states with dominant ethnic cores are secure enough to give concessions to peripheral regions while retaining the ability to suppress minority mobilization against the state. Lustick, Miodownik, and Eidelson use computer-based modelling of the hypothetical multicultural country 'Beita' to estimate the effects of centralized repression, decentralization, and devolution of power on secessionism.[13] They find that giving autonomy to and sharing power with regionally concentrated ethnic minorities does increase ethnic minority mobilization in the short-term, but also significantly reduces the risk of ethnic secession compared to centralization and repression.

Perhaps the most forceful argument in favour of ethno-federalism has been made recently by Liam Anderson.[14] According to him, ethno-federal critics have improperly generalized lessons derived from the breakup of post-communist states to all ethno-federal systems. Furthermore, they have not considered that ethno-federalism was, in many if not most cases, not a cause of ethnic conflict that could have been avoided but often an unavoidable negotiated solution to pre-existing conflicts. Only in the case of the creation of the Soviet Union could early Bolshevik state-builders have conceivably developed alternative political arrangements that might have avoided collapse in 1991. Anderson argues, however, that in the Soviet Union, it was not those units created by the Soviets, in Central Asia, for instance, that sought independence, but pre-existing units, such as the Baltic States, that had been forcibly incorporated shortly before and during World War II. Thus for Anderson, ethno-federalism is not a source of instability but a useful solution to pre-existing ethnic conflict that might otherwise appear intractable. It is not an ideal political arrangement, but rather a useful one to hold polities together that might otherwise split with the chance of a violent civil war. And if secession does occur, ethno-federal systems that fail are more likely to transition peacefully as compared to unitary states. But what about non-ethnic federations? Because of a lack of real-world cases of federal systems that do not reflect regionally concentrated ethnic diversity, Anderson argues that no useful comparison between ethno-federal systems and non-ethnic federation can be undertaken. Policymakers almost always choose ethno-federalism when confronted with ethnic diversity.

The question thus arises whether ethno-federalism has helped multi-ethnic Pakistan stay together or whether it has fanned the flames of social unrest and conflict. Formally speaking, Pakistan exhibits ethno-federal structures, as all provinces reflect an underlying ethnic homeland, even if further ethnic minorities are nested in each of them. Furthermore, Katharine Adeney argues that before Independence, Jinnah and Muslim League leaders consistently advocated for a loosely federated independent India with semi-autonomous constituent units based on religious identity.[15] However, faced with a Muslim-majority population and ethnolinguistic minority mobilization in the provinces, the Pakistani state moved away from their pre-Independence consociational plans, culminating in the elimination of ethno-federal structures in West Pakistan through the One Unit Plan. This failure to recognize linguistic identity through official representation at the national and provincial levels helped contribute to a sense of alienation of the non-Punjabi ethnolinguistic minorities by the early 1970s, even after the separation of East Pakistan. The official recognition of provincial languages in 1973 still could not overcome grievances against the real and perceived dominance of Punjab province.

The Eighteenth Amendment in 2010 helped re-empower both parliamentary rule and provincial autonomy by decentralizing political and budgetary control away from the centre and Punjab province. Another welcome step was the renaming of the North-West Frontier Province (NWFP) to Khyber Pakhtunkhwa—for the first time—officially recognizing the majority language group in the province. According to Adeney, however, changes have not gone far enough.[16] Pakistan's provinces only account for around 35 per cent of public expenditures, compared to 45–55 per cent in India and the US, and 60–70 per cent in Germany, Canada, and Belgium. Additionally, ethnic minorities from outside Punjab, particularly Sindhi and Baloch, are significantly under-represented in state institutions, including the military and the civilian bureaucracy. While provincial quotas for these institutions exist, better-educated Punjabi migrants in these provinces often take advantage of these opportunities. An increased effort to incorporate disadvantaged ethnic minorities, according to Adeney, would also lead to greater identification with the Pakistani state. Adeney also argues that creating more provinces, for instance a separate Saraiki/Siraiki-language province in southern Punjab, would generate much goodwill among population groups that have felt both culturally and economically disadvantaged vis-à-vis the centre.[17] The federation is still dominated by a core ethnic region, Punjab, which, as we have seen above, Hale associates with more instability and lesser likelihood of survival, particularly when compared to federations with a greater number of smaller subnational units.

But would the creation of a greater number of ethnically defined provinces endanger or improve national stability? This is a key question discussed by a number of contributors in this volume. Sultan Mahmood argues that renaming the North-West Frontier Province to Khyber Pakhtunkhwa in 2010 encouraged minority Hindko speakers to restart efforts to carve out Hazara division as a separate province. Hindko-speakers living in the Hazara division do not identify either with the Pashtun majority in KP, or with Punjab next door, even though their spoken vernacular is very similar to Punjabi. Their sense of identity has been shaped through exclusion: in Punjab they are associated with Pashtuns, whilst Pashtuns in turn regard them as Punjabi. Furthermore, before Partition, it was the Hindko-speaking areas that overwhelmingly supported Jinnah's Muslim League in the NWFP, while Pashtun-majority areas generally voted for Congress. Mahmood believes that the demand for a separate province has been long-standing, but did not take on serious traction until 2010, when the Pashto language, but not Hindko, was incorporated into the new province's name. While the demand for a new province was primarily a reaction against Pashtun nationalism, he believes that this would be a positive move to provide greater local democratic accountability. Politically, however, it remains a distant reality. While initially supported by political parties, particularly the PML-N and Q-League who opposed the strengthening of Pashtun nationalism, Hindko-speaking activists are split into several different movements. Furthermore, the Pashtun nationalist Awami National Party (ANP) government, which served as the main rallying point for the creation of a separate province, has been replaced by Imran Khan's Pakistan Tehreek-e-Insaf (PTI) as KP's governing party, with great support from the Hazara division. This has further taken momentum away from the movement.

Underlying, but not completely aligning with, the broader institutional debate on ethno-federalism exists a deeper theoretical argument between primordialists and constructivists about national and ethnic identity. Many proponents of ethno-federalism implicitly hold to the primordial assumption that ethnic groups have moved through history as coherent units with a distinct culture and language. Giving these pre-existing groups more autonomy in a decentralized federal setup would thus likely satisfy long-standing political and cultural demands for recognition and autonomy, and thus ensure long-term stability of the state. Arend Lijphart's discussion of consociationalism—a decentralized constitutional system designed to provide corporate group rights in multicultural societies—assumes the existence of historically stable and internally coherent ethnic groups.[18] Constructivists, on the other hand, argue that ethnic and national groups do not exist in and of themselves.[19] Instead, they are socially imagined entities that have developed as a result of socioeconomic processes of modernization like print capitalism[20] and industrialization,[21] as well as political institutions and manipulation by ethnic entrepreneurs.[22] Of particular relevance here is *The New Central Asia: The Creation of Nations* in which Roy argues that political identity in Central Asia was ambiguous and multidimensional before the October Revolution of 1917 and the rise of the Bolsheviks.[23] The Soviets assumed the region was populated by coherent but socioeconomically backward national groups that had to be supported and developed before their working classes could join the broad transnational proletarian revolution. The Soviet practice of naming its constituent states and provinces (oblasts) after their putative ethnic majority, and establishing official provincial languages, alongside Russian, helped instil a sense of national identity that did not exist beforehand. As a result, when the centripetal ideological framework of socialism fell away, the Soviet Union fragmented into its nationally delineated constituent units.

Consequently, constructivist critics of ethno-federalism argue that ethno-federal institutions structure the political interests of elites in ways that endanger the stability and future viability of multi-ethnic states. Ethnic identity would be politicized by ethnic entrepreneurs who would take advantage of the decentralization of power and resources, which in turn would raise the likelihood of ethnic conflict and even civil war.[24] If they already exist, then non-recognized ethnonational aspirations should be vigorously discouraged so as to avoid the domino effect of ethnolinguistic fragmentation and disintegration. Other constructivists, however, have made the argument that since ethnic identity is not uni but multidimensional and can be moulded and shaped, ethno-federalism can be designed in such a way as to encourage small and emerging ethnic movements, since they might undercut larger ethnic and religious mobilization that could threaten the state. Kanchan Chandra, for instance, shows that the relative ease with which ethnic movements can successfully demand new states in India has undermined regional challenges to the central state, as well as undercut efforts by Hindu nationalists to enshrine an exclusionary Hindutva-based national identity against non-Hindu minorities.[25] Provincial fragmentation on the basis of ethnolinguistic identity can thus serve to preserve national unity and stability vis-à-vis religious and ethnic centrifugal forces, given the right institutional framework.

In this volume, only Rasul Baksh Rais explicitly draws on constructivist theory in his analysis of Siraiki ethnic mobilization. According to him, three generations of ethnic entrepreneurs have managed to construct a sense of Siraiki ethnolinguistic identity, whereas before people identified their vernacular in more local terms. Residents of Multan, for instance, used to refer to their spoken language as 'Multani', whereas now it is connected with Siraiki. According to Rais, the crystallization of a distinct Siraiki cultural identity group making political demands ultimately has political roots. This development has its roots in the unequal distribution of economic resources across and within Pakistan's provinces. In addition to igniting ethnic minority mobilization in other provinces, residents of southern and western Punjab have similarly felt neglected in favour of central Punjab, particularly Lahore and its environs. Political grievances, therefore, were channelled by cultural entrepreneurs to create a broader sense of ethnic inequality and, in some cases, agitation for a separate province. These demands increased particularly in the wake of the Eighteenth Amendment and its devolution of powers to the provinces, as well as the renaming of the NWFP to Khyber Pakhtunkhwa.

According to Rais, however, the Siraiki movement for the establishment of a separate province faces insurmountable obstacles. First of all, it does not have very deep historical roots to draw on, as pre-existing political entities in south Punjab, like the princely state of Bahawalpur, were never organized along ethnic principles. Secondly, Siraiki speakers are spread across all four provinces, making it very difficult to carve out a province that encompasses all Siraiki-majority areas. Furthermore, due to a relative lack of socioeconomic development and a feudal agricultural structure in Siraiki-speaking areas, ethnic identification remains confined to a fairly narrow population segment. Also, a large influx of wealthier and more educated Punjabi settlers has created a constituency with little interest in splitting up the province. Lastly, and perhaps most importantly, the country's political establishment has on the whole little incentive to go through with the division of Punjab. Rasul Bakhsh Rais lauds Siraiki ethnonationalists for their achievements up until now, but believes they have not been able to establish a broad enough movement to achieve their political goals. He himself argues that, rather than splitting provinces through divisive ethnonationalism, more power and resources should be devolved to local governments to satisfy local demands. In essence, echoing the critics of ethno-federalism above, he argues that ethnonational mobilization is ultimately destabilizing and should be discouraged through political decentralization on a non-ethnic basis.

Unlike Rasul Bakhsh Rais, Nukhbah Langah argues that ethnic identity is essentially primordial and based on clearly distinct factors of language, culture, religion, and descent. In her telling, constructivists may be correct in pointing out the role of political events and instrumentalist entrepreneurs in politicizing ethnicity, but they do not explain the creation of such identities in the first place. According to her, the state's drive to create a uniform Pakistani identity based on the Urdu language and Islam backfired, because ethnic minority leaders interpreted this as an attempt by Punjabi and Muhajir-controlled centre to weaken regional cultures. Langah's focus in this chapter is on two cross-ethnic alliances of the 1990s, the Pakistan Oppressed Nations Movement (PONM) and the United Nations Alliance (UNA), what political pressures led them to fall apart, and how their failure has led to tensions between minority groups. Rather than mobilizing together to achieve greater minority rights and recognition, some ethnic entrepreneurs are encouraging violence against other minorities as an easy means to keep their movement going. Langah emphasizes the example of Siraiki-speaking migrant workers in Balochistan and Baloch insurgents, who view them as dominant Punjabis who need to be pushed out. Ironically, these migrant workers harbour the same socioeconomic grievances against Punjabi elite, and migrate precisely because of a lack of economic opportunities. In the end, she maintains that the best way to safeguard the interests of Siraiki speakers from economically underdeveloped south Punjab, to avoid violence among ethnic minorities and to strengthen Pakistan's federation, is to create a separate province in south Punjab explicitly reflecting a primordial Siraiki identity.

Conclusion

The contributors to this volume all engage in a discussion of the distribution of power in Pakistan's federal structure and how this distribution intersects with the question of ethnic identity in the country. Overall, all authors agree that decentralization of power increases democratic accountability, identification of the people with the state, and even economic productivity. Existing provinces should be given their full constitutional authorities, while the two regions of FATA and GB should be fully incorporated into Pakistan's federation, either as constituent units or by merging them into existing provinces. Only Rezvani and Flowerday differ here: Rezvani suggests that giving some regions special autonomy as partially independent territories may actually provide a long-term solution to intractable centre–periphery conflicts as well as the problem of socioeconomic development. Flowerday argues that geopolitical contingencies, and the clash of Pakistan's statist perception of boundaries with China's traditional notion of sovereignty based on concentric influence and tributary relationships, helps explain the inability to change the ambiguous situation for residents of GB.

None of the authors call into question Pakistan's ethno-federal setup, or argue that its provincial boundaries ought to be reorganized on a purely administrative basis. However, some authors, like Langah, argue that separate provinces should be carved out for ethnic minorities without a provincial homeland. This would satisfy their need for official cultural recognition, ensure better provision of governance and economic resources, and also greatly diminish the possibility of anti-state mobilization. Rais, on the other hand, believes that breaking up existing provinces on an ethnic basis would unnecessarily encourage future ethnic minority demands, and lead to a perpetual process of fragmentation and instability in the country. Creating more and smaller provinces might very well be useful, but this should be done on a purely administrative basis, or by taking into account historical and non-ethnically defined entities, like the princely state of Bahawalpur. Accordingly, Pakistan would move away from full ethno-federalism towards becoming a partial ethno-federation.

The aim of the conference, and this edited volume, is to present centre–periphery dynamics in Pakistan from a local perspective, while also grounding the discussion in the broader comparative literature on federalism and ethnic identity. No attempt has been made to force contributors to adhere to a particular description or policy proposal. Hopefully, this volume will lead to a greater understanding on the part of the reader of the local salience of decentralization and ethnic identity in Pakistan. By including a mix of international and well-established Pakistani scholars, as well as less well-known local authors, this volume should also provide a good mirror of the state of scholarship in Pakistan and serve as an inspiration to continue improving the culture of political and social science research.

Finally, I would like to thank the following people and organizations for making this volume possible. The Hanns Seidel Foundation (HSF) and the American Institute of Pakistan Studies (AIPS) provided the funding for the original conference. I want to thank Kristof Duwaerts and Omer Ali from HSF, and Nadeem Akbar and Kamran Asdar Ali from AIPS in particular. Our organizing committee at the Forman Christian College, which also included Muneeza Mirza, Shakila Sindhu, and Muhammad Younis, worked hard to put the conference together. Special thanks go to Rasul Bakhsh Rais for making the connection with the Oxford University Press, Pakistan (OUPP). I am particularly grateful to Fiza Kazmi and the team of editors at OUPP for helping improve the final shape of this volume. Lastly, I want to thank our student editors, Natasha Waseem, Hasnain Abbas, and Noor Nishan, for helping edit the manuscript.

Notes

1. Ronald Watts, *Comparing Federal Systems in the 1990s* (Kingston: Institute of Intergovernmental Relations, Queen's University, 1996).
2. John McGarry and Brendan O'Leary, 'Must Pluri-national Federations Fail?', *Ethnopolitics* 8, no. 1 (2009): 5–25.
3. Yaqoob Khan Bangash, *A Princely Affair: The Accession and Integration of the Princely States of Pakistan 1947–1955* (Karachi: Oxford University Press, 2015).
4. 'Win for Ex-Fata,' *Dawn*, July 23, 2019.
5. Henry E. Hale, 'Divided We Stand: Institutional Sources of Ethnofederal State Survival and Collapse,' *World Politics* 56, no. 2 (2004): 165–93.
6. Valerie Bunce and Stephen Watts, 'Managing Diversity and Sustaining Democracy: Ethnofederal versus Unitary States in the Postcommmunist World,' in *Sustainable Peace: Power and Democracy after Civil Wars*, eds. Philip G. Roeder and Donald Rothchild (Ithaca: Cornell University Press, 2005), 133–58.
7. Philip G. Roeder, 'Ethnofederalism and the Mismanagement of Conflicting Nationalisms,' *Regional & Federal Studies* 19, no. 2 (2009): 203–19.
8. Liam Anderson, 'Ethnofederalism: The Worst Form of Institutional Arrangement…?' *International Security* 39, no. 1 (2014): 165–204.
9. Bunce and Watts, 'Managing Diversity and Sustaining Democracy.'
10. Roeder, 'Ethnofederalism and the Mismanagement of Conflicting Nationalisms.'
11. Hale, 'Divided We Stand.'
12. McGarry and O'Leary, 'Must Pluri-national Federations Fail?'
13. Ian S. Lustick, Dan Miodownik, and Roy J. Eidelson. 'Secessionism in Multicultural States: Does Sharing Power Prevent or Encourage It?', *The American Political Science Review* 98, no. 2 (May 2004): 209–29.
14. Anderson, 'Ethnofederalism.'
15. Katharine Adeney, 'Constitutional Centring: Nation Formation and Consociational Federalism in India and Pakistan,' *Commonwealth & Comparative Politics* 40, no. 3 (November 2002): 8–33.
16. Katharine Adeney, 'A Step Towards Inclusive Federalism in Pakistan? The Politics of the Eighteenth Amendment,' *Publius The Journal of Federalism* 42, no. 4 (2012): 539–65.
17. Ibid.

18. Arend Lijphart, *Democracy in Plural Societies: A Comparative Exploration* (New Haven: Yale University Press, 1977).

19. Rogers Brubaker, *Ethnicity Without Groups* (Cambridge: Harvard University Press, 2004).

20. Benedict Anderson, *Imagined Communities: Reflections on the Origin and Spread of Nationalism* (London: Verso, 1983).

21. Ernest Gellner, *Nations and Nationalism* (Oxford: Blackwell, 1983).

22. Paul Brass, *Theft of an Idol: Text and Context in the Representation of Collective Violence* (Princeton: Princeton University Press, 1997).

23. Olivier Roy, *The New Central Asia: The Creation of Nations* (New York: New York University Press, 2000).

24. See, among others, Roeder, 'Ethno-Federalism and the Mismanagement of Conflicting Nationalisms.'

25. Kanchan Chandra, 'Ethnic Parties and Democratic Stability,' *Perspectives on Politics* 3, no. 2 (2005): 235–52.

1

Examining Autonomy Options in Pakistan's Federally Administered Tribal Areas and Balochistan: Federalism, Full Independence, or Partial Independence?

David A. Rezvani

He drew a circle that shut me out—
Heretic, rebel, a thing to flout.
But Love and I had the wit to win:
We drew a circle that took him in!

Edwin Markham

Since 2001, Pakistan has faced a number of insurgencies that have created grave political instability, economic disorder, and violence for the country. In 2014, among 177 sovereign states, the Fund for Peace ranked Pakistan as the tenth most fragile state in the world.[1] But, rather than being derived from generally stable and relatively prosperous parts of the country (such as the city of Lahore), much of this ranking is largely driven by the unfortunate economic, political, and security climate in regions in the country that have been the locus of violent insurgencies, such as the Federally Administered Tribal Areas (FATA) and Balochistan. These places are some of the poorest in the country, with relatively low literacy rates, inadequate infrastructure, high infant mortality, and poor access to education. Conflict in these regions has also produced large numbers of internal refugees. For example, after Pakistan Army's 2009 campaign in the northwest of the country, an estimated three million people fled. With their homes and cities destroyed in the wars, many of them took refuge in makeshift camps.[2] Since that time, approximately 1.4 million people have returned to their homelands. But as of December 2017, the United Nations High Commissioner for Refugees (UNHCR) reported that 249,000 individuals were still registered as internally displaced persons (IDPs). In addition to such turmoil, insurgent attacks, suicide bombers, and political assassinations have also wreaked havoc in other parts of Pakistan. Furthermore, FATA and Balochistan have also contributed to the destabilization of surrounding states (like Afghanistan) and threatened outside powers (like the US) by serving as bases for the mobilization of insurgent groups such as the Taliban. Because of threats to America's nation-building activities in Afghanistan as well as perceptions of lawlessness and pockets of warlord rule, the Obama administration waged a drone war on parts of FATA. According to the Bureau of Investigative Journalism, US drone attacks in FATA killed between 2,296 to 3,718 people, including 416–957 civilians from 2004–13.[3] These attacks also resulted in significant economic destruction and further injured between 1,089–1,639 people. Overall, it has been estimated that from 2003–15, as many as 20,076 civilians, 6,076 security forces, and 30,323 militants have lost their lives during the wars in the tribal areas.[4]

In light of these difficulties, a variety of alternatives have been suggested as solutions, including the maintenance of the status quo, allowing full independence, and providing rights within the context of Pakistan's federation. As distinct from each of these options, this chapter suggests that higher degrees of mutual benefit can be achieved for Pakistan and each of these territories through the creation of separate, partially independent territories. This chapter will begin by distinguishing partially independent territories from other political forms. Secondly, it will then discuss some of the reasons for their significance as well as their advantages over full independence. Thirdly, it will examine why partial independence for some regions may be beneficial in light of current conditions within Pakistan. Lastly, the chapter will conclude by addressing some of the challenges that remain for the establishment of partially independent territories.

The Distinction Between Partially Independent Territories and Other Forms

As discussed more extensively in *Surpassing the Sovereign State: The Wealth, Self-Rule, and Security Advantages of Partially Independent Territories*, partially independent territories (PITs) such as Scotland, Hong Kong, Puerto Rico, Iraqi Kurdistan, and nearly 50 other territories around the world, are nationalistically distinct and constitutionally unincorporated polities that divide and share some powers of sovereignty with a sovereign (core) state.[5] PITs possess a wide range of domestic powers (that apply to their own territory) as well as a limited range of foreign affairs capabilities, including some aspects of economic representation and membership in international organizations.

PITs tend to be nationalistically distinct because they have a culturally distinct population that believes that they ought to rule over themselves in certain respects within a specific territory.[6] They are also constitutionally unincorporated in the sense that they possess a distinctive set of rights and powers in some respects as compared to other parts of the core state with which they are associated. For example, the citizens of Scotland (UK) have different rights and powers with respect to issues such as education and local police powers, which they control, as compared to most citizens in the United Kingdom where the same rules do not apply.

Because PITs are constitutionally unincorporated, they are not member-units of federations which are an integral part of sovereign states. So, for example, unlike citizens of one of America's states, the citizens of the US territory of Puerto Rico cannot vote directly for the US President. At the same time, however, they also do not have to pay income taxes to the US federal government while still obtaining billions of US dollars in assistance and other benefits that are tailor-made to their interests. PITs are also distinct from member-units in federations because they have limited foreign affairs abilities. For example, the Åland Islands and Greenland are members of the Nordic Council with countries like Sweden and Norway. Hong Kong is a member of a wide range of international organizations such as the World Bank and the International Monetary Fund (IMF). Many PITs also have limited treaty-making capacity, as with the capability of the Channel Islands, Bermuda, and the Cayman Islands to negotiate their own Tax Information Exchange Agreements.[7]

Partially independent territories are also distinct from colonies within an empire or what can be described as sham autonomous regions, like the Autonomous Region of Tibet (China) or the historic Bantustans of South Africa during the apartheid administration. Unlike sham autonomous regions and colonies, partially independent territories are provided with powers that are entrenched, which means that there is a mechanism to make their powers guaranteed, defensible, and consequently very difficult to change.

Some sovereign states that have relatively high degrees of rule of law (for example with a World Governance Indicator Raking above 70) provide this type of entrenchment over the division of power between the core state and PIT by formal-legal or unwritten constitutional rules.[8] Formal-legal entrenchment includes legal mechanisms that require supermajority legislation, a referendum, or mutual agreement between the core and PIT legislatures before changes to their constitutional order.[9] Conventional entrenchment includes deeply held informal agreements, precedents, and principles that are informally acknowledged by a state's high court or head of state (such as those that prevail between the UK and its associated overseas and devolved territories).[10]

Still other states that do not have a relatively high degree of rule of law (as with the current condition in Pakistan) can also provide credible guarantees to a territory through political-formal means. This form of entrenchment exists when there is a recognized and discernible threat of war, territorial fragmentation, or economic catastrophe as a result of the usurpation of legal commitments. As compared to formal and conventional entrenchment, political-formal entrenchment is a historically more common credibility mechanism that has worked to integrate historic fiefdoms with monarchically ruled domains.[11] Such entrenchment is also a relatively common fixture in federal relations as discussed in the literature. Chad Rector, for example, discusses the concept of 'relationship-specific assets' in which assets that are shared between different polities (such as access to natural resources, military capabilities, and an expanded land and maritime economic zone) retain their value only as long as the relationship persists.[12] Dissolution of the political arrangement can threaten to bring economic disaster, secession, or war, which would in turn threaten such relationship-specific assets. Hong Kong's autonomous system is arguably entrenched because of the pivotal economic roles the territory plays for China—by, for example, being the source for over 40 per cent of the country's foreign direct investment.[13] Premature autonomy arrangements in nationalistically distinct and constitutionally unincorporated regions that do not have formal, conventional, or meaningful political-formal guarantees will result in sham partial independence, such as the condition that currently prevails in Pakistan's regions of FATA, Gilgit-Baltistan, and Azad Kashmir.

The Significance of Partially Independent Territories

Partially independent territories have advantages that often put them ahead of other competing political alternatives. The division of power between a territory and a core state in such arrangements often gives rise to compromise amidst difficult disputes. It also produces economic specialization and economies of scale that allow industries to flourish. Even as PITs have final authority and control over much of their own domestic affairs, core states furnish capabilities such as external defence, proxy diplomatic assistance, infrastructure investments, an economic safety net, and expert advice. Such conditions have provided PITs a much better set of opportunities for stability, burden sharing, and specialization that have in turn resulted in PITs becoming significant factors in international affairs in the areas of global finance, international security, and geostrategic capability.[14]

Sophisticated Offshore Financial Centres

Partially independent territories have capitalized on their credible autonomy and division of power with a core state through economic specialization. One area they have especially focused on is international finance. Partially independent territories like the Cayman Islands (UK), Hong Kong (China), and Liechtenstein (Switzerland) are some of the most sophisticated offshore financial centres (OFCs) in the world. These territories receive about $3.5 trillion of the world's cross border loans.[15] This amounts to approximately 15 per cent of all global lending. According to data from the Bank for International Settlements (BIS), partially independent territories also receive 76 per cent of all loans that go to the world's offshore financial centres.[16]

With regard to the international outcomes of such offshore financial centres, some have emphasized that their limited regulation and low taxes mostly play a beneficial role for global finance through business and governmental competition with other jurisdictions. By competing with firms that are domiciled in OFCs, financial institutions of other countries are forced to become more efficient. Similarly, developed countries are pressured to reduce their rates of taxation, lest businesses continue to flee to OFCs where governments have intentionally crafted lower degrees of regulation and lower taxes to attract international business. Others, however, including some G20 leaders, scholars, and international organizations—such as the Organization for Economic Cooperation and Development (OECD) and the IMF—have blamed OFC PITs for being a major cause for the 2008 global recession because of banking secrecy rules which prevented businesses and financial institutions from having information on the ability of banks to furnish credit and repay loans.[17]

Centrepieces of Compromise

Partially independent arrangements like those for Northern Ireland (UK) and the Kurdish Territories (Iraq) also serve as centrepieces of compromise for some of the world's most difficult nationalistic disputes. The issue of providing autonomous powers to nationalistically distinct territories has been one of the principle alternatives that has been debated and fought for in as many as 46 per cent of the world's conflicts internal to states after the end of the Cold War.[18]

Geostrategic Capability

Partially independent polities like Greenland (Denmark) and New Caledonia (France) also furnish military basing rights, an extended maritime economic zone, and preferential natural resource access to sovereign states.[19] Extended economic and military capabilities, and preferential access to vast natural resource—which were primary reasons for historic imperial control—are now available through the cooperation of a partially independent arrangement without the historic imperial problems of lost international legitimacy, high security costs, and violent rebellion. These problems are some that Pakistan still grapples with amidst its forcible territorial control without the consent of populations in a range of its territories. It is also noteworthy that, similar to Pakistan, many of the territories associated with other core states are really large. Consider, for example, the PIT of Nunavut which accounts for about 21 per cent of Canada's land mass. An even more striking example is Greenland, whose land mass is about 50 times larger than Denmark. Such differentials between the land mass of PITs, as compared to their core states, are relatively common even from a historic standpoint. The British Dominion PIT arrangements of Canada, Australia, New Zealand, and South Africa were all much larger than their UK core state. However, the size of these territories does not reduce the feasibility of the arrangement. On the contrary, the size of such territories enhances core state interests because it is able to maintain an extended economic zone, military capabilities, and preferential access to natural resources without the secessionist threats, high domestic security costs, and loss of international and domestic legitimacy that are associated with other forms of direct and indirect rule.

Why we should expect Partial Independence to Surpass the Alternative of Secession

For those who are considering the possibility of secession (whether in Pakistan or in other parts of the world), it is arguably worth noting that partial independence tends to surpass full independence when it comes to economic, security, and many self-rule issues.[20] We should expect relative success for partially independent territories relative to full independence for three reasons: the public goods that are available to them, the nationalistic compromise that they represent, and their security advantages.

Public Goods

First, partially independent territories benefit from a wide array of public goods that are furnished by a typically powerful core state. The quantity and quality of such services from another state is, in most cases, not available to fully independent states. This includes defence, customs unions, fiscal transfers, single market access, expert advice, shared reputational association, and proxy diplomatic representation. Such public goods allow local vested interests, specialization, accountability, and competition that the centralized rule of a sovereign state often cannot provide. It is arguably no accident that partially independent territories have an average GDP per capita (of $33,144) which is nearly four times higher than those of sovereign states (of $9,780).[21] Even with an apples-to-apples comparison while controlling for population, GDP, region, and core state, partially independent territories are associated with a GDP per capita that is $35,860 higher than sovereign states.[22]

Satisfying Core-territory Nationalism

Second, partially independent unions tend to do more to satisfy the distinct nationalism of core and territorial populations than the alternative of sovereign statehood. Nationalism is defined here as a principle in which a distinct population believes that it ought to rule over itself to some degree within a particular territory.[23] Partially independent territories satisfy core state nationalism by allowing distinct population benefits (such as preferential access to minerals, distant military bases, and an expanded economic zone) without the inconveniences of imperialism. In addition to the distinctive public goods that are available to them, partially independent territories better satisfy territorial interests by allowing powers of guaranteed self-determination that are usually not available to fully independent states.

Better Security

Third, as compared to sovereign states, partially independent unions tend to have improved security because they are the embodiments of compromise and the division of credible power between core and territorial societies. With shared institutions, disputes that may have otherwise been settled with street violence or on the battlefield are authoritatively resolved in the sober chambers of a parliament, courtroom, or through political negotiation.[24] In sum, as one political scientist once claimed, '"If you are interested in survival" amidst the dangers and challenges of the international system, the best way to survive is not necessarily "to have your own state and lots of power".' And as former US President Bill Clinton said in a different context, 'we're all in this together' is a better philosophy than 'you're on your own'.

Pakistan has attempted (and failed) to employ a variety of governmental options for ruling over contentious parts of its country. It has experimented with direct rule and annexation. It has tried to incorporate territories into its evolving federation (as with East Pakistan and Balochistan). It has attempted forms of indirect rule (as with its arrangements in the Tribal Areas or its weak autonomy commitments in Gilgit-Baltistan). These efforts have, however, failed. They have been met with secessionism, grave degrees of nationalistic violence, widespread insurgency, destruction of infrastructure, and, ultimately, loss of control. These should not be surprising outcomes. In addition to Pakistan, a wide range of other countries have also experienced devastating problems with such forms of governance. As the literature on nationalism and imperialism confirms, forms of core state direct and indirect rule over nationalistically distinct territories suffer from the local population's rejection of control by a foreign and alien national group.[25] Weak or sham autonomous arrangements, which are smokescreens for direct or indirect rule, often have similar outcomes. Such alternatives create unnecessary risks for insurgency. They are also costly because they require the core state to perpetually invest in repression and militarized rule. They also fail economically because the repression and militarized rule that is designed to crush ethnically rooted insurgency also tends to reduce local initiative, self-rule, and separate institutions that are critical for advances in industrialization and services.[26]

Partially independent territories, however, do not suffer from such deficits. The allocation of credible powers in some areas to local populations placates local nationalism. It boosts local economies because it empowers local political and entrepreneurial leaders to allocate resources based on their own particular circumstances, needs, and resources rather than the priorities of a distant and alien capital. Greater control over local conditions also provides powerful vested interests for local populations and leaders to maintain political stability, lest their gains be stolen from them by violence and extremists. All of these benefits are of course advantageous to the local populations. But the resulting stability and division of powers also allows the core state to cash in by providing advantages to it, such as access to vast resources.

Partial Independence Advantages as Compared to Federation Member-unit Status

Federations overall have huge benefits. Similar to partially independent territories, they profit from the compromises that can occur through the division and sharing of powers. For those who are considering federation member-unit status for territories in Pakistan (and other parts of the world), it is nevertheless noteworthy that federations tend to be less feasible than partially independent unions in some notable ways.

Symmetry Problems

Among these factors is the one-size-fits-all package of powers that federations tend to offer. For example, within Pakistan's federal union, one of the powers that is within the ambit of the federal government is control over shipping and ports. Balochistan's leaders have complained about the loss of control over their infrastructure, as with the federal government's control of the Gwadar Port in province's southeast.

As distinct from such conditions which ride roughshod over local interests, a tailor-made arrangement might result in a compromise between Pakistan's geopolitical interest of building a port that can accommodate Chinese warships (to deter India) with local economic interests of having greater control over commerce and infrastructure.

Still another example of the problems of a one-size-fits-all package of powers can be seen with the 2010 Eighteenth Amendment to Pakistan's Constitution which abolishes the concurrent (shared) list of 47 powers between the provinces and the central government. In practice, these wide-ranging powers were exercised by the centre and constituted the work of 17 central ministries with an estimated budget of PKR 190 billion.[27] While such an arrangement may be good for some provinces, it may be burdensome for others. A large province, like Punjab, may be more institutionally fit for administering and raising the necessary taxes for such tasks. By contrast, a smaller, much poorer region like Balochistan will have significant challenges.[28]

Some of Pakistan's greatest challenges to its territorial integrity, resource revenue, and internal and external security come from its smallest territories (like FATA) and provinces (like Balochistan). While federations tend to have trouble because of such efforts at legal symmetry, PITs provide a set of rules that are tailored to their specific needs. Rather than applying a package of powers to a local jurisdiction that was created for other territories with very different geographic, political, and economic needs, the bilateral nature of partially independent unions creates the opportunity for a core state and a local population to adapt a local jurisdiction's competencies to the peculiarities of local interests.

Member-unit Equality Problems

Federations also have feasibility problems because of the destabilizing demands for member-unit equality.[29] No federation has perfectly symmetrical member-units. But, according to scholars of federalism, those with highly asymmetrical units are in an especially difficult situation. Such asymmetry can manifest itself when federations have an ethnically distinct territory with over 50 per cent of the population (as with Pakistan's Punjab province). Such a populous, nationalistically-distinct federation member-unit is what Henry Hale calls a core ethnic region.[30]

The percentage of Pakistan's population[31] in its various territories and provinces is as follows:

- Punjab: 56 per cent
- Sindh: 23 per cent
- Khyber Pakhtunkhwa: 13 per cent
- Balochistan: 4.8 per cent
- FATA: 2.3 per cent
- Azad Jammu and Kashmir: 2.2 per cent
- Gilgit-Baltistan: 0.7 per cent

Hale argues that such regions tend to push countries toward internal conflict and ultimate fragmentation. Local nationalists distrust and fear the power the core ethnic region wields in government institutions. Meanwhile, citizens and leaders associated with the core ethnic region feel that their majority representation provides them with a unique mandate to implement their will on the rest of the country.

Accordingly, over time, Sindhis, Bengalis, and the Baloch in Pakistan have complained that they have been subjected to discrimination by the more populous Punjabis. These minorities are also under-represented in state institutions such as the parliament, army, and bureaucracy. Such perceptions result in alienation and more radicalized local nationalism. This can also lead to the eventual failure of federations.

In contrast to the dangerous threats of fragmentation that Hale predicts with the presence of a core ethnic region when a federation has a larger number of member-units, the likelihood that any one member will dominate in this way tends to decrease. Indeed, the number of federations that have failed decreases in direct proportion to the increase in member-units.[32] So, for example, federations between 1900 and 2006 with two to three units failed 69 per cent of the time. Those with four to seven units failed 67 per cent of the time. Those with 8–12 units failed 20 per cent of the time. And those with more than 13 units failed just 13 per cent of the time.[33]

One alternative to address these problems would be to reformulate Pakistan's federation so that it has more member-units, which would make them more equal and symmetric. Such changes would, however, require a revolutionary restructuring of Pakistan's constitution by carving up large provinces such as Punjab and, to a lesser degree, Sindh. New member-unit governments would need to be imposed on areas of Punjab that may not want them. Local nationalists may also emerge that vigorously (or violently) oppose the changes.

An arguably more feasible opportunity for such restructuring is, however, provided through the creations of PITs. As distinct from federations (with such member-unit equality problems) PITs thrive on inequality.[34] As Hale argues, federations tend to fail when there are high degrees of inequality between member-units. With PITs, however, the opposite is true: lower degrees of equality are associated with higher degrees of stability.[35] The more unequal, the more the core state is able to furnish public goods that can convince local leaders that their arrangement is worthwhile. Hence, rather than imposing on the majority of the country the one-size-fits-all changes that are often required by federations, it is sometimes more feasible to create tailor-made solutions for specific areas through the creation of a partially independent territory.

Partial Independence and Moving Beyond the Historic Status Quo in FATA

This section focuses on some of the reasons why FATA may be a good candidate for partial independence amidst the wars and instability that has prevailed in the region since 2001. The next section then discusses some of the hurdles that remain for partial independence to be established.

Some scholars contend that the source of instability in the Tribal Areas is rooted in the failure of Pakistan to extend its monopoly of control to these war-torn and poverty-stricken regions.[36] There is arguably some truth to these views since indirect rule distanced these territories from the powers of the central government and may have made them more susceptible to Taliban infiltration. There are, however, a number of reasons why partial independence may be more advantageous for both the Pakistani government, the local population, and outside actors (such as Afghanistan and the United States). First, the larger historic reality is that—all other things equal—the self-rule and formalized communication links with the core state that existed as a result of indirect rule facilitated peace and stability in the region for many decades.[37] Similarly, partial independence could also provide local leaders with control over their own internal affairs, which would satisfy desires for local self-determination, provide local vested interests, and deliver a context for further economic assistance. Just as has happened in other partially independent territories throughout the world, such factors could provide a context for greater security and economic stability. Second, continued military control over FATA will be difficult to sustain without exacerbating locally rooted desires for ethnic and tribal self-rule over time. Because partial independence provides local self-rule, it arguably reduces nationalistic tension by allowing local leaders and populations credible degrees of self-determination without the additional burdens of full independence. Third, in spite of the long peace that prevailed in the Tribal Areas until 2001, there were, nevertheless, some serious deficits of the arrangement that contributed to its vulnerability to capture by the Taliban, exacerbation of unrest at the hands of the military, and general unrest in light of the region's underdeveloped conditions.[38] These considerations include the fact that FATA was (and remains) cut off from the rest of Pakistan in many respects, languishes in its levels of infrastructure development and education, and many of the local laws, such as collective punishment provisions, remain deeply unpopular locally.[39] Negotiations between the core state and FATA for a new relationship under partial independence would presumably provide opportunities for both sides to work together to fix such deficits.[40]

FATA's Historic Experience with Self-rule

There is one policy that has a proven track record of creating decades of peace in the Tribal Areas: allowing the region to self-rule. FATA consists of seven agencies in North West Pakistan: Bajaur, Mohmand, Orakzai, Khyber, Kurram, North Waziristan, and South Waziristan. For nearly five decades, from Pakistan's independence in 1947 until 2001, the Tribal Areas have been largely stable.[41] Because subduing the Pashtun tribes proved very difficult for the British in the nineteenth century, measures of self-rule were provided to the Tribal Areas in a form of indirect governance under the direction of a political agent which represented the outside authorities. Under this system of governance, local tribes would mostly be left to themselves to manage their own affairs unless they took actions that threatened British interests, such as fighting among themselves or fomenting violence against British forces. The system was enshrined in the 1901 Frontier Crimes Regulation (FCR), which stipulated that British appointed commissioners would coordinate and supervise tribal *malik*s (chiefs).[42]

After Pakistan gained its independence in 1947, the central government appointed its own political agents in the Tribal Areas to continue this system of indirect rule under the FCR. While having a wide range of discretion, political agents were also incentivized to minimize military intervention. As one political agent confirmed:

> [We had] discretion in the sense that there were no hard and fast rules. You could do anything, as long as it worked, [the government] was happy. If you used force, it was a mark against you—you were not qualified to be a political agent ....[43]

The FCR also contained a number of controversial provisions, including the allowance of collective punishment. Instead of being directly applied to the Tribal Areas, the original purpose of the collective punishment provisions of the FCR was to support indirect rule and to prevent larger threats to British security in the region.[44] Direct rule was left to the self-governance of tribes and their own indigenous system of justice. As one of Pakistan's political agents confirmed in 1950:

> Mostly, since there was no 'Berlin Wall', and people were moving all the time, there were disputes between the tribals and the settled people. For these, you held conferences—what is called jirga. These settled people would say, 'These people kidnapped my son, or my brother, my relations.' So you held this big conference, these problems were brought up and amicably settled to the satisfaction of all concerned … It worked beautifully. Within the tribe, we never bothered. They had their own systems. We never interfered.[45]

Collective punishment was therefore a means to hold tribal leaders and the rest of their tribe to account for not being able to keep the crimes within their tribal jurisdiction in check.

After America's invasion of Afghanistan in 2001, however, this form of governance came under threat as the Taliban fled to the Tribal Areas. After the 9/11 attacks and America's subsequent invasion of Afghanistan in 2001, elements of the Taliban fled from Afghanistan to FATA. These developments were a catalyst for incremental Talibanization that was already underway after mujahedeen mobilization against the December 1979 Soviet invasion of Afghanistan as well as Pakistani President Ziaul Haq's encouragement of Deoband religious seminaries.[46] The consolidation of Taliban power in FATA resulted in the emergence of insurgent groups, such as the Tehreek-e-Taliban Pakistan (TTP), which disrupted the historic indirect rule in the region that had prevailed under the FCR.[47] Through a campaign of intimidation and assassination of Tribal *malik*s, they succeeded in usurping control of much of the region by 2004.[48] The TTP then used the region as a base from which they could launch insurgent attacks within Afghanistan and Pakistan. Over time, Pakistan responded by launching a series of devastating military campaigns and an ongoing military occupation, which mostly succeeded in reasserting control and removing the Taliban threat in the region. These offensives by the Pakistan Armed Forces include Operation Rah-e-Nijat (2009), Operation Koh-e-Sufaid (2011), and Operation Zarb-e-Azb (2014).[49] With these military offensives into the area, the FCR has been maintained as a means of direct (rather than indirect) rule. The transition to the direct forms of rule under the Taliban and the military, however, raises the spectre of local nationalistic opposition.

Challenges of Perpetual Military Control in FATA

According to a 2010 poll from the New American Century Foundation (NACF), 70 per cent of citizens in FATA approved of the Pakistan military pursuing al-Qaeda and Taliban militants in their area.[50] Additionally, 79 per cent of citizens supported the military governing their region. These are remarkable results, especially in light of the massive destruction and vast numbers of internally displaced people caused by the Pakistan military's successive campaigns against militants in the region. Much of the local support for the military may be an expression of relief after the ouster of elements of the Taliban from the region. According to the NACF poll, 60 per cent of residents opposed Afghan Taliban fighters and even more (69 per cent) opposed the Pakistani Taliban being present in FATA.[51]

But while the local population may have been expressing relief after the ouster of the Taliban, such sentiments are unlikely to last with continued Pakistani military occupation. Indeed, just after America's invasion of Afghanistan in 2001, local citizens had similar levels of approval of US forces, which significantly waned over time. Once hostilities have ended, militaries tend not to be well-suited institutions for critical roles such as extending civil and human rights, which are vital for the resumption of stable economic, political, and security affairs. Indeed, in 2012, Amnesty International reported that human rights violations 'continue across the Tribal Areas, in parts where there is an ongoing armed conflict and parts where there are no longer active hostilities between the Armed Forces and the Taliban and other armed groups'.[52] Amidst the ongoing efforts to stamp out insurgency, they reported summary execution, torture, enforced disappearances, and arbitrary detention. They also reported that such activities have been conducted without investigation, accountability, and prosecution of those that are responsible. If such conditions are allowed to persist, they will tend to give rise to the sentiments of rebellion and secessionism that they are designed to prevent.

Pakistani leaders such as former president Asif Ali Zardari as well as military leaders have therefore been wise to move in the direction toward reforming the pre-existing political order in the region.[53] Article 247(3) of the 1973 Constitution stipulates that 'no act of Parliament is applicable to the FATA or any part thereof unless the President of Pakistan so directs. The governor of Khyber Pakhtunkhwa acts as the "agent" to the President of Pakistan'. In August 2011, President Zardari announced a limited series of amendments to the FCR. Provisions in the FCR that allowed officials to engage in 'whipping' and corporal punishment were annulled.[54] The concept of bail was also introduced for detainees (except for those of whom there are 'reasonable grounds for believing that he has been guilty of an offence punishable with imprisonment for 10 years').[55] An appeals process was also set up for individuals accused of crimes (although the Political Agent would still simultaneously play both a policing and judicial role).[56] Surprisingly, however, the collective punishment provisions in the FCR, in which citizens are charged for crimes that their relatives commit, were not annulled. Instead, they were allowed to continue but limited to male citizens between the ages of 16 and 65.[57] Despite these amendments, however, human rights organizations confirm that the practice still continues even for children below the age of 16.[58]

As a senior lawyer and former president of the Peshawar High Court Bar Association (PHCBA), Advocate Abdul Latif Afridi, observed: 'Political agents have become non-entities ever since the army stepped into FATA … Ever since militancy began in the area, the FCR has become toothless'.[59] Indeed, two months before the enactment of these amendments in June 2011, the president also enacted the Actions in Aid of Civil Powers Regulation (AACPR), which codified the de facto military control and martial law in FATA. In many respects, the AACPR appears to trump the newer FCR changes. The AACPR grants the military sweeping powers over the territory in terms of 'law and order duties, to conduct law enforcement operations, to continue national calamities and for rehabilitation'.[60] Under Article 16(1) of the AACPR, even individuals that are 'suspected of an act of challenging the writ or authority of the Federal or Provincial Government' can be charged with a criminal offence. Freedom of speech is also curtailed in this context. According to Article 16(3) 'threaten[ing] in [any] manner whatsoever the peace and tranquillity of any area by subversion, spreading literature, delivering speeches electronically or otherwise thus inciting the people' is also considered criminal behaviour. The Preamble of the AACPR justifies these conditions by referring to Article 245(1) of Pakistan's Constitution which says, 'The Armed Forces shall, under the directions of the Federal Government, defend Pakistan against external aggression or threat of war, and, subject to law, act in aid of civil power when called upon to do so.'

In spite of the provisions in the Constitution preventing judicial jurisdiction over citizens in FATA, the courts have asserted themselves with respect to issues of *habeas corpus*. For example, in June 2012, the Peshawar High Court ordered the release of 1,035 individuals who were not considered to be involved with the Taliban or other militant organizations.[61] Amnesty International, however, asserts that even with such judgments by the courts, the authorities nevertheless do not consistently comply with court decisions on the release or trial of detainees.[62] In sum, perpetual military occupation, the attendant loss of individual rights, and the dangers such conditions entail for further rebellion gives rise to a costly role that Pakistan's military is presumably reluctant to play.

One of the challenges that Pakistan's leaders face with respect to these territories is strategic planning and a vision of how these territories might evolve in ways that create mutual benefit between the core state (Pakistan) and these regions. Interestingly, Pakistan's territories have already begun going through a type of evolution that mirrors the condition of some of the territories in America's federal union as it was in the beginning in accordance with the 1787 Northwest Ordinance (a US law).[63] America's federal union with its current geographic scale did not emerge instantaneously. Instead, it came into being in accordance with a step by step plan specified in the 1787 Northwest Ordinance.

The first phase involved military rule through a governor appointed by America's president (which is similar to FATA's current condition). Under this first phase, territories were under the 'plenary power' (or direct rule) of the US Congress. Similar to FATA, the rights that were guaranteed to citizens living elsewhere in the country were not provided to citizens in such territories. Basic rights available to citizens elsewhere in the country such as trial by jury and *habeas corpus* were suspended for territorial citizens.[64] Similarly, Article 247(2) of Pakistan's Constitution specifies that Pakistani courts do not have jurisdiction in FATA. The fundamental rights mentioned in Pakistan's constitution are therefore unenforceable in FATA by the courts.

Phase two of America's federal union was to allow degrees of decentralized powers. Under such decentralization, the territories were allowed to elect local legislators and appoint judges. Ultimate authority would, however, still be in the hands of the US Congress and the president. In the third and final phase, the territory would be admitted to America's federal union, with powers protected by the

Constitution from arbitrary usurpation by the central government. If such a sequence of stages is applied to FATA, the third phase could equally result in a PIT arrangement.

Feasibility of FATA and Balochistan for Partial Independence?

While federations may be more infeasible than the establishment of PITs, partial independence nevertheless has its own emergence hurdles. Even if central and local governments are convinced by the advantages of a partially independent union, sadly this is often not enough for their emergence. From the perspective of state authorities, the fact that a partially independent arrangement might make sense from an economic, political, and security standpoint is often not sufficient to cause their emergence. Many potential core states and weaker polities (such as many of the world's fragile states) could greatly benefit from the division of powers embodied in a partially independent union yet, in many cases, they do not emerge. Powerful norms of state cohesion and nationalism within states mitigate against sharing and dividing sovereignty. It is very difficult for sovereign states to transfer their sovereign powers to territories within their international legal space. Powerful norms of power monopolization rooted in centuries of history and perceptions of political interests tend to bar the way and prevent the degree of constitutional commitments that are necessary for their creation. The tendency of Pakistan's government and military to centralize and monopolize power is generally a common feature of sovereign states.

Overcoming these powerful norms usually requires cataclysmic events that weaken such norms in favour of forms of government that can prevent further disruption.[65] In spite of the harm that they unleash, wars, threats of state fragmentation, economic disaster, and other constitutional revolutions allow leaders and citizens to set aside pre-existing norms that prevent divisions of power. Under such circumstances, the vested interests and ideology that previously blocked the consideration of new solutions are reset. Within such a constitutional vacuum, partially independent territories are often born.

All partially independent territories have their roots in such cataclysmic events. Countries like the United Kingdom, France, the Netherlands, Spain, and others established partially independent territories only after a history of terrible wars and territorial fragmentation. The secession of the Thirteen Colonies led to partially independent arrangements for Canada in 1846 and ultimately other British Dominions like Australia, South Africa, and New Zealand. France's loss of empire, including its inability to retain Algeria and its sham partial independence failures in Indochina, helped give rise to more serious commitments to New Caledonia and French Polynesia. Denmark's loss of Iceland after 1918 (and formally in 1944) underscored the need for renewed commitments to prevent the possible secession of Greenland and the Faroe Islands. The Netherlands' loss of the Dutch Antilles helped produce a greater willingness for associated PITs in the Caribbean. Moldova's war with the nationalistically distinct territory of Transnistria helped give rise to a PIT with Gagauzia. After much foot-dragging, the United States allowed Puerto Rico's new constitutional order because of the disaster of WWII and the strategic role the territory would play in protecting the mainland. And after a history of broken promises, Canada divided powers with the Inuit territory of Nunavut after experiencing the near secession of Quebec in 1995.

Similarly, Pakistan has also experienced a range of cataclysmic events that could have provided opportunities for leaders to overcome norms against the monopolization of control. Such events include the 1947 war of secession with India and especially the 1971 secession of East Pakistan (Bangladesh). Furthermore, the secessionist threats the country continues to face in the Tribal Areas, Balochistan, Gilgit-Baltistan, and Azad Kashmir provide ongoing reminders of further fragmentation disasters that may lie ahead. Hence, in light of the experience of other countries around the world, there is hope for the establishment of partially independent territories in Pakistan. First, as argued here, they make sense from a political, economic, and security standpoint—especially when compared to the other political alternatives that Pakistan has previously tried. Second, Pakistan has already experienced more than enough cataclysmic events which Pakistan's population and leaders are naturally eager not to repeat.

Conclusion

In spite of the emphasis here on their advantages, partially independent territories are certainly not panaceas for Pakistan or the problems of poverty, insecurity, and nationalism faced by the world's population. In order for such arrangements to be established in Pakistan, some of the key hurdles that remain include the capacity to commit to forms of entrenchment. As Pakistan's commitment to the rule of law increases over time, formal and conventional entrenchment mechanisms can become a more viable option. Political-formal entrenchment also remains a viable alternative in the short term if linked to relationship-specific assets.

In spite of such hurdles, however, no solution will be perfect. Pakistan has tried other political alternatives (such as direct rule, indirect rule, federation member-units, and sham autonomy) and they have failed. Forcible rule (whether direct or indirect) of nationalistically distinct territories incites resistance and insurgency. Federation member-unit status also suffers from infeasibility problems, such as crudely applying a one-size-fits-all solution that can be vastly inapplicable and irrelevant to the specific circumstances and conditions of a territory (as with East Pakistan and Balochistan). PITs, however, do not suffer from such problems. Their credible division of powers eliminates nationalistic resentment. When compared to the alternative of full independence, PITs tend to be wealthier, more secure, and have more credible forms of self-determination.[66] In the case of Pakistan's territories such as FATA, a partially independent arrangement would provide opportunities to remove the legacy of military occupation, isolation, poor infrastructure, and nationalistic radicalization. And unlike federation member-units, their powers and capabilities are tailored to their unique circumstances. For example, much like the case of Iraqi Kurdistan, Pakistan could greatly benefit from doing more to decentralize local police and security powers to its territories whose local leaders also have a vested interest in eliminating violent and destabilizing insurgency. Much like the case of the relationships between other core states with territories that have vast natural resources (like Canada-Nunavut, Denmark-Greenland, and France-New Caledonia), Pakistan could also improve its exploitation of the vast natural resources of its territories by doing more to share power with territorial leaders and entrepreneurs. Extracting resources under the conditions of mutual agreement and power-sharing reduces local antagonism. It can also unlock local entrepreneurial incentives to increase local productivity. Partial independence would also offer ways to accommodate Pakistan's reluctance to make Gilgit-Baltistan and Azad Kashmir part of its federation because of the territorial disputes with China (as with Gilgit-Baltistan) and India (as with Azad Kashmir).

Notes

1. The Fund for Peace Fragile States Index, 2014. This ranking is based on the use of 12 different political, security, and economic indicators. The social indicators that they examine include: 'mounting demographic pressures, massive movement of refugees or internally displaced persons, legacy of vengeance-seeking group grievance or group paranoia and chronic and sustained human flight'. The economic indicators that they examine include: 'uneven economic development along group lines' and 'sharp and/or severe economic decline'. The political and military indicators that they examine include: 'criminalization and/or de-legitimization of the state, progressive deterioration of public services, suspension or arbitrary application of the rule of law, and widespread human rights abuse, security apparatus operates as a "state within a state", rise of factionalized elites and intervention of other states or external political actors'.

2. Internal Displacement Monitoring Centre, 2015.
3. 'Where the Drones Strike Data,' *Bureau of Investigative Journalism*, 2013.
4. Ibid.
5. David A. Rezvani, *Surpassing the Sovereign State: The Wealth, Self-Rule, and Security Advantages of Partially Independent Territories* (Oxford: Oxford University Press, 2014).
6. Michael Hechter, *Containing Nationalism* (New York: Oxford University Press, 2000).
7. Michael Foot, 'Final report of the independent Review of British offshore financial centres,' October 2009, https://www.gov.im/media/624053/foot report.pdf.
8. Daniel Kaufmann, Aart Kraay, and Massimo Mastruzzi, *The Worldwide Governance Indicators: Methodology and Analytical Issues* (Washington D. C.: World Bank Group, 2010), http://info.worldbank.org/governance/wgi/pdf/WGI.pdf.
9. Rezvani, *Surpassing the Sovereign State*.
10. Geoffrey Marshall, *Constitutional Conventions: The Rules and Forms of Political Accountability* (Oxford: Oxford University Press, 1984).
11. Hendrik Spruyt, *The Sovereign State and its Competitors* (Princeton: Princeton University Press, 1994).
12. Chad Rector, *Federations: The Political Dynamics of Cooperation* (Ithaca: Cornell University Press, 2009).
13. Rezvani, 'Dead Autonomy, a Thousand Cuts, or Partial Independence? The Autonomous Status of Hong Kong,' *Journal of Contemporary Asia* 42, no. 1 (2012): 93–122.
14. See Rezvani, 'Partial independence beats full independence,' *Territory, Politics, Governance* 4, no. 3 (2016): 269–96.
15. '81st Annual Report,1 April 2010–31 March 2011,' *Bank for International Settlements*, 2011.
16. Ibid.
17. On the role of OFCs, see, for example, Gregory Rawlings, 'Taxes and transnational treaties: responsive regulation and the reassertion of offshore sovereignty,' *Law & Policy* 29, no. 1(2007): 51–66; Ronen Palan, 'Tax Havens and the Commercialization of State Sovereignty,' *International Organization* 56, no. 1 (2002): 151–76; and Michael Webb, 'Defining the boundaries of legitimate state practice: norms, transnational actors and the OECD's project on harmful tax competition,' *Review of International Political Economy* 11, no. 4 (2004): 787–827.
18. Rezvani, *Surpassing the Sovereign State*.
19. Alexander Cooley, *Base Politics* (Ithaca: Cornell University Press, 2008).
20. Rezvani, *Surpassing the Sovereign State*.

21. Data converted to constant 2005 US$ using the United Nation's Implicit Price Deflator (United Nations Statistics Division, 2009).
22. Rezvani, 'Partial independence beats full independence.'
23. For a similar definition, see Hechter, *Containing Nationalism*.
24. Rezvani, 'Partial independence beats full independence.'
25. See Hechter, *Containing Nationalism*.
26. Stephen Van Evera, 'Primed for Peace: Europe After the Cold War,' *International Security* 15, no. 3 (1990/1991): 7–57.
27. Mehtab Haider, 'Concurrent list spending is Rs190b, are the provinces ready?' *The News*, September 28, 2009.
28. Katharine Adeney, 'A Step Towards Inclusive Federalism in Pakistan? The Politics of the Eighteenth Amendment,' *Publius The Journal of Federalism* 42, no. 4 (2012): 16.
29. Rector, *Federations*.
30. Henry E. Hale, 'Divided We Stand: Institutional Sources of Ethnofederal State Survival and Collapse,' *World Politics* 56, no. 2 (2004): 165–93.
31. Pakistan Bureau of Statistics, 2011.
32. Katharine Adeney, 'Between Federalism and Separatism,' in *Managing and Settling Ethnic Conflicts: Perspectives on Successes and Failures in Europe, Africa, and Asia*, eds. Ulrich Schneckener and Stefan Wolff (London: Hurst, 2003), 173.
33. Ibid.
34. Rezvani, *Surpassing the Sovereign State*.
35. Ibid.
36. Peter Chalk, 'The Pakistani-Afghan Border Region,' *Ungoverned Territories: Understanding and Reducing Terrorism Risks* (Santa Monica: RAND Corporation, 2008).
37. Thomas H. Johnson and M. Chris Mason, 'No Sign until the Burst of Fire: Understanding the Pakistan-Afghanistan Frontier,' *International Security* 32, no. 4 (Spring 2008): 41–77.
38. Mariam Abou Zahab, 'Kashars against Mashars: Jihad and Social Change in the FATA,' in *Beyond Swat: History, Society and Economy along the Afghanistan-Pakistan Frontier*, eds. Benjamin D. Hopkins and Magnus Marsden (New York: Columbia University Press, 2013), 51–60.
39. Brian Fishman, 'The Battle for Pakistan: Militancy and Conflict Across the FATA and NWFP,' *Counterterrorism Strategy Initiative Policy Paper* (Vancouver: New America Foundation, 2010).
40. Shuja Nawaz, 'FATA—A Most Dangerous Place,' *Centre for Strategic & International Studies* (Washington, D. C.: New American Century Foundation, 2009).

41. Adnan Naseemullah, 'Shades of Sovereignty: Explaining Political Order and Disorder in Pakistan's Northwest,' *Studies in Comparative International Development* 49, no. 4 (2014): 501–22.
42. Kimberley Marten, Thomas H. Johnson, and M. Chris Mason, 'Misunderstanding Pakistan's Federally Administered Tribal Area?', *International Security* 33, no. 3 (Winter 2008/2009): 180–89.
43. Quoted in Naseemullah, 'Shades of Sovereignty.'
44. Ibid.
45. Ibid., 513.
46. Muhammad Moj, *The Deoband Madrassah Movement: Countercultural Trends and Tendencies* (London; New York: Anthem Press, 2015).
47. Marten, Johnson, and Mason, 'Misunderstanding Pakistan's Federally Administered Tribal Area?'
48. Naseemullah, 'Shades of Sovereignty'.
49. Saman Zulfqar, 'An Overview of Pakistan's Security Situation after Operation Zarb-e-Azb,' *Journal of Current Affairs* 2, no. 1 (2015): 122.
50. New American Century Foundation.
51. Ibid.
52. 'Amnesty International Report 2012: The State Of The World's Human Rights,' *Amnesty International*, 2012, 13.
53. FATA has 12 representatives in Pakistan's National Assembly. But according to Articles 246 and 247 of Pakistan's Constitution only the President has the right to create rules for the territory.
54. Former FCR Article 6.
55. FCR Article 11A.
56. FCR Articles 47–8, 50, 55, and 55A.
57. FCR Article 21.
58. 'Amnesty International Report 2012,' 47.
59. Zulfiqar Ali, 'Structural subjugation,' *Dawn*, July 6, 2014.
60. AACPR Article 3(4).
61. 'Amnesty International Report 2012,' 43.
62. Ibid., 44.
63. Arnold H. Leibowitz, *Defining Status: A Comprehensive Analysis of United States Territorial Relations* (Boston: Martinus Nijhoff Publishers, 1989).
64. Ibid.
65. For more on this, see Rezvani, *Surpassing the Sovereign State.*
66. Ibid., Rezvani 'Partial independence beats full independence.'

2

Federalism in Pakistan:
Past and Present

Muhammad Younis and Irtiza Shafaat

Introduction

This chapter details the trajectory of the negotiation of the State of Pakistan with the idea of federalism, focusing upon the empirical realities of various power-sharing mechanisms employed by the ruling elites since the country's inception in 1947. The purpose of this chapter is to provide a broad outline of the historical journey of Pakistan in terms of the power configurations which ruled her, rather than sketching an all-encompassing narrative that holistically explains every complexity. Keeping in mind the dissonance attached with how federalism is imagined in theory and how it is operationalized in practice, especially in postcolonial developing states, attempting to posit a linear developmental trajectory of federal power-sharing in Pakistan historically would be an exercise in futility. On one hand, historical evidence points to the fact that federalism as an idea of power-sharing between the centre and the federating units, as opposed to confederal and unitarian arrangements, was never challenged in Pakistan. On the other hand, the performance of the ruling elites, including the political parties, civil-military bureaucracy, among other key actors in terms of paying deference to federal principles, has been sketchy at best. After looking at the historical factors which necessitated the power-sharing dynamics to be federal in nature, the chapter will enlist Pakistan's rollercoaster ride with federalism, including the passage of the 1956 Constitution, arrangements made prior to the 1958 martial coup, Ayub Khan's autocratic façade and the Presidential Constitution of 1962, the civilian-led PPP's constitutional democratic period, Ziaul Haq's martial law, the hybrid troika of 1988–98, Musharraf's martial law and subsequent state sponsored democracy, and finally the post-2008 era with its semblance of civilian primacy which culminated in the passage of the Eighteenth Amendment to the Constitution of Pakistan. Constant upheavals at the macro level of power-sharing, necessitated by extra-constitutional coups, have constantly undermined the growth of a healthy, civilian-led, political process in Pakistan, and their impact on the project of federalism will also be discussed.

A Historical Overview

The general structure of government in Pakistan was federal from the onset. This arrangement was necessitated by at least three socio-historical factors, according to Professor Jaffar.[1] Firstly, the All-India Muslim League (AIML), the founding political party of Pakistan, always championed the case of provincial autonomy in British India and, consequently, in any future administrative settlement for major groups. While the group identity envisioned by the Muslim League was solely based on religion, ethnic divisions within these groups were completely ignored. This misreading of the ethnic divisions within the areas that were to comprise Pakistan has had severe adverse consequences over the years. The common strand of strong commitment of the Muslim League to the provincial autonomy project can be observed in the positions assumed by its top leadership at the Lucknow Pact (1916), Jinnah's Fourteen Points (1929), subsequent arguments during the Round Table Conferences (1930–2), rhetoric employed in the 1937 provincial election campaigns leading up to the historic Lahore Resolution in 1940, and the acceptance of the Cabinet Mission Plan (1946), among other critical historical junctures. Simultaneously, the Muslim League always advocated a group identity based around religion, which ultimately led to a separatist freedom movement.

Secondly, the modulation of the partition of British India also necessitated that both newly independent states, India and Pakistan, would benefit from operating under a federal form of government. In the Partition plan, different provinces and princely states of British India were given the option to join any of the two nascent states or remain independent. Various modes ranging from referenda (as was the case in the North-Western Frontier Province) to the resolutions passed by representative bodies, among others, were adopted. The legislative assembly of Sindh opted for Pakistan, while voting in the limited franchise-based assembly was organized in Punjab separately, on the basis of Muslim and non-Muslim majority districts, resulting in the fateful partition of Punjab. As a consequence, the eastern parts of Punjab, predominantly Sikh majority areas, went to India, whereas western areas of Punjab were included in Pakistan. A massive, albeit chaotic, migration of people took place as a result of the decision of the communities in Punjab Assembly and the Boundary Commission. A humanitarian disaster ensued, with mass communal infighting and millions lost their lives in the resultant carnage. However, the vagaries of Partition, no matter how important as an issue that deserves deliberation, are beyond the scope of this chapter.

Thirdly, the heterogeneous nature of the Pakistani society—if observed at the time of Partition in terms of ethnicity, language, and cultural diversity—itself necessitated a federal arrangement in matters of power-sharing. Only a decentralized federal setup could accommodate the socioeconomic imbalances between the federating units and within the units themselves.

On the other hand, Ayesha Jalal's postulation that the Government of India Act 1935—which was federal in nature but paradoxically highly centralized—automatically assumed itself as the constitutional basis for the newly independent states of Pakistan and India, in her nuanced understanding of the historical context of politics in South, has its merits.[2]

Although Pakistan became a federation in letter, the ruling elites, in spirit, failed to run the state according to the established norms of federal constitutionalism. We will now view some explanations by different scholars on the reasons for the debacle of the concept of federalism in the Pakistani context.

The democratic aspirations of the founding fathers of the nascent state were crushed by the juggernaut of the civil and military bureaucracy who assumed a preponderant role in the power configurations that ruled the country. The interests of the civil-military bureaucratic elite ran contrary to the interests of a political leadership trying to emancipate themselves and the people. The fact that the overdeveloped bureaucracies were already entrenched in the power dynamics historically, through instruments employed by the colonial elites, aided this development.

Jami Chandio and Amjad Bhatti sturdily argue that the anti-federalist and Punjab-centric mindset of the ruling elites, coupled with the aforementioned dominance of the civil-military bureaucratic oligarchy, curtailed the evolution of federalism in Pakistan in the institutional context.[3]

Difference of opinion and dissidence in the nascent state were outrightly rejected by the ruling elites under the hypocritical garb of an attempt to protect the Islamic nationalism project. Religious groups, marginalized in the political sphere and with meagre populist support, were pitted against ethnic demands to support the self-serving ends of the ruling establishment. The Objectives Resolution (1949) provided that space by institutionalizing the role of Islam in the body politic of the country. The state was indirectly centralized through the use of Islamic rhetoric. The voices of the weaker federating units and marginalized societal groups were crushed as space for democratic dissent was curtailed. The constitution-making process was delayed for nine years, significantly reducing the representative and legislative role of the elected institutions of the state.

According to Dr Waseem, unlike many postcolonial states, Pakistan lacked continuity in terms of a political centre. Everything ranging from establishing the seat of government to the provision of institutional structures for financial stability, government coordination, tax collection and distribution, to name only a few, had to be constructed from scratch. Moreover, there was a perceived, and to some extent real, security threat from neighbouring India. This facilitated a decisive role for a central government equipped with strong military muscle. The security problems coupled with newly emerging realities of the bipolar dynamics of the Cold War severely affected the governance strategy, making Pakistan a highly centralized, and often paranoid, state immediately after independence.[4]

Ayesha Jalal mentioned that, in the beginning, there was no single all-encompassing and omnipresent institution. Therefore, there was considerable choice to tread upon either the representative institutions or administrative institutions path. The state opted for the latter as it was easier—the administrative machinery enjoyed a comparative advantage since there existed an infrastructural base at the time.[5] Dr Waseem gave a convincing argument for the predominance of central government over the provinces. According to him, it was the politics of the immediate pre-independence period that paved the way for a centralized state.[6]

The Muslim League, and especially its political elite from non-Pakistan areas, and the Muslim members of the Indian bureaucracy who chose to join Pakistan were none too pleased about the increased role of the smaller provinces, especially when the modalities for Pakistan were put into practice. This mistrust was one of the major reasons for the enhancement of the power of the central government as opposed to the provincial autonomy project. The politics of a few months preceding Partition substantially determined the governing arrangements of the new state which were essentially centralized and autocratic.

The role of the first Governor General could also point towards the preponderance of the central government. Jinnah, according to Hamza Alavi, did not trust the elected members of the provincial government and instead was giving more weight to the opinion of his select coterie of bureaucrats. He had opened secret channels of communication with the secretaries of provinces who would convey all important information to him. Most of his decisions were based on this information.[7]

Delay in constitution-making and subsequently in holding general elections also contributed towards enhancing the powers of non-elected institutions. Mohammad Ali Jinnah, the first Governor General of Pakistan, was very powerful, both constitutionally and politically. He was the President of the Constituent Assembly, the President of the Muslim League, and also headed the Ministry for the Rehabilitation of Refugees. Constitutionally, he had the power to amend any article of the Constitution until March 31, 1949.

Khalid Bin Sayeed opined that, being Governor General, he could enforce emergency in any province, overrule the decision of the provinces, or even dismiss the provincial government. This power was actually used to dismiss the ministries in Sindh, NWFP, and Bengal. He also had many constitutional powers to subordinate the prime minister and the federal cabinet. This huge concentration of power in one institution was a clear negation of the spirit of federalism in terms of checks and balances and the separation of powers.[8]

The Objectives Resolution can also be considered as one of the root causes for strengthening central government. It institutionalized the role of religion in the politics of Pakistan. Religious parties, completely marginalized owing to their anti-Pakistani role during the independence movement, were emboldened by the passage of the resolution. In the backdrop of this resolution, they presented their charter of demands to be incorporated in the new Constitution while presenting themselves as the sole authorities which could interpret religion. They started openly interfering in matters of running the state while negatively influencing the political discourse in the constituent assembly through the back door.

Jinnah himself disliked provincial factionalism as it was against his utopian ideal of an Islamic state. This is evident from his dealing with the Bengalis' demand for a national status for their language. Jinnah categorically rejected that demand by emphasizing the importance of one language for the unity and solidarity of a nation. The language issue was resolved after it took a violent turn. The Constituent Assembly in 1955 passed the language bill whereby both Urdu and Bengali were declared national languages. The bill also recognized the importance of regional languages by empowering the provincial governments to take necessary steps for the promotion of regional cultures and languages.

The accession of Balochistan, especially the State of Kalat, to Pakistan also raised many questions as to the nature of federalism in Pakistan. Many Baloch intellectuals still believe that it was a coerced rather than a voluntary accession. The unfortunate saga took a violent turn when the brother of the Khan of Kalat took up arms against the State of Pakistan. The way he was treated scarred the memories of the Baloch people. Though a commission was constituted on the Balochistan issue, its recommendations were never given due consideration. Many Baloch nationalists regard their history with Pakistan as a tale of broken promises and blatant state aggression by the centre. Balochistan has experienced at least four full-fledged military operations.

The 1956 Constitution

After nine years of its inception, Pakistan finally succeeded in framing its first Constitution in 1956, promulgated on March 23. Under the Constitution of 1956, Pakistan was a federation of two units, the provinces of West Pakistan and East Pakistan. It provided for a parliamentary and federal form of government—one of the unique features of the Constitution was that the central legislature was unicameral, which was not common practice in most federations. Essentially, after the creation of One Unit, albeit quite an unnatural one, Pakistan became a federation of two units with roughly equal populations and therefore bicameralism was not adopted. Both federating units were given equal representation in the central legislature through the Second Constituent Assembly. Under the 1956 Constitution, Pakistan adopted most of the fundamental characteristics of a federal state such as dual polity, distribution of powers between the centre and provinces, a written and partly rigid constitution, and a potent judiciary equipped with the power of judicial review.[9]

Theoretically, it seemed that the Constitution provided for an impressive mechanism for provincial autonomy but in practice the situation was highly skewed in favour of the central government. In addition to the inclusion of almost all the important subjects in the federal list, the federal government was provided with different mechanisms to intervene in provincial affairs. It had the right to guide and advise a provincial government. It could form a law for any part of the country to implement a treaty. The laws made by the federal legislature on any of the concurrent subjects were given preferential treatment in the event of a conflict with any of the provincial laws on the same subject.

Most importantly, the federal government had the power to proclaim an emergency in any province. During a period of emergency, the provincial governments could be dismissed, the legislature suspended, and the governor could be handed over all the executive responsibility of the province concerned. In the case of a financial, administrative, or constitutional emergency, the effects were the same.

The power distribution dynamics, in effect, had subordinated the provinces to the central government. In a country like Pakistan which was in the early stages of its democratic and federalist development, this unbridled power could have unforeseen complications for the development of true federalism.

The central government used its power to shuffle the provincial ministries without reasonable justification. Moreover, though the Constitution provided some mechanism for interprovincial coordination and conflict resolution such as an interprovincial council for coordination and a tribunal consisting of one or more judges from the Supreme Court for conflict resolution, none of these institutions could be established during the lifetime of the 1956 Constitution. The distribution of resources was also not equitable and West Pakistan held significant advantage.

The Constitution of 1962—Federalism through Central Autocracy

The Constitution of 1956 remained in force for less than two years. It failed to bring national unity or political stability due to its inherent weaknesses and an inadequate and underdeveloped political sphere. Finally, martial law was imposed with Ayub Khan as Field Marshal and Iskandar Mirza as President. Neither could get along well with the other and eventually the former dismissed the latter. Ayub's contempt for parliamentary democracy was quite clear. He did not like it as, in his opinion, it did not suit the genius of the people of Pakistan and introduced a system of sham basic democracies. This step was hailed by many scholars of international repute, including Samuel P. Huntington.[10]

As the Constitution of 1956 had been abrogated and the system of government was being run under martial law regulation, Ayub wanted to give the country a constitution inclusive of his bigoted vision of democracy. A constitutional commission headed by Justice Shahab-ud-Din was established. The commission was to present recommendations for the Constitution along with some other duties. The commission recommended a presidential system with checks and balances, federalism with equal provincial autonomy, and bicameral central legislature, to name a few.

Ayub's remark upon receiving these recommendations—to the effect that the commission was not supposed to guide us about what to do as we already know what to do—indicates the commission's lack of an autonomous mandate. In the end, the Constitution provided for a presidential form of government with almost no checks and balances. In other words, federalism was provided with a very strong central government. The aforementioned analysis of the constitution-making process is quite helpful in understanding the devious contours of federalism envisioned by the framer. In the opinion of a number of political analysts, the true nature of a federal setup cannot be grasped completely without knowing the procedure of constitution-making—a spirit reflected in subsequent governance arrangements.

The Constitution of 1962 provided for a federal form of government. Pakistan continued to be a federation of two units. The central legislature (including the National Assembly and the Senate) was bicameral, with representation from both East and West Pakistan. There was only one list for the distribution of powers between the centre and provinces. Residuary powers were given to the provinces. Almost all the important powers were given to the central government. The distribution was also meaningless on another account because the centre retained the power of policymaking and regulation even on provincial subjects.[11]

Moreover, the governor was appointed by the president exercising his discretionary powers. The governor was not a nominal figurehead; he was the real provincial executive. He had the power to disregard any of the recommendations of provincial legislature. The governor was responsible to the president, and henceforth could only be removed by him. The centre was where all the authority lay and the provinces were not partners in the running of the state. Instead, there was a relationship of command and subservience and the central government was controlling the provinces indirectly.

According to Dr Waseem, military rule and federalism are not compatible with each other as they are motivated by two antithetical ideological frameworks. Militaries prefer centralization, whereas federalism is all about sharing and distributing, i.e. decentralization. While the 1962 Constitution maintained the federal structure, the spirit behind it was essentially unitary. According to data compiled by Waseem, the distribution of resources was highly schemed in favour of the centre and, to some extent, in favour of West Pakistan.[12] In the early 1950s, 80 per cent of total government expenditure was on West Pakistan and only 20 per cent on East Pakistan. In the late 1960s, Ayub Khan tried to make some amends by enhancing the share of East Pakistan to 36 per cent, but it was too little too late.

East Pakistan's Grievances—Rationalizing the Fall of Dhaka from the Federal Perspective

The military had a predominantly Punjabi character, in both numbers and outlook. However, from 1947, when the Bengalis accounted for only 1 per cent of the armed forces, the recruitment had been increased to 5 per cent in the army, 16 per cent in the air force, and 10 per cent in the navy by 1963. With only two out of 32 generals belonging to East Pakistan in 1968, that province was understandably alienated from the armed forces of Pakistan. Similarly, the civil servants who now dominated both wings of Pakistan had a predominantly non-Bengali character. No Bengali was appointed Chief Secretary of East Pakistan for 22 years after Independence. Among the civil servants in influential positions at the centre, there was not a single Bengali officer as late as 1968, as opposed to seven from Punjab, two from Urdu-speaking refugees from India, and one from NWFP.

Given the acute inequality in all the major fields, an extreme reaction from East Pakistan was both natural as well as logical. In these circumstances, the Awami League presented its own vision of federalism based on six points, allocating only defence, foreign affairs, and currency (under certain conditions) to the centre. These points attracted huge public support and manifested themselves in an impressive victory in the general elections of 1970. The Awami League won 160 out of 162 seats allocated to East Pakistan but failed to win even a single seat from West Pakistan. On the other hand, the most popular party of West Pakistan, won 81 out of 135 seats but did not contest even a single seat from East Pakistan. The election results depicted the extreme political polarity and cultural disconnect between East and West Pakistan. These election results and subsequent desperate military manoeuvres culminated in the separation of East Pakistan.

The Constitution of 1973—A Step Forward towards Federalism

The East Pakistan debacle changed the thinking about federalism in Pakistan. Smaller provinces decided to put the majority of Punjab to the test and limit it. Zulfikar Ali Bhutto from Sindh accommodated this demand by creating a bicameral central legislature, i.e. the Senate becoming the upper house and the National Assembly becoming the popularly elected lower house.

The Constitution of 1973 was different from the previous ones on many fronts. There were four federating units, a bicameral legislature, and no need for the principle of parity, among other things. The Senate, the upper house or the 'house of units', had almost equal legislative powers with the National Assembly but was very weak in fiscal matters. The Constitution was preceded by an accord between the Pakistan Peoples Party (PPP), Jamiat Ulema-e-Islam (JUI), and the National Awami Party (NAP). In this accord, JUI-NAP's right to form governments in NWFP and Balochistan was acknowledged. The appointment of a governor in the provinces was required to be made after consulting the provincial governments.

The issue of centre-province relations had always generated great controversy. The Constitution of 1973 attempted to resolve this controversy by dividing the powers between the centre and provinces on an equitable basis. Two lists, central and concurrent, were provided to distribute powers between the two tiers of government. The central list consisted of 67 subjects, whereas the concurrent list was given 47. Residual powers were given to the provinces. The parliament had exclusive jurisdiction over the matters delimited in the federal list, whereas both the centre and provinces had jurisdiction over the concurrent list. But if a provincial law on a concurrent subject conflicted with the central law on the same subject, the latter prevailed. The provinces, especially the smaller ones, always remained dissatisfied with the concurrent list, demanding its abolition. The list was abolished through the Eighteenth Amendment in 2010.

The Supreme Court of Pakistan, being the guardian of the Constitution as well as of the federation, was given a powerful role to resolve intergovernmental disputes. The power of judicial review to protect the Constitution and the power to appoint an arbitrator to resolve intergovernmental or interprovincial disputes were also assigned to the apex court.

Zia's Martial Law—The Military Strikes Back and Subsequent Path Dependence

The enactment of the Eighth Amendment by General Zia in 1985 gave birth to an era of complete negation of federalist principles, and instability ensued. It was an antidote to the federal character of the original constitution of 1973. The president became all-powerful and was legally authorized to remove the prime minister and dissolve the National Assembly at his discretion. The provisions to nominate the prime minister in a house elected on a non-party basis further strengthened his hold over the house, where he could force the members to elect his nominee or face the consequences.

The amendment led to an era of rule by weak political governments who were subservient to the military establishment, and culminated in another martial law in 1999.

A desperate attempt to rid the Constitution of this aberrant provision was made through the Thirteenth Amendment, withdrawing the clauses related to the presidential discretionary powers but, in essence, during these 15 years, the federal structure of the country had to undergo unbearable stress, resulting in weakening of the very basic legitimacy of the institutions of the state.

General Pervez Musharraf's martial law and his restoration of clause 58(2b) and the subsequent elections did not contribute at all in furthering the cause of federalism. The prime ministers functioned as long as they enjoyed the pleasure of the president or the military establishment. The provinces looked to the centre for all kinds of policies and finances. The provincial governments were ruled by the hand-picked politicians whose performance depended only on their proximity to the federal government and the office of the president. His local government reforms, in retrospect, were a façade employed by the military establishment to deeply entrench their grip over policy matters and power by operationalizing patronage networks. The lack of observance of the democratic principles in running the state resulted in lopsided policymaking, particularly in matters of security.

The Eighteenth Amendment to the Constitution of Pakistan—Federalism Returns

Eventually the Eighteenth Amendment, which was enacted and promulgated after the elections of 2008 by the coalition government led by the PPP, provided a return of pure federalism in the Pakistani context, at least in spirit. According to Khan, the amendment brought with it significant constitutional changes, particularly by devolving more responsibilities to the provinces, and shifting 18 federal ministries from the centre to the provincial level. Furthermore, federal and provincial responsibilities were clearly demarcated through two federal legislative lists so as to avoid informal centralization as in the past.[13] On the other hand, a semblance of parliamentary preponderance was also achieved through ridding the Constitution of the tampering done to it by military dictators.

The concurrent list was abolished and all its items were devolved to the provinces. All residuary or unlisted items of power were also shifted to the provinces, leading to unprecedented decentralization. The National Economic Council, an advisory body which tries to harmonize the economic ties between the centre and units as well as among units, was also restructured. With regards to operationalizing an emergency in a province, the constitutional mechanism was altered—the provincial assembly had to pass a resolution to legitimize such a course of action. Otherwise, if the president chose to impose an emergency in a province, the decision would need to be approved by both the houses of parliament within 10 days. Economic and fiscal autonomy of the provinces was greatly increased as a consequence of a review of Article 172(2), by adding that mineral and natural gas within a province or the territorial waters adjacent to it would be jointly and equally owned by the province and centre.

Fiscal Federalism under the Eighteenth Amendment

The National Finance Commission (NFC) Award under the Pakistan Muslim League-Nawaz (PML-N) and PPP governments (1991 and 1996) was agreed on the basis of consensus. In 1996, Nawaz Sharif enhanced the share of the province from 28 per cent to 45 per cent of the national divisible revenue. Punjab received 57.88 per cent, Sindh 23.28 per cent, NWFP 13.54 per cent, and Balochistan 5.3 per cent. Musharraf's regime failed to develop the much-needed consensus and therefore chose to impose it in 2006. Under that arrangement, the provincial share was kept at the same 45 per cent of the divisible pool while providing for one per cent increase per annum, rising to 50 per cent in the following five years.

A major breakthrough in fiscal federalism was achieved under the coalition government led by the PPP. The share of provinces under the 7th National Finance Commission Award was increased from 47 per cent to 50 per cent of the divisible pool for 2010–11 and 57.5 per cent for the following four years. Progressive criteria for the award benefited the provinces immensely. Factors such as poverty, revenue generation, and inverse population density, in addition to population, were recognized for the determination of the award. The award also changed the ratio of the provincial share: Punjab received 51.74 per cent, Sindh 24.55 per cent, NWFP 14.62 per cent, and Balochistan 9.09 per cent.

The Eighteenth Amendment has made it obligatory for the share of a province in the new award to never be less than what it was receiving earlier. There is also a provision for the annual monitoring of the implementation of the award. The Monitoring Report has to be presented to national and provincial assemblies and the provinces can raise loans to expand their revenue generation base. The Seventh NFC award has paved the way for rebuilding and strengthening fiscal federalism in Pakistan.

There is a provision for the National Finance Commission under Article 160 of the Constitution of Pakistan to transfer resources from the federal divisible pool to the provinces. The commission is not only responsible for vertical distribution, i.e. the total share of all the provinces in the divisible pool, but also the horizontal distribution, i.e. the share that each province enjoys.

The Council of Common Interests

The Council of Common Interests (CCI) was created in the 1973 Constitution and was proposed because it could harmonize relations between the centre and the units, serving as an intergovernmental institution for negotiation. However, with the rollercoaster ride between civilian and military rule, the institution remained ineffective at best, if its performance is gauged through the lens of conflict resolution, with only 11 meetings being held from 1973–2009. In theory, the Eighteenth Amendment empowered the CCI in ways never before imagined. According to Khan, the CCI supervises and regulates 22 matters specified in Part II of the Federal Legislate List (FLL).[14] These include national economic planning, the coordination of scientific and technological research, oversight of public debt, energy policy, and educational policy. The federal government can only legislate on these subjects after consulting with the provinces. The prime minister (who cannot delegate his role to a minister), the chief ministers of the 4 provinces, and 3 federal nominees are members of the CCI, whose meetings are scheduled every 90 days. The Council's secretariat is also supposed to be staffed in a manner representative of all provinces and regions, ensured through a quota system.[15]

Consequences of the Eighteenth Amendment

The massive devolution of items of power on the central list to the provinces created further challenges. The performance of the provinces in this regard has been sketchy at best—their lack of capacity in handling education, health, energy, and other important sectors related to public sector development has been exposed. The main victim has been law and order, where the provinces failed to allocate adequate resources.

The failure to create empowered local government institutions through devolution of fiscal powers, even after the election of these bodies, reflects a structural democratic deficit in formal constitutional terms. All provincial governments have amended their respective Local Bodies Act in an attempt to render them totally ineffective. Local bodies do not have any real autonomy in matters such as education and health. This approach of the legislators is itself a sign of the hangover being suffered as a result of historically operating under the tutelage of non-democratic forces and being resistant to change.

Conclusion

The journey of the project of federalism in Pakistan has been tumultuous—and the performance of Pakistan, if gauged under federal indicators, has been historically terrible—but its validity as the basic governing mechanism has never been questioned. Pakistan, to many scholars, took a wrong start by promoting the administrative institutions such as the military and bureaucracy at the expense of representative and political institutions. In the historical milieu of a glaring democratic deficit in the founding political party, and the decisions taken by the founding father after the inception of the state among other factors, Pakistan's experience with federalism was severely tortuous.

By the time the country was divided as the Eastern Wing parted ways, the overwhelming preponderance of Punjabi-centric ruling establishment was deeply entrenched, with the smaller provinces marginalized and their grievances heightened. The 1973 Constitution, which is still the basic constitutional framework for Pakistan, albeit with massive overhauls through amendments, was based around a broad political consensus and went a long way in rationalizing federal contours for state-running. In the decades that followed, extraconstitutional martial laws and hybrid quasi-democratic regimes enjoyed power—to the detriment of the federal project. It was only in 2009, after the passage of the Eighteenth Amendment to the Constitution of Pakistan, that a semblance of civilian and parliamentary preponderance could be observed, in relative terms, as provincial autonomy was increased, the project of fiscal decentralism moved in a progressive direction, and intergovernmental and representative institutions were empowered. But there is no endgame in the democratic consolidation project or federalism, and the

Pakistani state still needs to negotiate carefully with the challenges as well as the opportunities provided by the major overhaul post the Eighteenth Amendment. While this Amendment can be lauded for its spirit, its implementation has been sketchy at best. And that is where the real battle lies—for legislators as well as the citizenry of Pakistan.

Notes

1. Syed Jaffar Ahmed, *Historical Evolution of Federalism in Pakistan* (Islamabad: PILDAT, 2014).
2. Ayesha Jalal, *Democracy and Authoritarianism in South Asia: A Comparative and Historical Perspective* (Cambridge: Cambridge University Press, 1995), 18.
3. Jami Chandio, 'Features on Federalism,' *Strengthening Participatory Federalism and Decentralisation: Centre for Civic Education in Pakistan* (December 2013): 8.
4. Mohammad Waseem, *Politics and the state in Pakistan* (Lahore: Progressive Publishers, 1989).
5. Jalal, *Democracy and Authoritarianism in South Asia*.
6. Ibid.
7. Hamza Alavi, 'The State in Post-colonial Societies: Pakistan and Bangladesh.' *New Left Review* 74 (1972).
8. K. B. Sayeed, *Pakistan: The Formative Phase, 1857–1948* (Karachi: Oxford University Press, 1968).
9. Refer to the 1956 Constitution of Pakistan for an in-depth analysis.
10. Samuel P. Huntington, *Political Order in Changing Societies* (New Haven: Yale University Press, 1968), 251.
11. Ahmed, *Historical Evolution of Federalism in Pakistan*, 8.
12. Waseem, *Politics and the state in Pakistan*, 265.
13. D. L. Khan, 'Federalism and the Eighteenth Amendment: Challenges and Opportunities for Transition Management in Pakistan,' *Forum of Federations* 1 (2012).
14. Ibid.
15. Ibid., 6.

3

The Future of FATA and the Federation of Pakistan: The Ethnic Dimension

Rashid Ahmad Khan

Introduction

According to the Indian Independence Act of 1947, the federation of Pakistan was to consist of the Governor's provinces of East Bengal, Punjab, NWFP, Sindh, and the Commissioner's Province of Balochistan (Section 2, Subsection 2, Clause a, b, and c). Pursuant to the signing of instruments of accession by the states with the new dominion, the states of Bahawalpur (Punjab), Khairpur (Sindh), Kalat, Mekran, and Lasbela (Balochistan), and the states of Amb, Dir, Chitral, and Swat (NWFP) became part of the federation of Pakistan. The Interim Report of the Basic Principles Committee constituted by the First Constituent Assembly of Pakistan on March 12, 1949, presented in the Assembly in 1950 by Prime Minister Liaquat Ali Khan, described the federation of Pakistan as comprising the Governor's Provinces, the Chief Commissioner's Province of Balochistan, the capital of the federation, and such states that had acceded or might accede to the federation of Pakistan.

As far as the Tribal Areas of Pakistan were concerned, they were never considered as an integral part of British India and were variously referred to as 'excluded areas' or 'protected areas'. The British exercised control over these areas on the basis of mutually agreed treaties under which these areas were granted internal autonomy and financial assistance in exchange for peace and tranquillity on the border regions. On the eve of Independence, these treaties lapsed and the Tribal Areas became technically independent. However, the people of these areas, through their traditional decision-making mechanism, jirga, voluntarily joined Pakistan in 1947.

Under One Unit (1955), all these administrative units were merged into the province of West Pakistan to frame the 1956 Constitution on the basis of the principle of parity, except the Tribal Areas. The 1956 Constitution, while declaring the Tribal Areas as part of the federation of Pakistan, specified their special status (Article 1, Subsection 2, and Clause c) by identifying them as 'the territories, which are under the administration of the Federation but are not included in either province'. Under Article 103 of the 1956 Constitution, the Tribal Areas are designated as 'Excluded and Special Areas', to which neither an Act of Parliament nor that of a Provincial Legislature was to apply. Article 104 of the 1956 Constitution specified the manner in which these areas were to be administered by the Federation (President) through the provincial governor as his agent. Under this Article, sweeping powers were given to the provincial governor to administer the Tribal Areas. According to Article 104, Subsection 2:

> The Governor may, with the previous approval of the President, make regulation for the peace and good government of a Special Area, or any part thereof, and any regulation so made repeal or amend any Act of Parliament of the provincial legislature or any other law in force in the Area.

It is to be noted that the governor was to exercise these powers on behalf of and under the direction of the President. According to Subsection 4:

> The President may, from time to time, give such directions to the Governor relating to the whole or any part of the Special Area as he

may deem necessary and the Governor shall, in the exercise of his functions under this Article, comply with such directions.

Tribal Areas under the 1973 Constitution

The 1973 Constitution describes the Tribal Areas under Article 246 as:

(i)   the Tribal Areas of Balochistan and Khyber Pakhtunkhwa;
(ii) the former states of Amb, Dir and Chitral;

As far as the constitutional status of the Tribal Areas was concerned, the Article makes little change. However, it does make a distinction between the provincially administered and federally administered Tribal Areas. According to a senior civil servant of Pakistan, who also had long experience of working in the Tribal Areas as Political Agent, it was a partial reversion to the pre-1901 position (before the creation of NWFP as a separate province) when the governance in the Tribal Areas was the domain of the provincial authority in Punjab. Lord Curzon, famous for pursuing an aggressive 'Forward Policy' towards the Afghan frontier, had changed this arrangement and brought the Tribal Areas under the direct control of the Centre.[1] According to Article 246 of the 1973 Constitution, the Provincially Administered Tribal Areas (PATA) are:

(i)   The districts of Chitral, Dir, and Swat (which includes Kalam), the tribal areas in Kohistan district, Malakand Protected Area, the tribal areas adjoining Mansehra district and the former state of Amb; and
(ii) Zhob district, Loralai district (excluding Duki Tehsil), Dalbandin Tehsil of Chaghi district and Marri and Bugti tribal territories of Sibi District;

The Federally Administered Tribal Areas are:

(i)   Tribal Areas, adjoining Peshawar district;
(ii) Tribal Areas, adjoining Kohat district;

(iii)   Tribal Areas, adjoining Bannu district;
(iv)   Tribal Areas adjoining Dear Ismail Khan district;
(v)   Bajaur Agency;
(va)   Orakzai Agency;
(vi)   Mohmand Agency;
(vii) Khyber Agency;
(viii) Kurram Agency;
(ix)   North Waziristan Agency; and
(x)   South Waziristan Agency;

From this, it appears that a totally incongruent pattern of federalism has emerged in Pakistan since its independence in 1947. Balochistan was denied provincial status until 1970. It was ruled directly from the centre through the Agent to the Governor General. It was only when the second military ruler of Pakistan, General Yahya Khan, dissolved the One Unit on the unanimous demand of almost all political parties from West Pakistan that Balochistan was given provincial status. Since then, the province has had an administrative and political setup similar to other provinces of the country, but there are still certain areas where the provincial government does not enjoy direct powers. For the sake of administrative control and maintenance of law and order, the province is divided into two categories: A and B.

The tribal areas of Khyber Pakhtunkhwa (KP), formerly NWFP, present a more confusing picture. Here, there are areas which are in part federally controlled and in part provincially controlled. For example, the former Malakand Agency, which included Bajaur, Chitral, Dir, Swat, and the Malakand Protected Area, is now split up into Bajaur, which constitutes a tribal agency under federal control, as well as Chitral, Dir, and Swat as districts of the KP province. The position of Malakand Division is even more interesting. As a Protected Area, it is something in between a regular district of the KP province and a political agency under federal control. However, practically, it is the province which exercises full control over it. Darra Adam Khel, inhabited mostly by the Afridi tribe, suffers from an even greater anomaly. It is connected with two regular districts of Peshawar and Kohat by a 40-mile-long road passing through it for a few miles. This area is a federally controlled area where famous gun-making factories are located.

Article 247 of the 1973 Constitution provides the mechanism through which the Tribal Areas of Pakistan are to be governed. In continuation of the British tradition, the Article says that no Act of the Federal Legislature (Parliament is applicable to FATA unless the President so desires) or any Act of the Provincial Assembly applies to the areas unless the Governor so desires—and for that he must secure the prior consent of the President. This Article also authorizes the President to modify or amend any laws in force in the Tribal Areas. Both the President and the Governor have the authority to enact regulation with respect to the Tribal Areas under their respective jurisdictions. As provided under Article 104, Subsection 4 of the 1956 Constitution, Article 247, 6 of the 1973 Constitution also says that:

> The President may, at any time, by Order decide that whole or any part of a Tribal Area shall cease to be Tribal Area, and such Order may contain such incidental and consequential provisions as appear to the President to be necessary and proper. Provided that before making any Order under this clause, the President shall ascertain, in such manner as he considers appropriate, the views of the people of the Tribal Area concerned as represented in a tribal *Jirga*.

The provisions of Article 247 of the 1973 Constitution are in continuation of the provisions of the Indian Independence Act of 1947 and the 1956 Constitution. All these documents provide that the President possesses the legal authority to decide whether a Tribal Area can cease to exist but only after ascertaining the views of the concerned Tribal Area as represented in a tribal jirga. Since independence, the Tribal Areas of Pakistan have undergone a number of changes under the Order of the President and new political agencies and regular districts have been created. But there is no evidence that before making these changes, the views of the people of the Tribal Area concerned were ascertained, as provided for under Clause 6 of the 1973 Constitution. The fact of the matter is that the residents of the Tribal Areas have never been consulted before making any administrative changes in the map of the Tribal Areas. In both KP and Balochistan, the policy has been similar. The Federal Government has used its authority directly without consulting the provincial government or the people of the Tribal Area concerned. In this way, only a legal fiction has been maintained by designating them as Provincially Administered Tribal Areas.[2]

Although the Tribal Areas are part of the federation of Pakistan, their people are not entitled to enjoy the political, civil, and legal rights to which the people in other parts of the country are entitled. They have representation in the National Assembly and the Senate—the lower and the upper houses of Parliament—but no act of Parliament can apply to their areas. Geographically, they form a part of KP, which also provides all the manpower and expertise to manage the affairs of the areas in terms of development and administration, but the provincial legislature has no jurisdiction over FATA. The Governor of KP controls the areas on behalf of the Federal Government (President) through the FATA Secretariat.

The legal framework for governance is provided by the Frontier Crimes Regulation (FCR), which were originally issued in 1872 when FATA was under the control of Punjab. Following the separation of the frontier regions from Punjab and the creation of the new province of NWFP, a fresh Regulation was issued in 1901. This Regulation is still in force in FATA, although it was lifted in Balochistan and other parts of NWFP in 1956. A much-abused provision of FCR (Section 38.1) was abolished in 1963, but other equally repressive provisions of the Regulation of the colonial era still form the law of the land in FATA despite repeated calls for its replacement.

For example, Section 21 gives extremely vast powers to the Political Agent, who is the linchpin of the whole dispensation based on FCR.

Under this section, once the Political Agent has determined that a person or a tribe has turned hostile, he has three options available to him:

(1) The seizure and arrest of the proscribed tribe members or any of them or their property.
(2) The confiscation of any such property and the imprisonment of the persons seized.
(3) Preventing the tribe or the individuals of the districts from any intercourse or communication with the proscribed person or tribe.

On one hand, the Political Agent has been armed with the most arbitrary of powers; on the other, there is no judicial oversight since there is a bar on the jurisdiction of the superior courts. The FCR not only negates the basic human rights of the people of FATA, it also violates the age-old traditions of the tribal people based on *Pashtunwali* and *melmastia*.[3]

Consequences of Exclusion

Such repressive laws and regulation were applied by the British only to the Pashtuns and Baloch. There is thus an ethnic dimension of the policy of discrimination and exclusion. But, unfortunately, these laws have been retained even after Independence. The continuous exclusion of the Tribal Areas from the mainstream national development strategy has kept the areas underdeveloped, not only economically but also socially. Women have suffered the most as a result of social underdevelopment. For example, according to the data collected under the 1998 Census, the literacy rate in FATA is only 17.4 per cent, with 29.5 per cent for males and only 3 per cent for females. In 5 out of 7 political agencies comprising FATA, the literacy rate is even less than 3 per cent for females, and in the Frontier Region (FR) of Bannu, the female literacy rate is even less than 1 per cent (0.64).[4] In the field of health, the areas face similar problems. With a total population of over 3.5 million, the total number of doctors in FATA is only 450. Only 43 per cent of the total population has access to clean water for drinking and other purposes. The overwhelming majority of the population of FATA lives in rural areas. Only 2.7 per cent of the population lives in urban areas. Communication infrastructure and road density in the areas is also very low. It is at 0.17 km per square kilometre of area as compared to the national average of 0.26 km. Although it is better than the average in KP, which is 0.13, it has still not led to the economic development or poverty reduction in FATA.[5] Access to vital services and facilities remains restricted. Transportation of products to markets is hampered not only by lack of roads but also due to the clashes between the security forces and the Taliban belonging to the TTP and other militant groups.[6]

Ethnic Dimension

The ethnic base for the vast majority of the people of FATA is provided by the Pashto language. Pashto is spoken as a first language by 15.5 per cent (28–30 million) of Pakistan's 170 million population, according to the 1998 Population Census. Pashto-speaking people reside mostly in Khyber Pakhtunkhwa. There are also Pashto-speaking people in Balochistan. Karachi, the largest city of Pakistan and its industrial hub, has also attracted a large number of Pashto-speaking people. In fact, they constitute the third largest group (20 per cent) after Urdu and Sindhi speakers. Successive military operations launched against the Pakistani Taliban in the South and North Waziristan Agencies of FATA has led to the inflation of the Pashto-speaking population in Karachi, although some of them have also moved into the interior of Sindh.

There are two major dialects of the Pashto language spoken in Pakistan, the harder Pukhto, spoken in the northern parts of KP (Peshawar variety), and the softer Pashto, spoken in the southern parts of KP, FATA, and Balochistan. Pashto-speaking people are also found in adjacent areas of Punjab, Sindh, and Balochistan, who court it as their second language. But these Pashto-speaking people are not counted in the overall percentage of Pashto-speaking people of Pakistan. It is, however, KP which is a predominantly Pashto-speaking region. Provincially, the Pashto-speaking ethnolinguistic group known as Pashtun or Pakhtun constitutes 73.90 per cent, according the 1998 Population Census of Pakistan.

FATA is almost completely ethnically homogeneous, with Pashto-speaking people constituting 99.10 per cent of the population. These Pashto-speaking people are divided into about a dozen major tribes and several smaller tribes and subtribes. Uttamkhel, Mohmand, Tarkani, and Safi are major tribes living in the Bajaur and Mohmand agencies. Afridi, Shilmani, Shinwari, Mulagori, and Orakzai are settled in the Khyber and Orakzai agencies; while the frontier regions of Peshawar and Kohat are inhabited by Afridis. Moreover, the Turi, Bangash, and Masozai reside in Kurram Agency. The major tribes of North and South Waziristan are Darvesh Khel Waziris, while Mehsuds live in the central part of the region. The Bhitani tribe occupies the frontier region of Lakki and Tank, while the Waziris belong to Bannu. Other tribes of the region include: Utmanzai, Ahmadzai, Dawar, Saidgai, Kharasin, and Gurbaz. Lastly, Ustrana and Shirani live in Dera Ismail Khan.[7] All these major and smaller tribes are bound together in a vibrant tribal structure that permeates the cultural heritage of FATA.

Pashtunwali

The tribes of FATA have an honour code known as Pashtun, or *Pakhtunwali/Pashtunwali*. This is a code that has combined the tribesmen into a collective whole, curbing their individualism. The main characteristic of *Pakhtunwali* is that it enforces a rigid standard of behaviour for guiding the life of the community and determines the standard of behaviour of individuals and the tribe. It is a mixture of Islamic and local traditions—*rivaj*. *Rivaj* or local traditions are so strictly followed in the tribal society that in certain cases, as for example in relation to inheritance, *rivaj* takes precedence over religion.[8] *Pashtunwali* consists of certain principles. The foremost among them is embedded in the concept of *badal*. It means revenge with no regard to cost or consequences. It amounts to an obligation placed on an individual or a family which has been made a victim of an insult or injury. Owing to tribal linkages at the level of a tribe, clan, or subtribe, the insult generates an obligation which is to be redeemed through the actions of an individual or group. *Badal* has no limit in terms of time or space and the obligation remains until the revenge is obtained.[9]

The second component of *Pashtunwali* is the principle of *melmastia* or hospitality and protection offered to every guest. The tribesmen follow this tradition with a very strong passion without any expectation that it will be returned. This hospitality can even extend to an enemy if he enters the home of the host and asks for protection. This tradition can sometimes cause problems not only for tribesmen but also for the members of the administration or the powers dealing with Pashtuns. The reason behind Taliban's refusal to hand over Osama bin Laden to the United States to try him for his role in the 9/11 terrorist attacks on the United States was this principle of *melmastia*.[10] After 2004, Pakistani authorities faced the same embarrassing situation when some of the tribesmen in South Waziristan refused to expel foreign militants from their areas because they insisted that they were staying in their land as their guests.[11] Even during the British period, whether or not someone had committed an offence, they were able to escape the law if they had taken refuge with a tribal chief who was honour-bound to protect them under *melmastia*.

Despite long-standing tribal resistance to imperial encroachment from Central Asia as well as the Indian subcontinent, modern Pashtun ethnonationalism is the product of developments initiated by the arrival of the British in this region after their conquest of Sindh and Punjab in the nineteenth century. Before the British takeover, the north-western parts of India were under the control of the Sikh Empire of Maharaja Ranjeet Singh. But there was a difference between Sikh rule and British rule. The Sikhs never sought to establish sovereignty over the areas. They never, for example, entered Swat, Bajaur, Buner, the Kohistan valley, or Waziristan. The Maharaja had made ad hoc arrangements with the Khyber tribes to ensure safe passage, but no administrative authority was exercised which could be called permanent. The tribes were left free to manage their internal affairs.[12]

The British, who entered Peshawar in 1849 after defeating the Sikhs and annexing Punjab in 1849, established direct political links with the tribes of the north-western region. It brought to an end the long period of Sikh connection with the tribes living in the north-western regions of India, including the areas which now constitute FATA. The only problem the British faced was the continuing interference by the Amir of Afghanistan in the affairs of the Tribal Areas. To put an end to the continuous interference from Afghanistan, the British concluded a border agreement with Amir Abdur Rehman of Afghanistan known as the Durand Line in 1893.[13]

Although successive Afghan regimes, including the Taliban (1996–2001) and President Hamid Karzai, have refused to recognize the Durand Line as the international border between Pakistan and Afghanistan, for all practical purposes, it serves and is observed as the international boundary between the two countries. But it did become an issue of Pashtun ethnonationalism. During the 1950s and 1960s, it became the source of serious tensions between Pakistan and Afghanistan.[14] These were the heydays of Pashtun nationalism, which was based on Pashtun ethnicity and fired by issues such as the Durand Line. However, during the Soviet occupation of Afghanistan (1979–89), the issue lost its significance because of the overriding importance to the people of FATA of a common holy war against the Soviet occupation which rendered the Durand Line irrelevant. Over three million Afghan refugees eventually crossed the Durand Line to take shelter in Pakistan. Even after the Soviets had left

Afghanistan, it continued to be crossed at will by the people of the two countries. When the Taliban took over control of Afghanistan by capturing Kabul in 1996, they refused to meet the demand of the Pakistan government to show passports or other travel documents while crossing the international boundary between Pakistan and Afghanistan. Modern Pashtun nationalism is the reaction of the people of the Tribal Areas to British colonial rule and the changes introduced by them in the land tenure system that created a new class of small 'khans' having private ownership of the land, and a vast class of landless peasants who blamed the 'khans' as well as the British for their woes.[15]

As explained earlier, the British had placed the Tribal Areas under a separate system of political and administrative control based on FCR. According to the generally prevalent view, it was deliberately done by the colonial authorities for geostrategic reasons to serve as a buffer zone between the British Indian Empire and the Czarist expansion into Central Asia (Great Game) in the middle of the nineteenth century and later as a bulwark against Bolshevik Russia during the first half of the twentieth century.[16] However, the ethnic factor has played a more significant role not only in keeping FATA separate from settled areas under the British but also after the Partition of India and the establishment of Pakistan in 1947. FATA is ethnically much more homogeneous (over 99 per cent Pashtun) than KP, and the tribal code of honour referenced above, *Pashtunwali*, is followed here much more rigidly. This factor continues to hinder various efforts undertaken by the successive governments of Pakistan aimed at mainstreaming the Tribal Areas in the federal structure of the country.

Political Reforms in FATA

Although amendments to the FCR were made from time to time since its promulgation in 1901, they were of a minor nature and had little impact on the status of FATA in the new federation of

Pakistan. As the provisions relating to FATA in all the constitutions of Pakistan indicate, the British pattern of keeping the Tribal Areas as 'special areas' or 'excluded areas' continued to be followed. From 1947 to 1970, the Tribal Areas suffered complete neglect at the hands of successive governments in Islamabad. No attention was paid to uplift the areas and build a social and physical infrastructure to ameliorate the lives of the tribal people. However, during the first government of the PPP under Zulfikar Ali Bhutto, some development works were undertaken, including the construction of roads and the provision of electricity.

The first real change was brought about by the introduction of the adult franchise in 1996. The decision was taken by the caretaker government of Prime Minister Malik Meraj Khalid in view of the persistent demand by the political parties to extend this facility to the people of FATA. The extension of adult franchise to FATA led to the replacement of *malik*s and tribal elders as the electorate of the eight National Assembly constituencies by all adult men and women of the areas. This decision to extend the adult franchise to the Tribal Areas was vehemently opposed by the *malik*s and the tribal elders of the areas on the grounds that the people of the region were not ready to accept it and the system was being imposed on the people of FATA against their will. Their contention was proved wrong when an unexpectedly large number of both men and women thronged to the polling stations to exercise their right to vote for the first time in their history. A total of 1.6 million voters were registered, of whom 0.4 million were female. The eligible voters also included about 37,000 *malik*s. The number of contesting candidates and large voter turnout demonstrated the keen desire of the people of FATA to elect their representatives in a direct method of elections. In one Tribal constituency—NA 28 (Tribal Area II, Kurram Agency)—there were as many as 102 candidates.[17] This showed that, contrary to the claims by the *malik*s and tribal elders, the people of FATA welcomed the extension of adult franchise to their areas. All the subsequent parliamentary elections, i.e. 2002, 2008, and 2013, have been held in FATA on the basis of adult franchise. The number of constituencies has, however, been increased from 8 to 12.

These elections were, however, held on a non-party basis. The demand for party-based elections was therefore building up. Most of the political parties favoured allowing political parties to operate in FATA. PPP, which emerged as the largest party in the National Assembly following the 2008 elections, had committed itself to introducing political reforms in FATA, which included amendments in the FCR and the application of the Political Parties Act. These reforms were announced by President Asif Ali Zardari on August 27, 2011. Although these reforms were still considered insufficient, they proposed substantive changes in the prevalent legal and constitutional structure of the Tribal Areas. For example, for the first time in over one hundred years of the history of the region, political parties were allowed to function in FATA through the extension of the Political Parties Act. As a result, political parties were allowed to participate in FATA during the 2013 elections.

Under the reforms package, FCR Regulation III was amended to provide exemptions to children below the age of 16 and citizens above 65 years of age from punishments, such as arrest and detention, under collective responsibility. The reforms also proposed checks on arbitrary arrests and strengthened FATA Tribunals, where appeals could be launched against the decisions of the Political Agent. An appellate authority consisting of two commissioners was to be notified by the governor of the province. The 2011 reforms may have been modest in terms of their impact on the FCR-based political, administrative, and legal structure in FATA. However, they provided common ground for the political leaders of Pakistan and the citizens of the areas to interact and jointly launch a struggle for further reforms and full restoration of their democratic rights. These reforms have generated further demands for mainstreaming FATA through comprehensive political and constitutional reforms. The signing into law of the 2011 political, legal, and administrative reforms in FATA were, however, preceded by the issuance of two acts. The Action Regulation for FATA as well as PATA gave unprecedented powers to the armed forces of Pakistan combating terrorism in the Tribal Areas with retrospective effect from February 1, 2008, and allowed them to detain terror suspects for 120 days. These two notifications have been criticized as draconian regulation which essentially nullify the subsequently issued August 2011 FATA reforms.

The demand for political reforms in FATA even predates the establishment of Pakistan. In his meeting with Jinnah in New Delhi in June 1947, Khan Abdul Ghaffar Khan, the founder of the anti-colonial Pashtun *Khudai Khidmatgar* movement, had asked for a merger of the Tribal Areas with NWFP in exchange for his support to Pakistan that was to come into being only a couple of months later. Jinnah had agreed in principle but asked to ascertain the views of people of the areas on the issue of merger.[18] This, however, never happened. Hence, the FCR were never replaced with a more democratic alternative, and FATA remained outside of the federal framework of Pakistan. The political reforms of 2011 have amply demonstrated that the people of FATA are fully capable of exercising their democratic rights if provided the opportunity. The 2011 reforms, despite being modest, are a watershed in the history of FATA, and they are being termed as a new deal. But pressure for fully mainstreaming FATA through bringing about radical change in the legal, political, and administrative structure of the areas is growing. In this respect, various options are being considered.

Future Options

Broadly speaking, three options are being considered:

(1) FATA should be constituted into a separate province. This demand has been voiced by a group of *malik*s and tribal elders,

who fear the loss of their privileged position as a result of the merger of the areas with KP. But in view of the small size of the population, close geographical proximity, and the fact that the administration of FATA is carried out completely with the logistical support of civil servants from KP, this option is ruled out. Moreover, on economic grounds, FATA as a fifth province of Pakistan cannot sustain itself because it is poor in resources. FATA has only a small portion of cultivable land.

(2) FATA should be merged with KP. The Awami National Party (ANP) is the most ardent supporter of this demand. Their demand is based on both historical and geographical grounds. FATA's close geographical proximity with KP cannot be refuted. For example, Bajaur Agency is linked to Dir district, Mohmand with Charsadda, Khyber with Peshawar, and South Waziristan and North Waziristan with Dera Ismail Khan and Bannu. This kind of geographical linkage does not exist even between and among FATA agencies. On these grounds, the proponents of a FATA merger with KP assert that it should be part of KP. The FATA Secretariat, which carries out the administrative and developmental work in the Tribal Areas, is fully staffed with members of the KP provincial service. The provincial Governor as Agent to the President of Pakistan is responsible for managing the affairs of the areas. According to ANP, the current position of FATA is completely anomalous and the areas have deliberately been kept separate from KP in order to prevent the unification of Pashtun areas, fearing that it may become the base for resurgent Pashtun ethno-nationalism.[19] It may be mentioned that FATA, as compared to KP, is ethnically more homogenous, with 99.1 per cent of the population belonging to Pashtun ethnicity, whereas Pashtuns make up about 73.90 per cent of KP's population.

(3) Owing to stiff opposition from quarters with entrenched vested interests in the complete merger of FATA with KP, a third

option is being advanced. This proposes to grant maximum autonomy to FATA and mainstream the areas by raising the socioeconomic profile of the people of the Tribal Areas through development involving the construction of roads, new schools, hospitals, provision of safe drinking water, introduction of local government system, and empowering the women. This was the approach adopted by the Musharraf regime under which a large number of development schemes were launched by establishing a FATA Secretariat. Instead of completely eliminating FCR and merging FATA with KP, this option favours incremental changes in the FCR to gradually bring the people on a par with the rest of the country, enabling them to enjoy all the legal, political, and constitutional rights.[20] But this option has not received the support of political parties.

Conclusion

The Federally Administered Tribal Areas of Pakistan have long suffered neglect and discrimination, first at the hands of the British and, since 1947, by Pakistan due to the failure of successive governments to shed the colonial legacy symbolized by the notorious FCR. At the time of the birth of Pakistan, the country had other Tribal Areas apart from FATA, and the FCR was in force not only in Balochistan but also in certain parts of former NWFP. But this draconian law was lifted from these areas gradually. FATA remained the only part of Pakistan to which the authority of the Supreme Court of Pakistan did not extend.

There have been demands for bringing about change in the status of FATA by political parties and civil society organizations in the country. Some steps such as the introduction of adult franchise in 1996 and the reforms package of 2011 have been undertaken. These reforms are, however, very modest and there is increasing pressure for further reforms in FATA and for deciding the future status of the territories. Among these demands, the call for merging FATA with KP is the loudest and supported on the grounds of ethnic, cultural, and socioeconomic links. For example, the people of Bajaur agency have blood and business relations with the people of Dir and Mardan. On the same grounds, the people of Khyber agency are inseparable from the people of Peshawar. Charsadda has a sizeable population which belongs to Mohmand Agency. In the same way, the people of South Waziristan and North Waziristan have close and frequent interaction with the people of Kohat, Bannu, and Dera Ismail Khan.

Despite its existence for over a century as a 'special' or 'excluded' and separate administrative and political entity, FATA has not been able either to acquire a common identity or produce genuine leadership. This has been due to the absence of a democratic process in the areas. Before the extension of adult franchise, the members of the National Assembly were elected by an electorate consisting of 37,000 *maliks*. Small wonder that the MNAs or Senators from FATA, instead of articulating the interests of the Tribal Areas, were always known for their loyalty to a sitting government. Secondly, although 99.10 per cent of the people of FATA speak Pashto, they vastly differ from each other in terms of dress, accent, behaviour, and lifestyle. In contrast, the people of the tribal agencies geographically adjacent to the respective parts of KP have similarities in accent, dress, behaviour, and lifestyle.[21]

The future place of FATA in the federation of Pakistan is therefore most likely to be as a part of KP, and not as a separate province or a territory with a special status like Gilgit-Baltistan. This conclusion is based on the existence of close ethnic links between the people of FATA and the people of KP.

Postscript

On March 2, 2017, the Federal Cabinet chaired by then Prime Minister Nawaz Sharif approved the plan for the merger of FATA with KP as recommended by a Committee on FATA reforms headed by Advisor to the Prime Minister for Foreign Affairs Sartaj Aziz. The Committee was constituted in November 2015 and suggested merging the Tribal Areas of Pakistan into KP under a phased programme spread over a period of five years. During this period, a number of reforms and changes would be introduced in FATA to facilitate its integration with KP under a new system called *rivaj*. The recommendations of the Committee were earlier approved by a meeting of parliamentary leaders and discussed by Parliament.

The merger plan comprises a 24-point package under which, among other measures, FCR would be repealed and replaced with legislation for the new system of *rivaj*; the jurisdiction of Peshawar High Court and the Supreme Court of Pakistan would be extended; necessary constitutional amendments would be carried out to enable the people of FATA to elect their representatives for the KP Provincial Assembly in the next elections; and the National Finance Commission (NFC) would be requested to consider allocating 3 per cent of funds from the federal divisible pool to accelerate the pace of socioeconomic development in the Tribal Areas, in addition to the special FATA development fund announced separately.[22]

However, the fate of FATA still hangs in the balance. The government of PML-N had not been able to fulfil its commitment to integrate FATA with the KP province. This is largely because of severe opposition from the Jamiat Ulema-e-Islam-Fazl (JUI-F) and Pashtunkhwa Milli Awami Party. Both these parties have their support base in Pakhtun areas of KP and Balochistan and are also coalition partners of the PML-N government at the federal as well as provincial levels in Balochistan. They base their opposition to the merger plan on the plea that the people of FATA must be given an opportunity to express their views on their future. It is strange to find the Jamaat-i-Islami and Awami National Party on the same page regarding the future of FATA. Both these parties are in favour of a merger with KP. The merger plan is also being opposed by tribal elders. It is also speculated that the army has its own reservations on the merger plan and talks more about mainstreaming the areas than of the immediate merger with KP.

Notes

1. Humayun Khan, 'The Role of Federal Government and the Political Agent,' in *Tribal areas of Pakistan: challenges and responses*, eds. Pervaiz Iqbal Cheema and Maqsudul Hasan Nuri (Islamabad: Islamabad Policy Research Institute, 2005), 104. The proceedings of the seminar organized by Islamabad Policy Research Institute (IPRI).

2. Ibid., 106.

3. Khalid Aziz, 'The Frontier Crimes Regulation and Administration of the Tribal Areas,' in *Tribal areas of Pakistan: challenges and responses*, eds. Pervaiz Iqbal Cheema and Maqsudul Hasan Nuri (Islamabad: Islamabad Policy Research Institute, 2005), 125.

4. Haider Zaman, 'Problems of education, health and infrastructure in FATA,' in *Tribal areas of Pakistan: challenges and responses*, eds. Pervaiz Iqbal Cheema and Maqsudul Hasan Nuri (Islamabad: Islamabad Policy Research Institute, 2005), 73–4.

5. Ibid., 80.

6. The difficulties faced by the people in moving or transporting their goods from one place to another have been widely reported by both print and electronic media.

7. From the following government website, see https://fata.gov.pk/Global. php?ild=32&fId=2&pId=28&mId=13.

8. Aziz, 'The Frontier Crimes Regulation,' 119.

9. Ibid., 120.

10. Brenda Shaffer, *The Limits of Culture: Islam and Foreign Policy* (MIT Press, 2006), 281.

11. Shuja Nawaz, 'FATA—A Most Dangerous Place,' *Centre for Strategic & International Studies* (Washington, D. C.: New American Century Foundation, 2009).

12. Khan, 'The Role of Federal Government,' 102.

13. Ibid., 102.

14. Ijaz Hussain, 'Is the Durand Line Dead?' in a *Tribal areas of Pakistan: challenges and responses*, eds. Pervaiz Iqbal Cheema and Maqsudul Hasan Nuri (Islamabad: Islamabad Policy Research Institute, 2005), 159.

15. Adeel Khan, 'Pukhtun Ethnic Nationalism: From Separatism and Integrationism,' *Asian Ethnicity* 4, no. 1 (2003): 67–83.

16. Azmat Hayat Khan, 'Federally Administered Tribal Areas of Pakistan,' in *Tribal areas of Pakistan: challenges and responses*, eds. Pervaiz Iqbal Cheema and Maqsudul Hasan Nuri (Islamabad: Islamabad Policy Research Institute, 2005), 88.

17. Rashid Ahmad Khan, 'Political Developments in FATA: a critical assessment,' in *Tribal areas of Pakistan: challenges and responses*, eds. Pervaiz Iqbal Cheema and Maqsudul Hasan Nuri (Islamabad: Islamabad Policy Research Institute, 2005), 44.

18. Ibid., 25.

19. Selig S. Harrison, 'The Fault Line Between Pashtuns and Punjabis in Pakistan,' *The Washington Post*, May 11, 2009.

20. For arguments in favour of merger of FATA with KP, see Mohammad Anwar Nigar, 'Merge FATA with Khyber Pakhtunkhwa,' *FATA Reforms*, https://fatareforms.wordpress.com/2014/10/29/merge-fata-with-khyber-pakhtunkhwa-muhammad-anwar-nigar/.

21. Ibid.

22. For further details, see 'Federal cabinet decides Fata merger with KP,' *The News*, March 3, 2017.

4

Gilgit-Baltistan: State Security and Federalizing a Non-Federal Territory

Julie Flowerday

Introduction

The vision of Pakistan as a constitutional federal state that one day will embody a unified identity eludes Gilgit-Baltistan. Unlike Azad Kashmir, the latter territory has no place in any of Pakistan's constitutions.[1] Instead Gilgit-Baltistan exists at the margins of the state. It is entangled in a political nexus foremost between Pakistan and China—not Pakistan and India. In the discussion that follows, I limit my focus to Gilgit because its history is politically separable from Baltistan and because it lies at the heart of an unfolding situation that touches on Pakistan's national security. India's first Prime Minister, Jawaharlal Nehru, when asked about the value of the vale of Kashmir said the real jewel was Gilgit. Gilgit remains a key strategic location to both Pakistan and India but belongs to neither. Its present position as a Pakistani protectorate anchors the territory to Pakistan, yet even then its strength is also its weakness. As Hilali points out, 'Problems in the respective processes of nation-building and economic development are among the factors that constitute the roots of internal threats to security and stability of a region.'[2] The complication deepens when two different states (here Pakistan and China) carry out nation-building by co-opting state identification or evading state-centredness and by scaling its economic development to the state or a supra-state arrangement.

Accordingly, this chapter has a three-fold purpose: first, to recap a little-known history of Gilgit, which links Gilgit's unresolved political status to China and not colonial Kashmir; second, to relate Pakistan's concentration on nation-building and China's focus on economic development in Gilgit-Baltistan to competing schemes of state security; and third, to address the importance of residents' sentiments. It is concluded that the situation at Gilgit (Gilgit-Baltistan) is a tinderbox. Residents are caught in a conundrum that is neither negotiable nor foreseeably resolvable by either Pakistan or China. In addition to Gilgit, Pakistan, and China, there is India. India's colonial claims to Gilgit may be debatable but it remains tangentially critical to any resolution.

Gilgit History

Gilgit's unresolved political status exposes a little-known colonial history that discounts Pakistan and India's perceived rights of inheritance over Gilgit. At the time of Partition, the former Gilgit Agency—although in itself a legal governing instrument of British India—operated in territory that was not British Indian. The former Agency spatially approached what is today the Gilgit District. Elsewhere I have discussed the formation of the Gilgit Agency, which unfolded over the contested political status of Hunza.[3] I need only mention here that in 1891, British-led troops captured Hunza in a military campaign (Hunza-Nagar Campaign) and attempted to cut off China's tribute connection to it. It failed. In 1894, China resumed its exchange with Hunza and, after 1896, Britain physically withdrew all its personnel including road builders from Hunza and neighbouring Nagar. Thereafter, the British government never again had a resident official nor standing Indian troops in Hunza. From Gilgit Town, Britain exercised influence in producing a small mountain kingdom-state and ally to British India, which they named Hunza. Hunza remained the centre of British intelligence-collecting for Central Asia. However, some 50 years later at Partition, the former Gilgit Agency was neither autonomous (self-governing) nor was it British sovereign territory.

Based on this history, the Maharaja of Jammu and Kashmir's claim to the Gilgit Agency is questionable. In 1901, the British Indian government expressly and officially disqualified the Maharaja from their Gilgit Agency, explaining, 'The only portion of the Gilgit Agency, which is under direct control of the Darbar[4] is the Gilgit Wazarat comprising the tehsils of Gilgit and Astor and the *niabat* (deputy governor) of Bunji.'[5] The Wazarat was by comparison very small,[6] and significantly, the Maharaja's placement outside the Gilgit Agency never changed in the colonial period. In 1934, on the eve of Britain's leasing of the Gilgit Wazarat, Britain produced Regulation No. 1 of Samvat 1991 to create the *Praja Sabha*. This was a State Legislative Assembly for Kashmir that could make laws for the whole state or any part thereof—with certain restrictions. *Praja Sabha* had no power over matters dealing with the security of British India and 'matters of Frontier Policy including those relating to Ladakh and Gilgit'.[7] Hence, according to colonial Kashmir's constitutional law, Ladakh and Gilgit at all times existed outside the legal jurisdiction of the Maharaja and his state of Jammu and Kashmir.[8]

The other issue that never changed was Britain's failure to gain sovereignty over the territory of the Gilgit Agency. The distinction between de facto possession (practice that is not necessarily ordained by law) and de jure possession (legal rule that secures practice) assumes the presence of an agreement at some point between those involved in a struggle for control. But China never recognized Britain's claim of sovereignty, i.e. exclusive dominion over the region. More critically, the British-Chinese stalemate ended in an impasse. At the close of the colonial period, no Imperial British road traversed Hunza (Britain's proclaimed purpose for the 1891 Campaign)[9] and no border separated

British and Chinese territory at Hunza. Members of the colonial public and those of the post-Partition period were and are generally unaware of the earlier British-Chinese struggle and how it extended into the post-Partition era.

To ask why this alternate version of colonial history is not known is crucial. Colonial Britain took great pains to hide and later eliminate evidence of its dealings with China. For them, China was a dissolute pre-modern state that lay geographically at the margins of the Great Game (the play of British-Russian strategies of domination in Central Asia); thus by perceived state ranking, China was no match for them. Yet, it was not only the disappearance of documents and concealed state secrets that buried this hidden history—[10] it was the highly articulated horrors of the Kashmir Dispute. How might a little-known, emotionally detached analytical account of the Gilgit Agency based on political deception compare to the deeply embedded enmity wedded in bloodletting atrocities commemorating Pakistan and Indian Independence? Hence, the Kashmir Dispute shifts the discourse and its centre to Pakistan and India arguing over their perceived colonial inheritance. You must ask how can thousands upon thousands of books, White Papers, articles, life histories, and personal entries on the Kashmir Dispute be wrong?

After so much time, contemporary experts rely on other experts who have already centred their careers and writings on the Kashmir Dispute. By way of example, Martin Sökefeld conflates Britain's Gilgit Agency with the Maharaja's Gilgit Wazarat, thereby advancing a British-Kashmir diarchy of control that never happened.[11] Altaf Hussain similarly asserts a British-Kashmir diarchy and claims incorrectly that Britain leased the Gilgit Agency from 'the Kashmir State Government'.[12] Hermann Kreutzmann, in contrast, provides careful documentation of Pakistan's federation of the Northern Areas (renamed Gilgit-Baltistan in 2009) in 1974 which, he was cautious to point out, does not rest on Pakistan's constitutions. He does not, however, address the complications of its non-constitutionality. Lastly, the Government of India unites the Gilgit Agency with the Wazarat and claims that Gilgit and Ladakh (Baltistan) formerly belonged to the Maharaja and hence, following the latter's accession to India in 1947, now belongs to India. Whereas the Islamic Republic of Pakistan has no legal place for representatives of Gilgit-Baltistan in their National Assembly, the Republic of India maintains two open seats in its parliament.[13] China is scarcely mentioned as a contender in the Kashmir Dispute other than as a bothersome marginal power taking what it can get of the pickings. Contemporary accounts thus conflate the Kashmir Dispute with a range of agendas.

In spite of such obstacles, a very different history continues to emerge. In it, Britain formed the Gilgit Agency to capture Hunza in order to close-out China; the Maharaja of Jammu and Kashmir never had legal rights over the Gilgit Agency; and Britain never resolved its stalemate with China during the colonial period, and at Partition, there was no international border with China and Britain had no sovereignty over the territory of the Gilgit Agency. The Kashmir Dispute typically obscures other interpretations,[14] and since 1949, new issues demand attention. In 1974, the disputed region known as the Northern Territories became the Northern Areas, which residents regarded as an unofficial fifth province of Pakistan, and in 2009, it became Gilgit-Baltistan, a semi-autonomous governing entity. Notwithstanding these changes, the unresolved issue of sovereignty persists in the twenty-first century, which is the flaw that cannot be erased.

State Security

Pakistan's fixation on nation-building and China's fixed focus on economic development in Gilgit result in competing schemes of state security. For all intents and purposes, Pakistan and China's activities in Gilgit appear mutually agreeable, but they also underlie alternative strategies to state security. These notions are very different and go beyond critiques of the 'modern' state that debunk modernity as natural or even progressive but see it instead as a phenomenon arising under specific European, historical conditions. It is not the nineteenth century philosopher, Ernest Renan, who challenged the [un]naturalness of the state that is relevant here, but anthropologist Clifford Geertz's question, 'What Is A State If It Is Not Sovereign?'[15] His question helps to spotlight the fetish of state bordered-territory[16] underlying a Euro-centric notion of sovereignty that persists as a legacy of colonial rule. International law defines sovereign states as having a permanent population, defined territory, one government, and the capacity to enter into relations with other sovereign states.[17] A bordered territory, moreover, contributes to managing defence, workforces, consumers, and citizens, which turns the discussion back to Gilgit as its international border is not fixed and it is not a constitutionally sovereign territory of Pakistan. The neighbouring country under consideration is China, whose notion of state sovereignty is very different. Whereas borders are essential to Pakistan, they are nuisances to China and its policy of economic development. This difference leads to competing, not complementary, schemes of state security at Gilgit. Pakistan orders itself alongside state bordered-territory; China systematizes itself by sustaining open alliances. A brief comparison follows.

Pakistan

Pakistan's policy of state federation is key to its attempt to incorporate Gilgit-Baltistan. Federation dictates producing the protectorate as a province and developing its residents' identity to default to state practices. Indeed, federation parallels Michel Foucault's notion of 'governmentality' whereby government constituted institutions become inseparable from people's daily lives.[18] A person's comprehensive identity is based on state laws and entitlements. People's actions, intentions, and sentiments become the scrutiny of the state, which disciplines through interiorizing people's lives. It happens 'naturally' by growing up in a school system, watching elders making a living, honouring a national flag, and patriotically standing for the national anthem. Federating a territory is subtle but effective in capturing people's worth and sense of belonging. Security is borne within and carried by its constituents. The flaw lies in Pakistan's lack of sovereign authority which governs federalization.

A full discussion of Pakistan's federation process at Gilgit is not possible here. Some highpoints include the initial landmarks made by Sir Sultan Muhammed Shah, Aga Khan III (1877–1957), followed by his grandson, Prince Shah Karim Al Hussaini Aga Khan IV (1936), in developing roads, schools, health, and education facilities. Prime Minister Zulfikar Bhutto (1973–7) led the government in efforts to incorporate the territory as a province by dismantling small colonial states and inducting them in the Northern Areas and by ending the Frontier Crimes Regulation (FCR) and instituting the Advisory Council governed by the Federal Minister of Kashmir Affairs (1974). Under Bhutto, the divisions of the Northern Areas comprised Gilgit, Baltistan, and two other districts of Ghizer and Ghanche.[19] President General Ziaul Haq (1977–88) succeeded Bhutto and reorganized the Northern Areas into three districts and imposed martial law. Under the later rule by Prime Minister Benazir Bhutto (1988–90 and again 1993–6) and Nawaz Sharif (1990–3), there were protests, demonstrations, and strikes that gave momentum to the formation of a regional movement.[20] The century ended with the Pakistan Supreme Court's verdict on local residents' attempt to make the Northern Areas an official province—which it deferred until there was settlement by Pakistan and India over the Kashmir Dispute.[21] In this period, the prescribed terminology within the Government of Pakistan was that: 'The areas constitute an integral part of Pakistan, but is not a federating unit'.[22]

Overall, Pakistan's policy of reproducing the state inside a non-sovereign territory appeared effective. Residents now hold National Identification Cards (NIC), carry Pakistani passports, use Pakistani credentials for driving vehicles, and define their professional and other qualifications by the state. District and Assistant District Commissioners reside in and represent the region; a Federal Minister oversees state matters; school children start their day by pledging allegiance to Pakistan and invoking the state prayer; and there is open access to Pakistan (that is, the area south, referred to as 'down-country'). Residents exist within a simulated state model of bordered-territory, but there remains a problem.

In August 2009, the Government of Pakistan introduced the Gilgit-Baltistan Empowerment and Self-Governance Order through a presidential order approved by its Federal Cabinet, and the government has used the Gilgit and Baltistan Legislative Assembly to develop parallel state institutions. The Order bears signification of presumed constitutionality (a presidential order approved by the Federal Cabinet); nevertheless, it fails in making Gilgit a sovereign part of Pakistan. Residents have no representation yet in the National Assembly, no right to vote in national elections, and no representation in Pakistan's Supreme Court. The contemporary circumstance approaches the situation faced by Britain at Partition. As international law governs sovereignty, any attempt by Pakistan to legitimate Gilgit (Gilgit-Baltistan) as de jure/de facto requires recognition by China and India. This has not happened.

China

It is interesting that in 1949 Chinese delegates of Chiang Kai-shek (Kuomintang) sat alongside the member state representatives of Great Britain and the United States of America in the UNSC that mandated a Pakistani protectorate. The undisclosed agreement prevents Pakistan from changing the political status of that protectorate. The issue here, however, is China's alternate and competing system of state security, a difference that arose possibly from China never having been successfully colonized. The Qing Dynasty, for example, had a complex order of relationships distinguished by Inner and Outer China. Outer China interlocked and interiorized other societies that came into contact with its empire. The Qing Dynasty's notion of ultimate supremacy, which it inherited from earlier dynastic practices, placed the emperor at a symbolic centre to which all other people of Outer China attached themselves through tribute relations described by *huiguan*. The practice was efficient. As dynasties changed, other relations at the margins fluctuated temporarily and conditionally. The outer margins never depended on fixed borders. In Xinjiang, for example, the closest tradition to a boundary was the *karun*, a Manchu term signifying guard-posts positioned on the routes and passes that were frequently used by travellers entering or leaving Qing territory.[23] Without intentionally oversimplifying, a pre-Qing notion of state was not generally about capturing, creating, and sustaining boundaries to territories over which they attached exclusive rights. Instead, China prioritized a metaphysical orientation to itself. It was 'the' centre, the hub that managed those in alignment to it through the extension of deep bonds of allegiance.

The difference of the colonial state and the Chinese state blinded Europeans from understanding divergent constructions. From a common Euro-progressive nineteenth century perspective, China was backward. It lacked 'modern' technological expertise, it had no industrial infrastructure, and had no interest in pursuing either. By European standards, China was evolutionarily inferior. Karl Marx premised that some forms of state, which ruled by tribute-collecting despots and depended on a system of production-property relations, were non-progressive. In particular, he said, 'Asia fell asleep in history.' The Asiatic states of China and India were decadent in their confrontation with Western capitalism and remained unchanged until stirred by the West.[24] Similarly, Sir Alfred Comyn Lyall (1835–1911) wrote, 'If Asians were organized, like Europeans, into sovereign nation-states, then it would not be legitimate for the "governing class" of another nation-state such as Britain, to impose "foreign rule" on them.'[25] For Europeans, the modern state left all other constructions lagging behind.

Hunza was caught between these two very different worldviews: Britain wanted to incorporate Hunza as a bordered sovereign territory. China wanted to maintain its tribute relations and open alliances. China's notion of 'tribute alliances' has been symbolically updated to other terminology but the imperial view of state and its ability to expand/contract persists. Unlike Pakistan, China's state security model is not based on bordered-territory. Its focus on economic development does not depend on borders; indeed, borders get in the way. As the late Owen Lattimore pointed out, China has an uneasy relation with bordering independent polities. It denies closure with an eye to opening, not closing off, territories. For lack of terminology, China's security system is a 'forward economic policy'. The Karakoram Highway (1960–78), which connects the capitals of Pakistan and China, is but one example of this forward policy. More recently, China's projected trans-communication line, the China Pakistan Economic Corridor (CPEC), passes from Xinjiang through Hunza to Gwadar (Balochistan), thus bisecting Pakistan from the high snowy Pamir, Karakoram, and Himalayan Mountains to the warm waters of the Arabian Sea. Such developments open, not close, China from its neighbour.

The question one may be asking is whether Pakistan attempted to establish a border with China. Commentators like Altaf Hussain say that it succeeded, but that cannot yet be substantiated. On March 2, 1963, Beijing released a document titled, 'People's Republic of China-Pakistan. Agreement on the Boundary Between China's Sinkiang [Xinjiang] and the Contiguous Areas'. In Article 6 of the agreement, China clearly stated that it would be signatory to a boundary treaty only after the resolution of the Kashmir Dispute between India and Pakistan.[26] That boundary does not yet exist. There is, of course, irony in this situation. Chinese officials at some level know that Pakistan and India cannot resolve the Kashmir Dispute without them. It makes China's agreement to agree on a border treaty seem false-hearted; or maybe, it is one more attempt on their part to force India to recognize China's territorial claims; or maybe it is their effort to grow inside Pakistan as an outside power in much the same way that Britain reproduced itself in the heartland of British India. Or maybe it reflects a very different worldview, one that does not support bordered-territory and is not encumbered by Euro-centric notions of state. In critiquing Beijing's released document, W. M. Dobell pointed out that the boundary on the map proposed by China was not the same as the boundary imagined by Pakistan which, needless to say, was not the boundary or map envisaged by India.[27]

China's state security system, moreover, dictates friendship alliances. Legacies of colonial sovereignty, constitutionality, and boundaries may be unnecessary constraints. Oneness lies at joining with the centre, not the centre replicating itself inside its units (as in federation). It is a very different way of thinking that draws from a Chinese historical image. The emperor lives. In place of the symbolic head, it is now the majesty of the nation-state that proclaims a timeless ideology of oneness of geography, people, and traditions of civilization.[28] This very different worldview of state security advances transit lines of communication that pass through Hunza and bisect Pakistan to open the country. Chinese state security creates thoroughfare alliances to its centre. It does practice state conversion of people by recruiting students and partnering businesses, but these efforts are presently at the low-end of its economic development. The high-end is the Karakoram Highway (KKH) (1978), its purported 50-year lease of tracts through Hunza and Gilgit-Baltistan (2013), and the ongoing construction of CPEC through Pakistan to Gwadar, Balochistan (2015–). Such roads and routes require constant vigilance, maintenance, repair, improvements, trained technicians, recruitment of workers, and such—rather like the radiating roads of Rome. Retrospectively, patience is crucial. Whereas China interrupted Britain's effort to build an imperial road through Hunza (1891 Campaign), it later succeeded in connecting Islamabad and Beijing (KKH).

Sentiments

In the pre-Partition period, Hunza was caught between two very different worldviews: Britain wanted to contain Hunza as a sovereign territory; China wanted to maintain its tribute relations and open alliances. The people of Gilgit (-Baltistan) are similarly trapped. Pakistan desires a border to be complete; China values open access. I began this chapter with Hilali's observation that problems in nation-building (Pakistan) and economic development (China) are among the factors that constitute the roots of internal threats to security and stability of a region. This is especially striking when there is more than one state involved in the affairs of a resident population which exercise different strategies for securing the area. Hilali adds yet another germane consideration that internal cultural threats 'pose greater threat to the internal stability of a country than do external threats or aggression'.[29] So what is happening inside Gilgit? What are people's sentiments?

Young scholar-researchers of Gilgit-Baltistan are interested in such questions as demonstrated by the following two examples. The first researcher visited Gilgit Town at the time of its regional elections a few years ago and found people shy about voicing their thoughts openly. They were, however, aware that the autonomous provincial assembly was not the same as the assemblies in Pakistan's proper provinces and believed that Gilgit-Baltistan was a puppet assembly of the federal government. There was also the suspicion that the timing of the election (winter) coincided with the time that the fewest members of the local intelligentsia were present.

The second scholar-researcher carried out a small investigation on stateless identity.[30] The investigator interviewed 13 students (men and women): eight attending universities inside Pakistan and five at a university and colleges in Gilgit-Baltistan. They came from different political divisions—Gilgit Town, Nagar, Hunza, Upper Hunza (Gojal), Ghizer, and a location in Baltistan. The researcher was surprised to learn that students studying inside Pakistan were more anxious about their stateless status than those living inside Gilgit-Baltistan. Those living inside Gilgit-Baltistan were little aware of state-non-state differences and did not feel the same stress. The researcher further confided that the situation was, for some students, highly embarrassing:

> when on media or anywhere else ... [people] are discussing the full-fledged four provinces and three non-provincial units, namely FATA, Azad Jammu and Kashmir, and the Islamabad capital territory, Gilgit-Baltistan is never named. The embarrassment for a citizen [resident] reaches its peak when the Pakistani person in front [of them] does not even know what on earth Gilgit-Baltistan is.

After a pause, the researcher continued,

> The still [continuing] statelessness of Gilgit-Baltistan may be the fault of its citizens [residents]. But if this is the case and the people of Gilgit-Baltistan realize it, the realization of this fact ... that ... if it is self-fault [means that] it is self-solution.[31]

According to the researcher, Gilgit-Baltistan would (if necessary) stand on its own independently but, if that were not possible, some looked on China not Pakistan favourably. That is, although some students in his study faulted Pakistan for Gilgit-Baltistan's statelessness, they did not necessarily look to Pakistan for a solution.

It was a small investigation but it deserves attention because, if the young scholar-researcher is right, grievances of regional identity are now spreading through villages and intensifying with literacy throughout Gilgit and Baltistan. Melancholy filled the researcher's thoughts in recounting:

> Neither it [Gilgit-Baltistan] is part of Pakistan nor is it not. Neither it is autonomous nor is it not. It has a separate legislative assembly of its own but it is governed by the federal directly at the same time. Neither it is not disputed like Jammu and Kashmir nor is it undisputed like

FATA ... Thus, neither is Gilgit-Baltistan a state, nor is it not ... It is a state and it is stateless at the same time. Gilgit is a paradox.[32]

Dilemmas of statelessness keep the Kargil War (1999) fresh in the minds of Gilgit-Baltistan residents. Beyond the abject sorrow that drained households of their young, the Pakistan government initially denied that those who fought and died in the war belonged to the state. For many years, the Pakistan government paid no homage to Gilgit-Baltistan heroes and troops lost in the Kargil War. The Pakistan Army insisted that none of its regular soldiers were involved in the hostilities of the war, but after 11 years, it added the names of 453 soldiers and officers killed in the Kargil War to 'a list of thousands of personnel killed while on duty [which has] been posted in the '"*Shuhada*'s Corner" (Martyrs Corner) on its website'.[33] A majority of those who died were soldiers from the Northern Light Infantry, an irregular regiment only recently 'made a regular regiment of the Pakistan Army because of its performance in the 1999 conflict'.[34] What are the narratives that people in Gilgit-Baltistan create to explain the Kargil War and to what other sources do they scale them? What are the narratives that residents will write of Gilgit-Baltistan? The discussion of sentiments of discontent is not reducible to an ethnic category, religion, language, or any other single or divisive category. At this broad scale, sentiments concern state identity at a time when states claim close to 99.9 per cent of the earth's land mass and seabed.

Conclusion

The situation at Gilgit (Gilgit-Baltistan) lingers indeterminately, which may produce a tinderbox as residents are caught in a conundrum that does not include their voice and does not appear, foreseeably, to be resolvable by Pakistan, China, and India. The interconnected issues of the unresolved conflict between colonial Britain and China, the present competing state security schemes of Pakistan and China, and the future of the people of Gilgit (Gilgit-Baltistan) now depend on three state players—Pakistan, China, and India—as well as the people of Gilgit-Baltistan. With hope, the present writing on state security systems contributes to exploring what can happen next in building pathways to peace and resolution.

Notes

1. Many state systems throughout the world hold territory that they do not mention in their constitutions and many also contend with unresolved political sites, which is particularly relevant in South Asia following the withdrawal of colonial powers.

2. A. Z. Hilali, 'Confidence- and Security-Building Measures for India and Pakistan,' *Alternatives: Global, Local, Political* 30 (2005): 55.

3. Julie Flowerday, 'Identity matters: Hunza and the hidden text of Britain and China,' *South Asian History and Culture* 10, no. 1 (2019): 46–63.

4. Darbar/Durbar: a feudal state council for administering the affairs of a princely state.

5. I. O. R. 'Gilgit Agency,' File No. 97-C, 1927, Letter No. 1800-F, July 24, 1901, Appendix I: 7. Darbar was alternately used for the Maharaja's Wazarat headquartered at Gilgit.

6. Rai Bahadur, Anant Ram, and Hira Nand Raina, *1931 Census of Jammu and Kashmir State*, Part I, Volume XXIV (Jammu: Ranbir Government Press, 1933), 59. According to the 1931 British Government Census, the Wazarat accounted for 3,112 square miles, 82 villages, and a population of 31,902, roughly 10 people per square mile. Only half a per cent of the area was under cultivation and wheat took up one-third of the total cultivation. The Wazarat comprised the *tehsils* (municipalities) of Gilgit and Astor and the *niabat* (deputy governor) of Bunji. Wazarat headquarters were Gilgit Town. By contrast, the agency covered 14,680 square miles, over three times as large as the Wazarat. The Agency comprised the political districts of Hunza (1891), Nagar (1891), the Shinaki Republics of Chilas and Gor (1893), Yasin (1895), Punial (1895), Kuh-Ghizar (1895), and Ishkoman (1895). It was also headquartered at Gilgit Town.

7. The *Praja Sabha* could make laws for the whole state but it was not lawful for it 'to consider or deal with any matter or enact any law relating to or affecting: (a) His Highness or any member of the Royal family or the management of the Royal household; (b) relations, treaties, conventions, or agreements between the State and His Majesty the King Emperor of India or with Foreign Powers or the Government of any State in India now subsisting or in force or hereafter to be

established or made; [and] (c) matters of Frontier policy including those relating to Ladakh and Gilgit'. Hilali, 'Confidence- and Security-Building Measures,' 50 and 55.

8. In the colonial period, the terms 'sovereign' and 'suzerain' were problematical as Native State rulers, chiefs, and Her Majesty's Government all used them. Viceroy Lord Dalhousie objected to both terms in 1904. He argued that 'the rights commonly associated with sovereignty [and suzerain] will be found, as time passes, to be increasingly incompatible with the future development of the Indian Empire' (I. O. R. L/P&S/18/D169: 1). The paramount power was British India. Accordingly, based on the 1889 Interpretation Act, (which adopted the phrase suzerainty), 'in every act where the word India occurs the statutory employment of suzerainty is involved' (Ibid., 2). Presently, some political scientists reserve 'sovereignty' for the territorial-based Euro-state that took root in fifteenth century Westphalia Conference.

9. On November 29, 1891, Colonel Durand sent a letter to the ruler of Hunza and another to the ruler of Nagar in which he claimed the right to build roads through their territories in order to safeguard the Empire against Russian advances. Durand gave them a 3-day ultimatum and added that 'the Supreme Government troops will enter your territory and the road will be constructed in spite of any opposition you may offer' cautioning that 'no refusal on your part to permit us its construction will be accepted. The road must be made' (I. O. R. P/L&S/18 A.83).

10. An eyewitness account tells of seeing documents at the colonial headquarters at Gilgit Town burned and the ashes emptied in the Gilgit River.

11. See Martin Sökefeld, 'From Colonialism to Postcolonial Colonialism: Changing Modes of Domination in the Northern Areas of Pakistan,' *The Journal of Asian Studies* 64, no. 4 (2005): 939–73.

12. See Altaf Hussain, 'Azad Kashmir is not the Islamic Republic of Pakistan,' *Gilgit-Baltistan Empowerment and Self-governance Order 2009* (December 2009). Hussain ignores Britain's partition of the Gilgit Agency from the Maharaja (1901) and erroneously claims that: '[The] British government took possession of Gilgit Agency from the Kashmir State Government through a lease agreement for 60 years on March 29, 1935 and returned back the area to the State Government on August 1, 1947, following the decision of British Government of dividing the subcontinent into two sovereign states of India and Pakistan. During the joint rule by British and Dogras the area was administratively divided into Gilgit Wazarat and Ladakh Wazarat'.

13. No seats are reserved for the region in the Pakistan Parliament. The Indian Constitution, on the other hand, includes Azad Kashmir and the Gilgit-Baltistan region in the Indian Union, and the state constitution of Indian-held Jammu

and Kashmir has reserved 25 seats for them. See Ershad Mahmud, 'Status of AJK in Political Milieu,' *Policy Perspectives* 3, no. 2 (2006): 105–23.

14. Accounts of the Kashmir Dispute typically include the Gilgit Rebellion (October 1947), the Maharaja's accession to India (October 1947), and what is commonly called the First Indo-Pak War (1949) that commemorated Pakistan and India's independence. On India's provisional accession of Kashmir and Pakistan's non-obligatory plebiscite, see Sumathi Subbiah, 'Security Council Mediation and the Kashmir Dispute: Reflections on Its Failures and Possibilities for Renewal,' *Boston College International and Comparative Law Review* 27, no. 1 (2004): 173–85.

15. Clifford Geertz, 'What Is a State If It Is Not a Sovereign? Reflections on Politics in Complicated Places,' *Current Anthropology* 45, no. 5 (December 2004): 577–93.

16. State-bounded territory approaches a system of containment, which I avoid using. I am grateful to Professor Hank Kennedy for pointing out that 'containment' belongs to the US and USSR's Cold War policies.

17. The Convention on Rights and Duties of States, December 26, 1933, http://www.oas.org/juridico/english/treaties/a-40.html.

18. Michel Foucault, *Power: The Essential Work of Michel Foucault 1954–1984*. Volume 2 (London: Allen Lane, 2000).

19. Hermann Kreutzmann, 'Kashmir and the Northern Areas of Pakistan: Boundary-Making along Contested Frontiers,' *Erdkunde* 62, no. 3 (2008): 209.

20. Ibid., 209–10: '… a Movement for the Determination of the Constitutional Position of Northern Areas was formed calling for constitutional integration of the Northern Areas into Pakistan and electoral rights for the population'.

21. It is curious why Altaf Hussain deceptively quoted the Azad Jammu and Kashmir High Court Decision (AJ&K HC May 29, 1999) and not the Pakistan Supreme Court. He writes that AJ&K HC recognized Northern Areas as a 'constitutional part of the state of Jammu and Kashmir … that the people of the Northern Areas are citizens for all intent and purposes'. See 'Azad Kashmir is not the Islamic Republic of Pakistan,' 3.

22. Kreutzmann, 'Kashmir and the Northern Areas of Pakistan,' 210.

23. Laura Newby, *The Empire and the Khanate: A Political History of Qing Relations with Khoqand c. 1760–1860* (Leiden; Boston: Brill, 2005), 14, 39, and 31–2. The guard-post that provided rights of protection in support of trade, tribute exchange, and sanctuary. It was positioned at strategic points within Xinjiang [Huijiang], for example, along the south of Tianshan in the border zone of the Qing Empire.

24. Later Lenin paved the way for the feudal interpretation of China in his statements at the Second World Congress of the Comintern in 1920. China and other Eastern countries, according to him, were no longer Asiatic but semi

colonial countries in which 'the oppressed masses [of colonial and backward countries] are not only exploited by a merchant capital, but also by feudal rulers, and by the state, on a feudal basis'. See K. A. Wittfogel, 'The Marxist view of China (Part 2),' *The China Quarterly* 12, no.1 (October–December 1962): 154.

25. Ronald B. Inden, *Imagining India* (Oxford: Blackwell Publishers, 1990), 176; and refer to Sir Alfred C. Lyall, *Asiatic Studies* (London: John Murray, 1899), 221–2. Lyall was rebuking Edmund Burke's critique of the East India Company being like the German Empire in its 'forcible domination of one clan or family over other races or tribes'.

26. Article 6 states, 'The two Parties have agreed that after the settlement of the Kashmir dispute between Pakistan and India, the sovereign authority concerned will reopen negotiations with the Government of the People's Republic of China, on the boundary, as described in Article Two the present Agreement, of Kashmir, so as to sign a Boundary Treaty to replace the present Agreement,' The People's Republic of China-Pakistan. Agreement on the Boundary Between China's Sinkiang and the Contiguous Areas, Peking, 2 March 1963, *The American Journal of International Law* 57, no. 3 (July 1963): 716.

27. W. M. Dobell, 'Ramifications of the China-Pakistan Border Treaty,' *Pacific Affairs* 37, no. 3 (Autumn 1964): 288. It is noteworthy that Altaf Hussain, like many earlier commentators, confuses Treaty and Agreement and presumes that no further deliberation would be needed.

28. Zhang Xiaomin and Xu Chunfeng, 'The Late Qing Dynasty Diplomatic Transformation: Analysis from an Ideational Perspective,' *Chinese Journal of International Politics* 1, no. 3 (2007): 409. Xiaomin and Chunfeng argue that *huiguan* (a Sino-centric world view) was the keystone of the tributary system.

29. Hilali, 'Confidence- and Security-Building Measures,' 74.

30. The researcher asked the following questions: How do you define your identity? How do you associate Gilgit-Baltistan residents by identity? How important is it to belong to a nation? What kind of problems do residents of Gilgit-Baltistan face because of statelessness? And why is Gilgit-Baltistan stateless?

31. Interviewed May 2014, Lahore, Pakistan.

32. M. A. C. (pseudonym), May 2014.

33. Press Trust of India, 'Pakistan Army admits to Kargil martyrs,' *NDTV*, November 18, 2010.

34. Ibid.

5

Autonomy-seeking Movements in Balochistan and the Role of the Federal Government

Mussarat Jabeen

Introduction

Balochistan, a land of diverse cultures and traditions, is the largest province, with 44 per cent of the total area and 5 per cent the population of Pakistan. Its coastline stretches 770 kilometres, sharing borders with Afghanistan and Iran. It is dominated by three major ethnic groups. Among them, the Baloch are in the majority, closely followed by the Pashtuns. There is also a significant Brahui-speaking community in Balochistan to which the Khan of Kalat, Mir Abdul Kurd, and Mir Ghaus Bakhsh Bizenjo all belonged.[1]

However, Brahui-speakers, like the last Khan of Kalat, generally include themselves within the broader Baloch ethnic framework, even though linguistically significantly different from Balochi-speakers.[2] Other scholars, such as Janmahmad,[3] also mentioned Brahui as a subtribe of the Baloch.

Apart from these groups, settlers from Northern India, Sindh, and Punjab reside in Balochistan. In pre-Independence Balochistan, economic activities were controlled by non-Baloch peoples. The vacuum created by the emigration of Hindus was filled with these settlers. An increase in the number of settlers was resented by the locals, which later provoked feelings of animosity between the two, manifesting itself in different movements. The non-Baloch tribes and natives were never given the equal status in the tribal setting. Despite the fact that many of these tribes had assimilated to Baloch culture and co-existed with them for centuries, they are still considered as inferior races.[4] Many Baloch and non-Baloch inhabitants were forced to adopt nomadic pastoralism due to the scarcity of resources centuries ago. Nevertheless, there are sedentary peasant populations which serve as the backbone of feudal culture.[5]

A Brief History of Balochistan

Baloch political and ethnic identity draws on unique cultural values and a deep historical narrative centring on large tribal confederations contending and co-existing with powerful neighbouring empires. A confederation of 44 Baloch tribes dominated this territory starting from the twelfth century under Mir Jalal Khan, a tribal chief. It later came under the control of Rind Lashkari in the fifteenth century. Some Baloch scholars argue that the foreign invasions of the Moguls and Tatars and mass migrations in the thirteenth and fourteenth centuries helped birth the idea of a national identity.[6] The first full-fledged state, the Khanate of Kalat, was established by Mir Ahmed Khan in 1666 and it was limited to the divisions of Sarawan and Jhalawan in the central part of today's Balochistan.

Nasir Khan (1749–95), the sixth Khan of Kalat, organized the major tribes (Marris, Mengals, and Bugtis) through a political and military system in the eighteenth century.[7] Some argue that he was the first ruler to claim sovereignty over the territory on the basis of a common Baloch identity.[8] Today's Karachi and a major part of Iranian Balochistan were also included in his domain.[9] Nasir Khan used the term Balochistan in official contacts with his neighbours, giving recognition to his country.[10] This first Baloch state embraced all the Baloch regions such as Makran, Western Balochistan, Derajat, Sistan, and Lasbela. All these areas were integrated into a single entity under a central authority.[11] The Khanate generated unity and patriotism, providing an unwritten constitution (*Rivaj* or *Dastur*). Another was a skilful domestic policy, which also supported the long reign of Nasir Khan. This policy was implemented without distorting the tribal and pastoral nature of the society. Nasir Khan also introduced a central bureaucratic apparatus to an area that had heretofore relied on indirect tribal rule. He gave the Khanate a modern outlook and established a 'proto-parliament' along with a kind of constitution based on Baloch cultural traditions.[12] His achievements made him the most influential Khan of the Khanate and even Baloch nationalist circles sometimes equated him to Peter the Great of Russia.[13]

The death of Nasir Khan weakened the Khanate. However, it remained independent until the mid-nineteenth century after the British had occupied much of the Indian subcontinent. The rivalry between the British and Russian empires led to the British attack on Afghanistan and British reinforcements stationed in Balochistan. The area also had strategic importance due to the access it provided to Kandahar and Herat. Furthermore, it shaped British policy toward Central Asia as a safe passage was required from Sindh to Afghanistan to control the supply lines, making Balochistan a buffer zone.[14] In 1839, an agreement was signed between the Khan and the British which permitted British-Indian troops to pass through Balochistan without any obstacle. The British wanted the support of the Khan against the local tribes, but he refused to be part of foreign aggression against the Afghans. He did not prevent the local tribes from attacking the British army. Consequently, the British attacked Kalat in November 1839 and killed him. The British justified their attack, blaming the Khan for the violation of the treaty and dismembering the state.[15] Subsequent rulers were installed at the behest of the British which at times resulted in local tribes rebelling against them. The British did recognize the Khan's sovereign rule and even increased the Khanate's territory by handing over largely Pashtun

Quetta and Mastung to the north, but also started interfering in its internal affairs and state affairs, which lasted until 1947.[16]

The people of Balochistan violently opposed the foreign occupation, but the British managed to control the region through exploitation of its tribal character. The British strengthened the institution of the tribal leaders, or sardars, while keeping the masses in a state of deprivation. Moreover, the British succeeded in creating differences between the Khan and the sardars under the Sandeman System. The system was introduced by Robert Sandeman, Agent to the Governor General and in charge of the Agency for Balochistan. It was based on direct relations with the sardars and tribal leaders, bypassing the authority of the Khan. This system provided a powerful weapon for the British to exploit the state and control any uprising.[17]

Unlike the Khanate of Kalat, British-controlled Balochistan remained under the direct supervision of the Agent of the Governor General who was also an administrative head. However, the tribal leaders were autonomous in their internal affairs and the agent was to intervene only in case of strategic need. The British wanted an economically and politically weak Balochistan, which would be easy to control through the tribal 'sardari' system. They divided Balochistan territories into three political divisions: British Balochistan comprised Pishin, Chaman, Shera Rud, Duki, and Shahring; the Khanate's state territories consisted of Kalat, Lasbela, Kharan, and Makran; and the Tribal Areas consisted of Zhob, Kohlu, Marri, Bugti areas, Chaghi, and Sanjrani territories.[18] There were also leased areas such as Quetta, Noshki, Nasirabad, Bolan Pass, and a corridor that connected British Balochistan with other territories. Apart from British Balochistan, the western and northern parts were under Iranian and Afghan control respectively. After Independence, the district of Makran was included in Balochistan, excluding an area of 800 kilometres around Gwadar, which remained under the Sultanate of Oman until 1971.[19]

By the end of the nineteenth century, the British constructed roads, railway lines, post offices, rest houses, and cantonments for their troops. This development was only to use the area as the supply routes for the British troops, which kept Balochistan underdeveloped. To support the British army, wheat and other commodities were usurped in the name of taxes, which further deteriorated the economy. This exploitation led to the creation of a huge class of landless labourers and tenants who were unable to execute the demand of the British soldiers.[20] To fulfil the needs of the British garrison and the vacuum created by landless persons, a new mercantile class known as settlers was brought from Punjab and Sindh, and land was allocated to them. Construction on the new rail line and the development of a coal-mining industry attracted further migration from more economically developed areas of British India. Being the landowners, the British controlled the resources and maintained their monopoly. All this shaped modern economic relations in Balochistan and increased wealth disparity.[21] Above all, the British did not develop industry and agriculture in Balochistan as they did in Sindh, Punjab, or other Indian provinces. It might have been a case of benign neglect, but it created economic disparity, and the Baloch people perceived it as discriminatory. Such deprivation triggered ethnic-based discontent against the central government even before the independence of Pakistan in 1947.

Baloch Nationalism

Nationalism is a phenomenon where feelings of a group of people are linked to ethnicity and territorial bond. Generally speaking, nationalism is based either on ideological affinity or on ethnic markers. Ideological affinity is accepted when nationalism is based on a perceived common history or belief of a political group that unites them. On the other hand, others view common ancestry, language, or ethnic markers as the basis of nationalism.[22] Ideological affinity is found in the Middle East, where traditional religions are a source of loyalty to a group.[23]

Baloch nationalists generally reject traditional religion as a source of loyalty for their group or community. Unlike their Iranian, Pakistani, or Afghan neighbours, they were never incited in the name of religion. At the time of Partition in 1947, there were dreadful massacres in various parts of the subcontinent between the Muslims and the Hindus in the name of religion. However, Balochistan remained peaceful and calm in communal terms, except in Quetta, where a little trouble was created for the Hindus in largely Pashtun neighbourhoods.[24] Baloch activists support their claim of composing a complete national community with their occupation of a relatively well-defined area, which is an essential requirement for the right of self-determination.[25] Apart from the common ethnic bond, they claim to have a shared past with historical struggle and experiences, as well as a common cultural heritage, living style, language, and religion. Since the foundation of the Khanate in the seventeenth century until its forced partition and union respectively with Iran in 1928 and Pakistan in 1948, the region preserved its autonomous status even in 1839 when the British occupied it. In this era, the Khanate signed different treaties with the British, which deprived it of its area and eroded the Khan's sphere of action, but its independence remained intact. It had diplomatic relations with the Mughal Empire, the Ottomans, Qajar Iran, Afghanistan, and the Sultanate of Oman.[26]

Modern Baloch nationalism is rooted in the anti-colonial struggle of the mid-nineteenth century. The growth of national identity and dominance of Baloch cultural values provided the essential ideological foundation for a state. However, while different tribal unions and confederations tried to establish their hold on various regions, they failed due to certain reasons, including the absence of clear rules of succession, fragile state institutions, intertribal rivalries, regional animosities, and lack of financial sources. The arrival of the British made the creation of a sovereign independent Baloch state impossible, but at the same time served as a rallying point against which Baloch nationalist sentiment could be mobilized.

Beginning of the Tensions between the Central Government and Balochistan

Conflicting narratives of Kalat's accession to Pakistan have resulted in considerable controversy. After Partition, the Khan of Kalat argued that Balochistan was never part of British India and it must maintain its independent status like Nepal.[27] On August 15, 1947, the Khan declared the independence of the state and offered to maintain special relations with Pakistan in the areas of defence, foreign affairs, and communications. In the coming months, negotiations were held between the Khan and the Governor General of Pakistan, Quaid-i-Azam Mohammad Ali Jinnah, on the basis of the agreement of August 4, 1947. The talks were not smooth and Pakistan demanded annexation of Kalat. The British High Commissioner in Pakistan is said to have warned the government about the danger of recognizing Kalat as a sovereign state.[28]

Crucially, Pakistan's leadership was committed to a centralized state structure bound together by religion. In spite of the Khan's claim, the areas under direct British rule were ceded to Pakistan and the decision was ratified by the municipality in Quetta and Shahi Jirga. Baloch leaders claimed that the majority of the municipality consisted of non-Baloch settlers who ignored the interests of the Baloch tribes.[29]

In October 1947, Ghaus Bakhsh Bizenjo, the leader of the lower house of the Kalat state, represented the Baloch people in the assembly and stated:

> We have a distinct civilization and a separate culture like that of Iran and Afghanistan. We are Muslims but it is not necessary that by virtue of being Muslims we should lose our freedom and merge with others. If the mere fact that we are Muslims requires us to join Pakistan, then Afghanistan and Iran, both Muslim countries, should also amalgamate with Pakistan. We were never a part of India before the British rule [...] We are not ready to merge with Pakistan [...] We want a honourable relationship not a humiliating one.[30]

Ignoring these claims, the Government of Pakistan insisted on accession, using different tactics including the threat of military action. The rulers of Kharan, Lasbela, and Makran districts acceded to Pakistan on March 21, 1948. The position of Kalat state was further weakened by a broadcast of All-India Radio claiming that Kalat had applied for the mergence with India two months earlier, but India turned down the request due to its geographical location. Later, Indian Prime Minister Jawaharlal Nehru apologized for the false news. However, the statement worsened the situation and the Khan of Kalat was forced to sign an instrument of accession on April 1, 1948 as the Pakistan Army captured Kalat.[31]

The Khan's act of relinquishing sovereignty was taken as a great blow to Baloch identity. This act ignited the spark to set in motion the Baloch insurgency. The Khan was held by the government for nine months.[32] This event enraged the people and the military entered the area to control the situation. Furthermore, the leaders of the Kalat State National Party (KSNP), Ghaus Bakhsh Bizenjo, Mir Abdul Aziz Kurd, and Mir Gul Khan Naseer were also arrested.[33]

The Khan's younger brother, Agha Abdul Karim Khan, refused to accept the forced accession of Kalat and fled to Afghanistan with 700 followers. Basing himself in Afghanistan, he launched a rebellion against Pakistan in May 1948. In response, a farman was issued by the Khan of Kalat on May 24, 1948, distancing himself from Prince Karim and his party. It was also stated that Karim and his party would not get any material or moral support, and would be penalized for defiance of the orders. Although this was done under pressure from the government, it discouraged Karim, and he returned to Pakistan. On his return, he and his 102 men were ambushed and arrested near Harboi Mountain.[34] In a trial held by a tribal jirga constituted by the Agent to the Governor General and headed by a district magistrate of Quetta, Prince Karim and his men were sentenced to varying terms in prison. The prince himself remained in captivity until 1956.[35]

Prince Karim was said to have had a personal grudge against the Government of Pakistan for removing him from the governorship of Makran and putting Sardar Mir Bai Khan Gichki in his place, who only served for a short time as the seat was abolished by the government. Karim continued his movement for the liberation of Balochistan and tried to enlist the support of tribesmen and members of KSNP. Among these prominent political figures, Malik Saeed Dehwar (secretary of KSNP), Qadir Bakhsh Nizamani (member of the Baloch League), Mohammed Hussain Anka (secretary of the Baloch League), and Muhammad Afzal Mengal of Jamiat-Ulema-i-Balochistan, joined this struggle and moved to Afghanistan. They crossed the border in order to strengthen this movement with the help of Afghanistan. Karim assembled ex-soldiers and officers of the Khanate's army, organized a force under the name of Baloch Mujahedeen, and became its commander. He also tried to get help from Kabul-based foreign embassies, but failed because the Afghan government was unwilling to involve itself and asked him to either stay as an asylum seeker or go back to Pakistan.[36] In spite of its apparent failure, the resistance conveyed the message to the Baloch people that their survival as a nation depended on armed struggle.

Second Insurgency and Issue of Provincial Autonomy

The One Unit Scheme, introduced in 1955, merged the four provinces into one West Pakistan. This was a great blow to provincial autonomy. Its aim was to maintain parity with East Pakistan. After the forced union of Kalat, Baloch nationalists resisted the One Unit, perceiving it as domination by Punjab. In 1957–8, Iskandar Mirza, the President of Pakistan, raised the possibility of the restoration of the Khanate and suggested the Khan get legal advice from British lawyers for Kalat's withdrawal from West Pakistan. The Khan consequently went to London and, on his return, mobilized demonstrations on a large scale. In response, the military stormed his palace and arrested him on October 6, 1958.[37] General Ayub Khan, who took over as military ruler in October 1958, imposed martial law for fear that the Khan wanted to secede with the support of Afghanistan and Iran. At that time, Khan was very vocal in criticizing the One Unit and wanted to restore the original status of Kalat.[38] Ghaus Bakhsh Bizenjo and Gul Khan Naseer were also arrested along with a large number of nationalist activists. They were imprisoned in Quli Camp in Quetta, a prison notorious for torture.[39]

In reaction to the Khan's arrest, the people of Balochistan assembled under the command of Nauroz Khan, a 90-year-old chief of the Zarakzai tribe, and the Chief of Jhalawan. In the hierarchy of the Kalat confederation of 1666, this position was third after the Khan of Kalat and Chief of Sarawan. Nauroz Khan had three demands for the government, including the release of the Khan of Kalat and the abolition of One Unit.[40]

This conflict is generally known as the Jhalawan disturbance. It was confined to the districts of Kalat, Khuzdar, and Kohlu. The guerrilla war continued for more than a year, but the army was able to crush it, albeit with considerable difficulty.[41] Nauroz Khan finally surrendered on May 15, 1959 along with 163 companions. His surrender was the result of a deal brokered on the Holy Quran by Doda Khan Zarakzai, another tribal leader, but the government did not honour the deal. He came down from the mountains with his companions to negotiate with the government, but was arrested and sentenced to death, later charged to life imprisonment.[42] Due to his age, his sentence was commuted to life imprisonment, and he died in the Hyderabad jail on December 25, 1965.[43]

In Balochistan, Nauroz Khan's struggle is regarded as a fight against tyranny and injustice. In this era, Baloch nationalism expanded further in Balochistan, including the Brahui-speaking area as well as the Marri and Bugti tribes that had previous abstained from involvement in politics. The initial focus of the nationalist movement had been the Kalat state, where a number of nationalist organizations had been founded back in the 1930s, first to gain recognition for, and promote, a distinct Baloch identity and culture, and then to struggle for provincial autonomy.[44]

Third Insurgency—Ayub Khan Era (1963–9)

In the 1960s, the government was fearful of tribal power. The chiefs of three major tribes, Akbar Bugti, Khair Bakhsh Marri, and Attaullah Mengal, were removed from their positions of tribal headship. Attaullah Mengal was an emerging nationalist and chief of the tribe when he was replaced by his uncle. His uncle was killed within 10 days of becoming the chief and, as a result, Attaullah and his father were imprisoned on suspicion of his murder.[45] Akbar Bugti spent most of the 1960s in prison on a similar murder charge.[46] Ghaus Bakhsh Bizenjo was charged with supporting the previous insurgent leader Nauroz Khan, who was demanding the dissolution of the One Unit. Increasing sentiments of nationalism in Marri and Mengal paved the path for a renewed insurgency, known as the Parari guerrilla movement, in 1963 which continued until 1969 under the leadership of Sher Mohammad Bijarani Marri, who was a close ally of Khair Bakhsh Marri.[47] Its aim was to back the Baloch demand for the withdrawal of the Pakistani Army from Balochistan, cancellation of the One Unit, and restoration of Balochistan as a unified entity. This insurgency also gave birth to leftist and radical groups. In this period, military garrisons were constructed in the interior of Balochistan.[48] The military regime claimed that its aim was the development of the area in order to curtail the aggressive activities of tribal leaders.[49]

In 1967, the government tried to defuse the situation by announcing a general amnesty, releasing Attaullah Mengal and Akbar Bugti from prison, and reinstating their positions.[50] However, the situation turned volatile again in 1968 when the government took the decision to curtail the powers of the tribal sardars. The insurgency continued in Kalat, Khuzdar, Kohlu, and Dera Bugti. Even though an Infantry Division was employed during the operation, the insurgency ended only after Ayub Khan stepped down as president. General Yahya Khan, who succeeded Ayub Khan, dissolved the One Unit and announced a general amnesty. He also held talks with Baloch leaders. After the dissolution of the One Unit, Balochistan got the status of a separate province and witnessed a brief spell of peace with the formation of the Baloch Nationalist government in 1972.[51]

Dissolution of Provincial Government and Armed Conflict (1973–7)

After the secession of East Pakistan (now Bangladesh), unrest returned to the province as Prime Minister Zulfikar Ali Bhutto gave Pakistan a democratic constitution, but he did not value the importance of political decentralization. The National Awami Party (NAP), a coalition of Baloch and Pashtun nationalists, won the largest number of seats in the NWFP (renamed Khyber Pakhtunkhwa) and Balochistan, but its government in Balochistan was dismissed in February 1973 after 10 months. Initially, Ghous Bakhsh Raisani was appointed as governor but the NAP showed great resentment, and talks between the PPP and NAP brought in Ghaus Baksh Bizenjo as governor and Attaullah Mengal as the chief minister of Balochistan. Bhutto made it clear to the governor that he would remain in office as long as he retained the confidence of the president.[52] However, Bhutto did not trust the NAP, which led him to dismiss the provincial government on the allegation of conspiracy.[53] The nationalist parties were also blamed for colluding with the Soviet Union against the federation.[54] In an unexpected alliance with Bhutto, Nawab Akbar Bugti, who had heretofore opposed the central government, blamed the nationalist parties for colluding with a foreign power against the federation. Rather than ideology or separatism, Bugti seems to have largely been driven by personal ambition in making this allegation.[55]

Bhutto appointed Akbar Khan Bugti as the new governor and G. M. Barozai, a Pashtun, as the chief minister of the province. The former provincial government was accused of sabotaging the democratic process and starting an insurgency against the state. Baloch students and political workers formed the Baloch Peoples Liberation Front (BPLF), headed by Khair Bakhsh Marri, leading a huge number of Marri and Mengal tribesmen into guerrilla warfare against the federal government.[56]

The guerrilla war initiated by the Marris and Mengals involved more fighters ideologically committed to the Baloch nationalist movement as compared to the previous conflicts, which also intensified the war. A total of 80,000 military troops supported by combat helicopters and the Pakistan Air Force were pitted against 55,000 poorly armed Baloch guerrillas in different phases of the war.[57] The conflict resulted in the loss of 3,000 military troops and 5,300 Baloch guerrillas, while the number of civilian casualties was probably higher.[58]

The conflict ended in 1977 when Bhutto was overthrown in a military coup by General Ziaul Haq. Zia announced a general amnesty, removed the army from Balochistan, and freed several thousand Baloch nationalist leaders and activists.[59] He wanted to solve the problem in his own unique way. He called on the Baloch leaders in Rawalpindi on May 8, 1978 and negotiated with Ghaus Bakhsh Bizenjo on the political and social issues of the province. Khair Bakhsh Marri avoided the meeting due to sickness[60] while Attaullah Mengal was in self-imposed exile in London. Bizenjo complained that the military operation had caused a heavy loss of human life and property in Balochistan. He also told Zia that the formation of a national government at the centre was not the solution to the problem and insisted that an elected government be put in place after conducting general elections.[61]

Not all Baloch leaders heeded the government's call for reconciliation. After his release from prison in 1977, Khair Bakhsh

Marri flew to London and then took refuge in Afghanistan, where thousands of his tribesmen joined him on his order. The Marris believed they had suffered the most and refused to return from Afghanistan, showing their mistrust of the political authorities, state, and government. They returned only after the fall in 1992 of the Najibullah regime, which had sheltered them.[62]

The government and the tribal sardars did not find a joint solution to their differences, particularly the issues of repatriation of Punjabi bureaucrats and Punjabi *abadkar*s (settlers) from the province, who they claimed had grabbed fertile land in the Pat Feeder Canal area development schemes. Another area of disagreement was the issue of autonomy in internal affairs without Islamabad's involvement, or the presence of military and paramilitary troops from the area. In the end, the biggest obstacle was that the federal government was not fully implementing the Constitution, as it sought to keep the province under its control. The tribal leaders themselves remained divided on the issue of autonomy as a few were demanding full sovereignty. Additionally, the Shah's government in Iran had strongly opposed the nationalist provincial government in 1973, fearing that it could set a precedent in Iranian Balochistan.[63]

The BPLF did not succeed in its plans but Baloch nationalists, and particularly the younger generation, became more alienated and radicalized as a result of the 1973–7 confrontation, and now increasingly supported outright separation. Individual leaders, like Khair Bakhsh Marri, also showed considerable inclination toward Marxist-Leninist ideology. Marri continued to fight for the recognition of the rights of ethnic minorities and was consistent and unwavering in his demand for an independent Baloch homeland till his death in June 2014.[64] Significantly, Ghaus Bakhsh Bizenjo, among other Baloch leaders, denied that they were seeking an independent 'Greater Balochistan' in an interview in 1975. To him, such terms were devised by the Islamabad-based bureaucracy because, 'having destroyed all democratic institutions, they hurl such terms as accusations against their political opponents in order to suppress opposition'.[65]

From the end of the conflict in 1977 until 2004, the major trends underlying the current Baloch national movement gradually emerged. In the 1990s, democratic institutions were able to mollify ethnic tensions to a certain extent. Furthermore, national level political parties such as the Pakistan Muslim League and Pakistan Peoples Party (PPP) became powerful. In the 1988 elections, the total combined votes of nationally oriented parties was 47.8 per cent, and 51.74 per cent in the elections of 1990. In 1997, once again, centrally-oriented parties came into power.[66] The centre-province relations remained normal with occasional tension, but the overall situation remained peaceful in Balochistan. The situation changed in 2002 with the rigging of elections by the military.[67]

Unrest in Balochistan since the Musharraf Era

There are three major factors distinguishing the new militancy from the previous ones. First is the emergence of a middle-class leadership; the second is easy access to sophisticated weapons; and third is a unity among various tribes and groups on different issues such as the central government's involvement in provincial affairs, and share of natural resources. In the past, nationalist parties led by tribal chiefs organized armed resistance against the government. They fought with the military from hideouts in the mountains as weapons were not easily available. Today, the situation is changed and no single group or party can be blamed for violence because all of them have armed troops. Violence prevails equally in both rural and urban areas due to the existence of the middle-class leadership at both places. Government installations and personnel are the main target. Huge reserves of gas, oil, copper, and gold are in Balochistan and the Baloch nationalists want control over these natural resources. This has been denied to them since the creation of Pakistan.

On October 17, 1999, one week after the military coup, Musharraf announced a 7-point reform agenda including the restoration of democracy and devolution of power. The Baloch leaders rejected the devolution plan and termed it suppression of provincial autonomy. Attaullah Mengal stated on August 22, 2000 that the 'regime's blueprint of local government is a mode of imposing a unitary form of government in the name of decentralization'.[68] Comparing it with the One Unit plan, he said, 'It would revive the bitter experiment of the 1950s and 1960s, which was the major cause of the break-up of Pakistan in 1971.'[69] He was right in his assessment as the system transferred power from the provinces to districts but not from the centre to the provinces, thus weakening provincial authority.

Local Baloch and Pashtun parties gained only 21 out of 124 seats in the Balochistan Assembly. Other seats were won by a coalition of religious parties named Muttahida Majlis-e-Amal (MMA) and the Pakistan Muslim League-Quaid (PML-Q). In comparison with the 1970–1 elections, in 2002, the Baloch parties lost a lot of political ground.[70] The military regime chose those Baloch leaders for cooperation who had traditionally aligned themselves with the centre.[71] The Election Observation Mission of the European Union (2002) in its report exposed vote tampering before, during, and after the elections. The Election Commission of Pakistan (ECP) was allegedly involved in gerrymandering electoral constituencies in order to weaken parties opposed to the regime.[72] Additionally, the Musharraf government added a Bachelor's degree requirement to the list of eligibility criteria for electoral candidates, while at the same time granting university degree equivalency to madrasa diplomas. This act benefited the MMA and deprived prominent nationalist leaders including those who once served and held the highest offices, such as Akbar Bugti.[73]

In January 2000, a judge of the Balochistan High Court was killed by unknown assailants. The federal government accused and arrested Khair Bakhsh Marri and kept him under detention. In those days, the Baloch Liberation Army (BLA) emerged and took responsibility for a number of killings, bomb blasts, sabotage activities, and rocket attacks on official installations.[74] The BLA, with its stronghold in Kohlu while having influence in Jafarabad, Nasirabad, Khuzdar, Lasbela, Chaghi, Bolan, and Sibi, is said to have taken ideological guidance from Khair Bakhsh Marri. The son of Khair Bakhsh Marri, Mir Balach Marri, became the head of the BLA in 2000, but was later killed in Afghanistan on November 21, 2007. His brother, Hyrbyair Marri, is leading the group in exile from London. Initially, the BLA targeted transportation routes, which gradually changed to attacks on gas pipelines. Its key grievance is custody of the natural reserves of Balochistan and the Gwadar seaport project in the hands of non-Baloch.[75]

In June 2002, military troops were deployed in the gas fields of Dera Bugti with a warning for Nawab Akbar Bugti and his tribesmen to surrender as they were accused of providing shelter to terrorists and criminals who were destroying gas installations with rocket attacks in the Sui area.[76] Despite this, the province remained peaceful until 2005 when an unfortunate rape case of a female doctor, Shazia Khalid, worsened the situation. The case came to the surface in January 2005. She was working at the Sui Hospital Complex in Dera Bugti when an army officer committed this heinous act and was not arrested.[77] The issue triggered a series of attacks by members of the Bugti tribe against security guards and the Frontier Constabulary (FC). In return, paramilitary forces raided locations in Kohlu District and other places.[78] The issue escalated first into a war of words and then armed conflict between the Bugti tribe and the federal government. President Musharraf even went on TV to announce to the Baloch, 'Don't push us … it is not the 1970s … and this time you [the Baloch] won't even know what has hit you.'[79]

In 2005, Akbar Bugti also joined the Baloch nationalist movement, leading to a heightening of tensions, including the exchange of rocket fire by both sides in March 2005. In this encounter, 8 paramilitary personnel died, while 62 tribesmen were killed. An attack was also made on President Musharraf in Kohlu City on December 14, 2005.

The next day a rocket fired from a helicopter injured the inspector-general and deputy inspector-general of FC in Kohlu. In the resulting unrest thousands of people, mostly women and children, were displaced. The conflicts in Dera Bugti and Kohlu alone forced 84,000 people to leave their homes.[80] All this worsened the relations between the military and the province for months, resurrecting old grievances such as provincial autonomy, allocation of resources, and protection of local culture and language.

The tension was at its peak in the Bugti area, rich in natural gas reserves. Nawab Akbar Bugti claimed a major share for his tribe in gas royalty as these reserves were discovered in the Bugti-controlled area. The government rejected this demand and the official sources depicted the dispute of royalty as that of 'greedy' local leaders who were opposed to development to preserve their status, and this demand was taken as part of an outdated relic of the feudal system.[81] Akbar Bugti was also blamed for keeping a private militia and leading a guerrilla war against the state.[82]

Pakistan's military did not take the matter seriously. The situation worsened and resulted in the killing of Akbar Bugti on August 26, 2006. Bugti and two other nationalist leaders were labelled 'troublemakers'. Along with Bugti, 37 tribesmen, 21 security personnel, and 4 military officers lost their lives. There are two narratives about his killing. According to the first source, which blames the military, a helicopter gunship dropped bombs at Bugti's hideout cave, which was located in Kohlu, about 150 miles east of Quetta.[83] The second recounts the entrance of 4 officers inside the cave where he was hiding. They asked him to surrender and an explosion was heard following which Bugti and the officers was buried inside the cave. It was conjectured that the explosion was from a 'planted explosive device or a rocket being fired'. Musharraf called it a self-inflicted casualty.[84] To condemn the killing of Bugti, Baloch nationalists held a grand jirga which was attended by more than 380 leaders, including 85 tribal chiefs, belying Musharraf's claim that he enjoyed the support of all except three tribal chiefs. The killing sparked widespread protest rallies in Balochistan and some parts of Sindh.[85]

The killing of Bugti proved to be a catalyst for the intensification of the situation in Balochistan. Earlier, it was the Marri tribe who used to talk about political action beyond the constitutional bounds, but in practice they participated in the elections and took the oath of allegiance to the Constitution. After the killing of Bugti, his tribe began thinking about engaging in contentious politics to pursue their objectives. Prior to the conflict of 2005, only 7 per cent of the area in the Kohlu and Dera Bugti districts was affected by unrest, whereas from 2006 onwards, more than half of the area of the province was afflicted. This turmoil further encouraged the disgruntled and unemployed Baloch youth to join the rank and file of insurgent groups, like the BLA and Baloch Republican Army (BRA). The BRA was founded in 2006 by Brahamdagh Bugti, the son of Akbar Bugti. Brahamdagh Bugti resides in Switzerland and, from time to time, demands independence. Many of the group members are living in the Gulf, India, and Afghanistan, and have expertise in arms and ammunition handling. With its centre at Dera Bugti, the BRA operates in Quetta and Baloch/Brahui-dominated areas. The organization is uncompromising in its demand for an independent Balochistan and opposes any type of dialogue. This in turn attracts young people who are already blaming the federal government for their economic problems and lack of opportunities.[86] President Musharraf justified the exercise of oppressive tactics in Balochistan, pledging to end the province's deprivation at the hands of a few tribal chiefs who were allegedly responsible for the underdevelopment of the area. The military sources also argued that only 7 per cent of the province was involved in the insurgency. This of course raised the question why the majority of the population under military control were still experiencing significant socioeconomic backwardness.

In 2005, once again, the issue of the construction of additional military cantonments surfaced along with two other problems: one was the price of natural gas explored in the southwestern part, and the other was the development of the Gwadar seaport for the benefit of external powers. The former President Musharraf ordered the construction of three new military cantonments at Kohlu, Dera Bugti, and Gwadar. The first two areas were the strongholds of Marri and Bugti sardars respectively. Both strongly resented the decision and demanded a cessation of the construction of these cantonments. To the Baloch people, these bases were not to counter any foreign power, but to control the locals and suppress the Baloch dissenters as all three locations have no adjacent international border. According to Baloch nationalists, 'There must be no army cantonment in any area of Balochistan and departments of civil administration should control the situation of security in [the] province.'[87]

The Baloch leaders demanded that the federal government withdraw the army from these areas, transferring responsibility to the Frontier Constabulary. They also viewed the construction of the cantonments as the rulers' intention to continue exploitation of the resources of the province. These leaders wanted greater Baloch representation in state institutions, demanding at least 75 per cent employees in the Coast Guard and a 30 per cent share in the navy.[88] Attaullah Mengal criticized the army in his meeting with the PML-N leader, Nawaz Sharif, on December 19, 2011: 'This is not Pakistan Army. Rather it is Punjabi army that is indulging in inhuman acts against the Baloch people'.[89]

Apart from the construction of military bases, the other two issues are the Gwadar seaport and utilization of natural resources.[90] The initial decision to build the port was taken by the elected government of Nawaz Sharif in 1992, which was welcomed by the locals and Baloch nationalists. However, due to a change in the situation, suspicions have increased with regard to the design and intention of the central state. Without local involvement, the Baloch people view the army as a mafia operating in the port area, falsifying records in order to grab land.[91] The plight of the local people is miserable as they have been there for centuries, but there is no documented evidence of their possession of the land.[92]

The Eighteenth Amendment to the 1973 Constitution in 2010 provided more powers to the provinces, but it kept ports and shipping under a Council of Common Interests (CCI) that has the authority to make decisions. The CCI consists of all the four chief ministers and the prime minister. Baloch leaders are critical of this control.[93] Simultaneously, natural resources are a source of both prosperity and tension for Balochistan. The discovery of gas reserves in Sui (Balochistan) in 1952 was estimated to account for 23.37 per cent of the total gas reserves of Pakistan. The gas was supplied to the major cities of Pakistan in 1964, but Quetta only received it in 1986.[94] Currently, Balochistan receives a 12.4 per cent share in gas royalty. In other words, the poorest province subsidises the richer provinces.[95] The late Akbar Bugti demanded a revision in the rates of gas royalty, bringing them on a par with those of Sindh and Punjab, but the military regime refused to revise the rate.[96] A large amount of the gas royalty goes to specific people, while common citizens derive no benefits. The Saindak project for copper exploration has been handed over to China with a 50 per cent share in profit. The remaining 48 per cent goes to the central government and the province receives only 2 per cent.[97] The Reko Diq project follows the same pattern with no representation of the Baloch people. No proper formula has been devised for distribution of income.[98]

Apart from this, the Baloch people do not have proper representation in the civil and military bureaucracies or in decision-making. According to Sial and Basit, there is no single Baloch at the head of more than 200 corporations of Pakistan. All federal secretaries are non-Baloch.[99] There is no Baloch ambassador in Pakistani embassies abroad. Of the 10 directors of Pakistan International Airlines (PIA), not one is a Baloch. Among the 342 members of the National Assembly, 16 are Baloch parliamentarians (number according to population) to look after their province. They have equal representation with other provinces in the Senate, but that house is less powerful. All this led them to think of themselves as a marginalized group. The federal government is playing a key role, not only in financial matters but also in the politics and administration of the province. Politically, the provincial government has been at the mercy of the federal government for its survival. The appointments to key posts in Balochistan, such as governors, chief secretaries, Inspector Generals of police and all others, are made by the centre.[100]

Measures of the Federal Government to Resolve Provincial Problems

The federal government took different measures to pacify the situation. First was the formation of a parliamentary committee on September 23, 2004 under the supervision of Chaudhry Shujaat Hussain, President of the PML-Q. The committee was assigned the task of exploring and addressing the grievances of the people of Balochistan. Two subcommittees were also constituted: one headed by Senator Mushahid Hussain Syed of the PML-Q, to make proper recommendations to improve the situation in Balochistan; the other, headed by Senator Wasim Sajjad, to prepare a constitutional reform package to fulfil the demand of provincial autonomy.[101]

At the first stage, the subcommittees heard the detailed views of the relevant official authorities and political parties of Balochistan and submitted reports to President Musharraf. The committees recommended concrete steps and measures, keeping in view the demands of the Baloch people. These recommendations include:

- Out of the total employment quota, 5.4 per cent to be allocated for Balochistan.
- An increased share in the gas royalty.
- Share in Gwadar seaport.
- Construction of the main roads and adjustment of funds from the provincial viewpoint.

All the recommendations were not approved by the federal government and the issue was referred to the representatives of the government and opposition for further recommendations.[102] The problem remained unresolved and Musharraf was blamed for not implementing the recommendations of the subcommittees. Even Mushahid Hussain himself complained of non-implementation of the reports and said that only 15 per cent implementation could bring change and improve the situation.[103]

The Eighteenth Amendment

On April 19, 2010, the Eighteenth Amendment became part of the Constitution of Pakistan after passing through different processes. It has brought changes in significant areas. It withdrew the powers of the President to dissolve the elected assemblies and reinstated the parliamentary system. The name of the NWFP was changed to Khyber Pakhtunkhwa. The structures of the CCI and the National Finance Commission (NFC) were also changed. All this was done to create better opportunities to accommodate the viewpoint of provincial governments on major financial issues and income from the natural resources of the provinces. Among many other reforms, the Eighteenth Amendment provided provincial autonomy, abolishing the concurrent legislative list and other related provisions. The 1973 Constitution has three lists of subjects for the distribution of powers between the centre and the provinces: federal, provincial, and a concurrent list with dual jurisdiction on 47 subjects. The authority to legislate on these subjects was given to both governments but, in the event of incompatibility, the federal law prevailed. It had earlier been decided that the concurrent list would transfer to the units in 1983, 10 years after the Constitution's implementation, but it was finally done through the Eighteenth Amendment after a lapse of 26 years.

The issue of provincial autonomy had been overshadowing centre-province relations since 1973. The Eighteenth Amendment is meant to resolve it, but autonomy is granted in theory only. The present government of Balochistan is the result of the 2013 Murree Agreement. It was decided in this agreement that the 5-year constitutional term of the chief minister would be divided between the Baloch National Party (BNP) and the PML-N. Dr Malik Baloch of the BNP was the first to complete half of the 5-year-term and his government was the first to implement the Eighteenth Amendment. PML-N Balochistan Chapter President, Sardar Sanaullah Khan Zehri, replaced Dr Malik as the chief minister. Well-informed sources in the federal government pointed out that the Prime Minister personally wanted his party's chief minister to implement the Murree Agreement as some circles had urged the PM to let Malik continue. Generally speaking, the federal government was managing the affairs of Balochistan. After nominating Dr Malik as chief minister, Nawaz Sharif settled the provincial affairs and ministers were appointed with his approval. It took 4 months as the PM was very occupied. At present, Balochistan has become the first province to conduct local government elections. But even the nomination of Quetta's mayor is done with the centre's involvement. No prominent change is visible and provincial autonomy is still a distant reality.[104]

Aghaz-e-Haqooq-e-Balochistan Package

On November 24, 2009, the PPP government approved a 39-point agenda for improving the situation in Balochistan. This step was taken to address the grievances of the province. The package consisted of initiatives for both politicians and youth to end their self-imposed exile, offering a better future except for those who were involved in terrorist activities. Both the package and the Eighteenth Amendment have positive measures for reviving a better relationship between the people of the province and the central government, but most important was to restore the trust of the Baloch people. The following is a summary of its five dimensions:[105]

- Withdrawal of the military from Sui and Kohlu districts.
- Halting the construction of military garrisons in Sui and Kohlu districts with no new cantonments in Gwadar district.
- Replacing of the Army by Frontier Constabulary.
- Judicial inquiry of the murder cases of Akbar Bugti, Lala Munir, Ghulam Muhammad, and all those who became victims of targeted killings in the province.
- The royalty worth PKR 120 billion, which goes back to 1954, will be paid within 12 years through defining a better formula in the current NFC award.
- The working and mechanism for the Gwadar Development Authority will be started under the supervision of the chief minister and a board of governors with seven members. All members will be from the province.

The carefully drafted package by the Parliamentary and Cabinet Committee was meant to overcome various contentious issues without disturbing the existing relationship between the provincial and federal government. Hence, some additional benefit was created for Balochistan in administrative and economic areas with commitments to pay pending dues of royalties which was a major irritant in centre–periphery relations. Unfortunately, this much-anticipated package was not implemented and the people did not get immediate relief. As a whole, the package was viewed very differently by different stakeholders. The ruling party termed it as a significant milestone, whereas the Baloch nationalists outrightly rejected it, considering it as no more than a piece of paper.

The package did not bring the Baloch leaders into a dialogue on key issues such as provincial autonomy or natural resource rights. Nothing changed and the nationalist leadership remained divided between the hardliners and the moderates: Brahamdagh Bugti and Hyrbyair Marri are included in the former group. Rejecting the package, Hyrbyair Marri called it a 'mockery and a cruel joke' on the people of Balochistan as it did not fulfil their expectations. He further stated in an interview with a TV channel: 'This package is misleading, it is another trap set for us to convince us that the federation pains for us and wants the solution of our miseries'.[106] He argued that the package did not provide any positive signal to them about the willingness of the federation and the mainstream political parties to resume talks on centre-province relations.

The Balochistan National Front, Jamhoori Watan Party (Talal), the Balochistan National Party, and the Balochistan National Party (Mengal) also rejected the package and conditioned the talks with the government through an international guarantee.[107] Senator Hasil Bizenjo, Senator Dr Abdul Malik, Sanaullah Baloch, and many others opined that, instead of solving the problems, the package would add problems for the people of Balochistan.[108] The government took 18 months to prepare the package while the Baloch leadership rejected the major part of it within 24 hours of its appearance. However, in 2010, Islamabad doubled the budget for Balochistan and released an additional grant of US$140 million for gas revenue debts.[109]

The Baloch people are not just offended over the economic 'plunder'; they are also resentful about the use of political and military means to 'rob' them politically and economically. They regard official attempts with doubt, as aiming to change their historical secular social culture with the help of madrasas and fundamentalist organizations under the guise of charity outfits, which were visible in Awaran after the earthquake of September 2013. Dr Abdul Malik Baloch, the former chief minister of Balochistan, argued in a seminar, 'If the Baloch people are not given a right to the resources of their province, we would be looking at yet another insurgency and no one will be able to control it.'

Conclusion

The issue of provincial autonomy in Balochistan is deeply rooted in history from the time the federal government pursued short-sighted policies, and successive governments followed them. The people resented the crude attempts by the central government to change the historical secular social ethos of the area. The parties in power branded the Baloch people as 'seditious' when, in reality, the Baloch had simply complained of being denied their legitimate rights. The actual tussle was political and administrative in its nature, but power-oriented solutions distorted the position. The government tried to suppress the demands of the people, imposing military solutions without accommodating them. The aggrieved party takes each attempt as the suppression of provincial autonomy as, for example, the One Unit scheme and dissolution of an elected government within 10 months of its formation. Natural (Sui) gas was supplied to Quetta in 1986 while it was discovered in 1952 and provided to the major cities in 1964. For the last 6 decades, Balochistan has been neglected and the basic requirements of life have not been provided to the people of the area. For the smooth running of affairs, the federation is responsible for aligning the units on matters of national interests and, in the event of failure or crisis, the prime culprit is the federal government. Violating the federation's norms and denial of power-sharing only led to a strong centre and weaker units. The centre feared that a weak government would strengthen the separatist forces in Balochistan and they would undermine the defence and security positions. This fear was further reinforced by the powerful role of the army in state affairs. The argument of uniform economic development worked equally for a strong centre. This policy was viewed as exploitation of natural resources as the government never bothered to take provincial authority into their confidence prior to a decision. This led the province to think that the federal government was robbing it of its resources. The central government also overlooked the ethnic and tribal peculiarities and the harsh economic realities that kept the people under the subjugation of tribal chiefs. The relationship between the two sets of government remained a victim of mistrust ranging from forced alignment to economic exploitation and repressive military operations. The government's failure to fulfil the demands of Baloch nationalists for cultural, economic, and political rights led them to think about secessionism instead of provincial autonomy.

The federal government's different measures such as the NFC award, the Eighteenth Amendment, cancellation of the concurrent list, share in natural resources, and the closure of military cantonments have by and large not been implemented. In the current situation, a negotiated solution is politically feasible as the resistance is weak and divided. It seems that the majority of the Baloch people favour autonomy, not the extreme position of independence, as only three of the 28 major tribal chiefs are regarded as incorrigible rebels by the federal government, whereas the others simply want provincial autonomy.

Notes

1. Farhan Hanif Siddiqi, *The State and Politics of Ethnicity in Post-1971 Pakistan: An Analysis of Baloch, Sindhi, and Mohajir Ethnic Movements* (Karachi: University of Karachi, 2009); and Adeel Khan, 'Renewed Ethnonationalist Insurgency in Balochistan, Pakistan: The Militarized State and Continuing Economic Deprivation,' *Asian Survey* 49, no. 6 (November/December 2009): 1071–91.

2. Taj Mohammad Breseeg, *Baloch Nationalism: Its Origin and Development* (Karachi: Royal Book Company, 2004).

3. Janmahmad, *The Baloch Cultural Heritage* (Karachi: Royal Book Company, 1982).

4. Ibid., 30.

5. Selig S. Harrison, *In Afghanistan's Shadow: Baluch Nationalism and Soviet Temptations* (New York: Carnegie Endowment for International Peace, 1981), 8.

6. Inayatullah Baloch, *The Problem of 'Greater Baluchistan': A Study of Baloch Nationalism* (Stuttgart: Steiner Verlag GMBH, 1987).

7. Harrison, *In Afghanistan's Shadow*.

8. Baloch, *The Problem of 'Greater Baluchistan'*, 20.

9. Breseeg, *Baloch Nationalism*, 165.

10. Shah Muhammad Marri, *Baloch Qaum Aed-e-Qadeem say Asre Hazir Tak* (Lahore: Takhliqat, 2000), 142.
11. Baloch, *The Problem of 'Greater Baluchistani'*.
12. Ibid., 84.
13. Marri, *Qaum Aed-e-Qadeem say Asre Hazir Tak*, 131.
14. Iqbal Ahmad, *Balochistan: Its Strategic Importance* (Lahore: Royal Book Company, 1992), xvii.
15. Breseeg, *Baloch Nationalism*, 175; and Harrison, *In Afghanistan's Shadow*.
16. 'Volume 6: Argaon to Bardwan,' *The Imperial Gazetteer of India* (1908), 279; Ayub B. Awan, *Baluchistan: Historical and Political Processes* (London: New Century Publishers, 1985), 62; and Breseeg, *Baloch Nationalism*, 175.
17. Breseeg, *Baloch Nationalism*, 176; Baloch, *The Problem of 'Greater Baluchistan'*, 14; and 'Volume 6: Argaon to Bardwan,' *The Imperial Gazetteer of India*.
18. Tahir Amin, *Ethno-National Movements in Pakistan: Domestic and International Factors* (Islamabad: Institute of Policy Studies, 1988).
19. Rafaqat Hussain, 'Gwadar in Historical Perspective,' *MUSLIM Institute* (2016).
20. Yu. V. Gankovsky, *The Peoples of Pakistan: An Ethnic History* (Moscow: Nauka Publishing House, 1971).
21. Breseeg, *Baloch Nationalism*; Khan, 'Renewed Ethnonationalist Insurgency in Balochistan.'
22. Max Weber, 'The Origin of Ethnic Groups,' in *Ethnicity*, eds. John Hutchinson and Anthony D. Smith (Oxford: Oxford University Press, 1996), 35–40.
23. G. Hossein Razi, 'Legitimacy, Religion, and Nationalism in the Middle East,' *American Political Science Review* 84, no. 1 (March 1990): 75.
24. Muhammad Akbar Notezai, 'NON-FICTION: THE UNKNOWN EXODUS,' *Dawn*, March 1, 2020.
25. Inayatullah Baloch, 'Resistance and National Liberation in Baluchi Poetry.' Paper presented at Balochi Symposium at the University of Uppsala, Sweden in August 2000.
26. Baloch, *The Problem of 'Greater Baluchistan'*, 9 and 164–5.
27. Alok Bansal, 'Factors leading to insurgency in Balochistan,' *Small Wars & Insurgencies* 19, no. 2 (2008): 184.
28. Baloch, *The Problem of 'Greater Baluchistan'*.
29. Bansal, 'Factors leading to insurgency in Balochistan,' 184.
30. Janmahmad, *Essays on Baloch National Struggle in Pakistan: Emergence, Dimension and Representation* (Quetta: Gosh-a-Adab, 1989).
31. Zubair Faisal Abbasi, 'Federalism, Provincial Autonomy and Conflicts' (Islamabad: Centre for Peace and Development Initiatives, 2010); and Siddiqi, *The State and Politics of Ethnicity in Post-1971 Pakistan*.
32. Daniel J. Lebowitz, 'Why has the Ethno-Nationalist Insurgency in Balochistan Endured for 66 Years?' *Geostrategic Forecasting Corporation*, 2015.

33. Breseeg, *Baloch Nationalism*.

34. Naseer Dashti, *The Baloch and Balochistan: A Historical Account from the Beginning to the Fall of the Baloch State* (Bloomington: Trafford Publishing, 2012).

35. Mansoor Akbar Kundi, 'Insurgency Factors in Balochistan,' *Central Asia Journal* 64 (2009); and Harrison, *In Afghanistan's Shadow*, 26.

36. Feroz Ahmed, *Ethnicity and Politics in Pakistan* (Karachi: Oxford University Press, 1998); and Kundi, 'Insurgency Factors in Balochistan.'

37. Mir Ahmad Yar Khan Baloch, *Inside Baluchistan: A Political Autobiography of His Highness Baiglar Baigi: Khan-e-Azam-XIII* (Karachi: Royal Book Company, 1975); and Siddiqi, *The State and Politics of Ethnicity in Post-1971 Pakistan*, 132.

38. Tahir Bizenjo, *Balochistan: Kia Huwa, kia hoga* (Karachi: Pakistani Adab Publisher, 1989).

39. Hasan Mansoor, 'Khair Bakhsh Marri: a fighter all the way,' *Dawn*, June 14, 2014.

40. Kundi, 'Insurgency Factors in Balochistan.'

41. Sheikh Asad Rahman, *Lack of Democracy and Socio-Economic Development of Balochistan* (Islamabad: Sungi Development Foundation, 2009); and Sasmita Tripathy and Saeed Ahmed Rid, *Democracy as conflict-resolution model for terrorism: A case study of India and Pakistan* (Colombo: The Regional Centre for Strategic Studies, 2009).

42. Rizwan Zeb, *Ethno-political Conflict in Pakistan: The Baloch Movement* (Routledge, 2019).

43. Kundi, 'Insurgency Factors in Balochistan.'

44. Dashti, *The Baloch and Balochistan*; and Siddiqi, *The State and Politics of Ethnicity in Post-1971 Pakistan*.

45. Janmahmad, *Essays on Baloch National Struggle*, 229.

46. Martin Axmann, *Back to the Future: The Khanate of Kalat and the Genesis of Baloch Nationalism 1915–1955* (New York: Oxford University Press, 2008).

47. Farhan Hanif Siddiqi, *The Politics of Ethnicity in Pakistan: The Baloch, Sindhi, and Mohajir Ethnic Movements* (Oxon: Routledge, 2012), 64.

48. Ian Talbot, *Pakistan: A Modern History* (New Delhi: Foundation Books, 2005).

49. Frederic Grare, 'Balochistan: The State Versus the Nation,' *Carnegie Endowment for International Peace* (April 2013).

50. Siddiqi, *The State and Politics of Ethnicity*.

51. Mir Gul Khan Naseer, *Tareekh-e-Balochistan* (Quetta: Rubi Publisher, 1986), 228–30.

52. Siddiqi, *The Politics of Ethnicity*, 65.

53. 'Balochistan Insurgency - Fourth conflict 1973–77,' *Global Security Organization* (2011); and Grare, 'Balochistan.'

54. Jason Heeg, *Insurgency in Balochistan* (Fort Leavenworth: The Foreign Military Studies Office, 2013).

55. Farhan Hanif Siddiqi, 'Nation-formation and national movement(s) in Pakistan: a critical estimation of Hroch's stage theory,' in *The Comparative Approach to National Movements: Miroslav Hroch and Nationalism Studies*, eds. by Alexander Maxwell (Routledge, 2012): 9–20.

56. Tripathy and Rid, *Democracy as conflict-resolution model*; and Farhan Hanif Siddiqi, 'Security Dynamics in Pakistani Balochistan: Religious Activism and Ethnic Conflict in the War on Terror,' *Asian Affairs: An American Review* 39, no. 3 (2012): 165.

57. Harrison, *In Afghanistan's Shadow*; and Grare, 'Balochistan.'

58. Ibid; and Kundi 'Insurgency Factors in Balochistan.'

59. Frederic Grare, 'Pakistan: The Resurgence of Baluch Nationalism,' *Carnegie Endowment for International Peace* 65 (2006): 1–14.

60. Shaikh Aziz, 'A leaf from history: Reclaiming Balochistan, peacefully,' *Dawn*, October 5, 2014.

61. Grare, 'Pakistan,' 1–14.

62. Mansoor, 'Khair Bakhsh Marri.'

63. Breseeg, *Baloch Nationalism*; and Harrison, *In Afghanistan's Shadow*, 35.

64. Mansoor, 'Khair Bakhsh Marri'; and Grare, 'Pakistan,' 7.

65. Breseeg, *Baloch Nationalism*, 349; and Janmahmad, *Essays on Baloch National Struggle*.

66. 'Pakistan: The worsening conflict in Balochistan,' *International Crisis Group*, South Asia Report 119 (2006): 6–7.

67. Mohammad Waseem, *Democratization in Pakistan: A Study of the 2002 Elections* (Karachi: Oxford University Press, 2006).

68. Breseeg, *Baloch Nationalism*.

69. Ibid.

70. Rasul Bakhsh Rais, 'The Balochistan Package: Redefining Federalism in Pakistan,' *Center for Civic Education Pakistan* (December 2009).

71. Pakistan National and Provincial Assembly election, EU Election Observation Mission Final Report (October 10, 2002).

72. Ibid.

73. Grare, 'Balochistan.'

74. Muhammad Feyyaz, 'Constructing Baloch militancy in Pakistan,' *South Asian Journal* (2013): 114–35.

75. Mahrukh Khan, 'Balochistan: The Forgotten Frontier,' *Institute of Strategic Studies* (2013).

76. Muhammad Ijaz Latif and Muhammad Amir Hamza. 'Ethnic Nationalism in Pakistan: A Case Study of Baloch Nationalism during Musharraf Regime,' *Pakistan Vision* 10, no. 1 (2009).

77. 'Raped doctor: I'm still terrified,' *BBC NEWS*, June 29, 2005.
78. 'Pakistan: The Forgotten Conflict in Balochistan,' *International Crisis Group*, Briefing No. 69 (October 2007).
79. *Dawn* - Letters; January 13, 2005.
80. 'Balochistan: Case and Demand,' *PILDAT* Briefing Paper (April 2007).
81. Grare, 'Balochistan.'
82. Grare, 'Balochistan.'
83. Wajahat Masood, 'The Murder of Akbar Bugti,' *Monthly Nawa-e-Insan* 279, no. 7 (2006): 22.
84. Pervez Musharraf, 'Understanding Baluchistan,' *AML US* (2011).
85. Marco Corsi, 'Internal Conflicts in Pakistan,' *Oriente Moderno* 23, no. 84 (2004): 39–49; and 'The State of Human Rights in 2005,' *Human Rights Commission of Pakistan* (2006).
86. 'Balochistan: Civil-Military Relations,' *PILDAT* Issue Paper (March 2012).
87. Ibid; and N. U. Haq, 'Balochistan, Disturbances: Causes and Response,' *IPRI* 6, no. 2 (2006).
88. Khan, 'Renewed Ethnonationalist Insurgency in Balochistan.'
89. 'Balochistan at point of no return, Mengal tells Nawaz,' *Dawn*, December 20, 2011.
90. The Gwadar seaport is one of the megaprojects of Balochistan with no local participation as no representative of the provincial government was present at the signing ceremony. Furthermore, the master plan was not discussed with the Balochistan government. President Musharraf signed the project agreement with Chinese vice premier, Wu Bangguo, on March 24, 2002. The work on the project started under the federal umbrella and China paid US $198 million out of US $248 million of the total cost of construction. Mussarat Jabeen, 'Developments in Pak-China Strategic Alliances,' *Berkeley Journal of Social Sciences* 2, no. 2 (2012): 1–16.
91. Robert D. Kaplan, 'Pakistan's Fatal Shore,' *The Atlantic*, May 2009.
92. Ibid.
93. Qaiser Butt, 'Provincial autonomy: "Gwadar port handover breaches Constitution",' *The Express Tribune*, March 4, 2013.
94. Until 1970, Balochistan provided 70 per cent of total gas of the country and after that Sindh began to contribute 48 per cent. Jobs were created in the area of gas supply but a small number of locals got jobs in this field. Balochistan receives only Rs. 27 for a unit of gas as compared to Rs. 170 and 190 per unit respectively by Sindh and Punjab. Grare, 'Pakistan,' 5 and 14.
95. Khan, 'Renewed Ethnonationalist Insurgency in Balochistan,' 1075.
96. Ibid.
97. Ibid
98. Ibid.

99. Safdar Sial and Abdul Basit, 'Conflict and Insecurity in Balochistan: Assessing Strategic Policy Options for Peace and Security,' *Conflict and Peace Studies* 3, no. 4 (2010): 6.

100. Rais, 'The Balochistan Package.'

101. Ibid.

102. Latif and Hamza, 'Ethnic Nationalism in Pakistan.'

103. Ibid.

104. Abdul Manan, 'Murree agreement: PM urged to let Malik continue as CM Balochistan,' *The Express Tribune*, December 5, 2015.

105. 'The Aghaz-e-Haqooq-e-Balochistan Package: An Analysis,' *PILDAT* Background Paper (December 2009).

106. 'Post and Update: Balochistan Package,' *The Researchers* (2009); and Sania Nishtar, 'The federation and provincial autonomy,' *The News International*, December 12, 2009.

107. *PILDAT*, 'The Aghaz-e-Haqooq-e-Balochistan Package.'

108. 'Post and Update'; and Nishtar, 'The federation.'

109. Grare, 'Balochistan.'

6

Ethnic Mobilization and Efforts to Establish New Provinces in Pakistan: Case Study of the Movement for a Hazara Province

Sultan Mahmood

Introduction

The Hazara division is the largest such unit in the province of Khyber Pakhtunkhwa (KP). The word 'Hazaar' is used for the figure 'thousand' in Urdu and Persian. According to the research of Major Wace, on his return to Kabul in 1398–99, the Turko-Mongol warrior King Taimur had stationed one thousand soldiers of the Turkic 'Qariq' tribe in this area to protect the important route between Kashmir and Kabul. Consequently, this area was named as 'Qariq Hazara'. The same name was used by Mughal King Babur in *Tuzak-i-Babari*. With the passage of time, the word 'Qariq' disappeared.[1] *Ain-i-Akbari* (1597 AD), *Tareekh-i-Farishta* (1605 AD), *Tuzak-i-Jahangiri* (1604–26 AD), *Khulasat-ul-Tawarikh* (1695 AD), and *Sair-ul-Mutakherin* (1771 AD) testify to this origin story of the region's name.[2]

The separate ethnic identity of the people of Hazara is embedded in the colonial history of this region. The British colonial government acquired the areas constituting the present Hazara Division from the Sikhs on March 29, 1849. Under the Sikhs and later under the

British, these areas were part of Punjab. Due to the distinctive culture of the people of this region, the British created a separate district of Hazara, and Major James Abbott was appointed as the first Deputy Commissioner of the district.[3] The formation of this district gave territorial identity and a sense of unity to the people of Hazara. There was an ethnic logic behind this decision. Hazara represented the grey area between Pathan and Punjabi cultural zones, having similarities and differences with both major cultures of the region. The majority of the people of Hazara claimed Pashtun origin. However, the dominant language of the region is Hindko, which significantly resembles Punjabi. When the North-West Frontier Province (NWFP) was formed from Punjab province in 1901, Hazara was attached to it as the only district east of the Indus River.[4] However, due to their distinct culture, the people of Hazara could never assimilate to the dominant Pashtun culture of the province.

The demand for a Hazara province has existed for a long time because of the separate cultural identity of this region. But it was the decision to rename NWFP as Khyber Pakhtunkhwa (KP) under the Eighteenth Amendment that created widespread resentment in the region and made the demand for a Hazara province popular and vigorous. The movement for the Hazara province is one of the significant sociopolitical movements of contemporary Pakistan but most of the available literature on the movement is piecemeal, covering only specific events, or representing writers' personal opinions in the form of newspaper articles. This demands a comprehensive scholarly and systematic study of the issue which does not exist. The present study is thus an attempt to fill this gap in the existing body of knowledge.

Ethnicity and Ethnic Mobilization: A Theoretical Perspective

Ethnicity is a sociopolitical phenomenon which creates unity among the individuals of a social group. Consequently 'such a group of individuals start to feel that they have common objectives and for achieving these objectives they have to initiate common efforts'.[5] This represents a social group possessing some degree of coherence and solidarity on the basis of common origin and interests. The feeling of coherence is fundamentally based upon some degree of commonality of race, colour, language, and territory. The *Oxford Encyclopedic English Dictionary* defines the word 'ethnic' as 'a social group having a common national language or cultural tradition ... denoting origin by birth or descent rather than nationality (ethnic Turks) ... relating to race or culture (ethnic) group; ethnic origins'.[6] An ethnic group possesses some degree of coherence and is composed of people who are, to some degree at least, aware of having a common origin. Because of the intense formation of in-group and out-group feelings associated with ethnic identity, it is often acknowledged to be a major driver of political mobilization and conflict, including international and civil wars.[7] In his study on the ethnic composition of the world, Walker Connor points out that in 1972, out of a total of 132 states, only 12 (9.1 per cent) could be considered ethnically homogenous states. In 31 states (23.5 per cent), the single largest ethnic group formed only 50–74 per cent of the population, and in 39 states (29.5 per cent), no single ethnic group could account for even half of the population. Another 25 states (18.9 per cent) consisted of one major ethnic group representing more than 90 per cent of the total population.[8] It is ethnic heterogeneity which often leads to ethnic conflict, especially in states with scarce and limited sources. In such states, ethnic feelings create the sense of deprivation, unrest, and consequent demand among ethnic groups for administrative control over resources. The Hazara province movement is an example of this fact.

Pakistan has a history of ethnic unrest. From its inception after Partition, Pakistan came to consist of five main provinces: the North-West Frontier, Balochistan, Sindh, Punjab, and Bengali-speaking East Pakistan. But after 70 years of independence, Pakistan has not been successful in either accommodating or eliminating ethnic divisions

and differences within its four provinces.[9] Dr Tahir Amin argues that
ethnic nationalism within smaller provinces remains a major unsolved
political issue in Pakistan.[10] This problem tends to make the process
of nation-building difficult.

There are ethnic and linguistic cleavages and conflicts in all four
provinces of Pakistan. Although the existing province names are based
on a regional ethnic identity, within each province there are various
ethnic minorities. For instance, in the province of Sindh, which
reflects the land of Sindhis, substantial non-Sindhi populations of
Urdu-speaking Muhajirs, Pashtuns, Punjabis, and Baloch exist. In
Balochistan, there is a substantial non-Baloch population including
Pashtuns and Brahvi speakers. Similarly, in the province of Khyber
Pakhtunkhwa, there is a sizeable non-Pashtun, Siraiki-speaking
population in the southern region of the province and Hindko-
speaking community in Hazara.

Ethnic feelings and subsequent ethnic mobilization in Pakistan
have been expressed in different ways. The people of East Pakistan
demanded provincial autonomy and then complete independence.
Similar feelings have developed in Balochistan. But there are also
non-secessionist ethnic movements which are not against the federal
government. These movements are demanding separate provinces
for themselves. The movement for a Hazara province is one of them.

In the different regions of Pakistan, voices have been raised to
reconfigure the provincial boundaries and create new provinces.
Supporters of the demand for the creation of new provinces think
that 'this division not only will [sic] solve the ethnic dilemma in the
province but it would help strengthen the federation of Pakistan'.[11]
But, keeping in view the multi-ethnic composition of the Pakistani
society, one can argue that creating new provinces may also aggravate
ethnic conflict and significantly harm national integration in
Pakistan. The Constitution of Pakistan provides the procedure to
create new provinces in the country. Clause 4 of Article 239 of the
Constitution says:

a bill to amend the constitution which would have the effect of altering the limits of a province shall not be presented to the President for assent unless it has been passed by the provincial assembly concerned by the votes of not less than two-third of the total membership.[12]

This means that after its passage in the two houses of Parliament, such a bill would have to be approved by the Provincial Assembly concerned with a two-thirds majority before its presentation to the President. As far as the number of provinces is concerned, neighbouring Afghanistan has 34 provinces while India has 28 states and seven union territories. Moonis Ahmar argues that, 'Pakistan is a multi-ethnic, multilingual, multicultural, and multireligious state but, despite its heterogeneous nature, the country maintained its provincial boundaries without accommodating new provincial units.'[13]

Formation of 'Hazarawal' Ethnicity: Historical Context

Stretching from Kohistan to Kaghan, Hazara division is inhabited primarily by Hindko- and Pashtu-speaking people. It is located east of the Indus River, comprising six districts: Haripur district, Abbottabad district, Mansehra district, Battagram district, and since January 28, 2011, the new Tor Ghar district. The division is allotted nine seats in the National Assembly and 20 seats in the Provincial Assembly. There are three public sector universities, one public sector medical college, three private medical colleges, and one semi-government university in the region. The Pakistan Military Academy Kakul, the Pakistan Ordinance Factory in Havelian, and the Tarbela Dam, which is the largest earth-filled dam in the world and second largest dam by structural volume, are situated in Hazara.

In Hazara, ethnicity is embedded in history, language, culture, and territoriality. According to J. Foltz, language and culture are important characteristics in forming the ethnic identity of any social group.[14] In Hazara, these factors play an important role: 'The Hazara model is one of ethnicity artificially created by colonial administrative arrangements which incorporated socially and economically distinct groups living in border zones between major cultural systems'.[15] These two dominant cultural systems are Punjabi and Pashtun. Under the Sikhs, these areas were part of their Punjab Empire. The British created a separate district of Hazara after acquiring the area from the Sikhs. When the NWFP was formed from Punjab province in 1901, a district of Hazara was made part of it. The district was about 8,300 sq. km and its population in the first census (taken in 1869) was 34,329.[16] The demarcation of administrative boundaries of the district of Hazara laid the foundation for the evolution of a distinct ethnicity. People in this area did not assimilate or absorb themselves in the neighbouring powerful Punjabi and Pashtun cultures, but maintained similarities and dissimilarities with both cultures. In the words of Akbar S. Ahmed, they 'have developed a new identity which they identify as "*Hazarawal*" or "person from Hazara"'.[17] This greyness has created 'irresolvable problems of cultural identification for the *Hazarawal*'.[18] The people of Hazara started to face a dilemma of identity outside the Hazara Division. Explaining this dilemma Ahmed writes:

> To the Pathan across the Indus, *Hazarawal* indicates non-Pathan identity and association with Punjab. Paradoxically, to Punjabis, *Hazarawal* means Pathan identity and association with the Frontier. *Hazarawals*, whether Pathan or not, confront this dilemma when they leave the Hazara Division. 'When we are in Punjab they call us "Khan Sahib" [a Pathan] and when we are in Peshawar they call us "Punjabis". We don't know where we really stand but both groups disown us. *Hazarawal* is neither Pathan nor Punjabi.'[19]

This sense of alienation has strengthened the separate identity and consequent ethnic feelings in Hazara. They have started to think: Why should we not have our separate province to recognize our identity?

The first major activity to realize the separate identity of Hazara surfaced in early 1980 when Qazi Azhar, along with a group of like-minded friends, founded the Hazara Student Federation in Karachi. Another significant development to organize the people of Hazara was the establishment of Hazara Qaumi Mahaz by the late Malik Asif Advocate in 1987. Separate organizations of the students of Hazara also existed in Quaid-i-Azam University, Islamabad, and Peshawar University which demonstrated their unity and cohesion.

Renaming the NWFP and the Demand for a Hazara Province

There is general agreement that renaming the NWFP to Khyber Pakhtunkhwa while passing the Eighteenth Amendment has given an impetus to the movement for a separate Hazara province. The Eighteenth Amendment of the Constitution of Pakistan was passed by the National Assembly of Pakistan on April 8, 2010. One of the articles asked for the provincial name change from NWFP to KP. While the Eighteenth Amendment was welcomed throughout the country as a whole, the renaming of NWFP remained a controversial issue. Although on one hand it fulfilled the dreams of Pashtun nationalists, on the other, the decision hurt the feelings of the people of Hazara division. The Awami National Party (ANP) had gained electoral support from Pashto-speaking areas on the promise to have the old colonial-era provincial name, North-West Frontier Province, changed in order to reflect Pashtun ethnic identity. According to them, if all other provinces of Pakistan were named after a majority ethnic community, their province should be treated the same.[20] But the people of Hazara division felt that they were being marginalized and ignored by the Pashtun majority of the province. These feelings created widespread anger, resentment, and unrest in the Hazara region, even leading to ethnic tension and a series of riots and protests in Hindko-speaking districts.[21] Such protests occurred in the past as well, most notably by the Hazara Qaumi Movement (HQM) in 1997 when a resolution was passed by the Provincial Assembly to change the provincial name.[22] In 2010, violent protests ensued once again, resulting in the killing of many people. The movement became aggressive when seven people were killed and over 100 sustained injuries on April 12, 2010 after police opened fire on a demonstration in Abbottabad. The people had been protesting against the renaming of NWFP as Khyber Pakhtunkhwa and demanding separate provincial status for the Hazara division. *The News* reported that 'the peaceful headquarter of Hazara Division turned into a battlefield'.[23] An all-encompassing strike was again observed in Hazara on May 2, 2010 in support of the demand for a Hazara province. Reflecting the anger of *Hazarawals*, a civil disobedience campaign was announced by the leaders of the movement.[24] Regularly organized public protest rallies in all of the major cities of Hazara and large public meetings reflected the emotional attachment of the people with the demand. People were chanting the following slogan throughout the Hazara region:

Ham lay k rahain gay Sooba Hazara
Hay Haq Hamara Sooba Hazara

We will achieve: Province Hazara
It is our right: Province Hazara

The movement's chief, Sardar Haider Zaman, vowed to continue to fight for a separate Hazara province. He emphasized that the people of Hazara would not accept further 'wrongdoings' of the provincial government led by the Pashtun nationalist ANP.[25] The movement also reflected strong feelings of resentment against the Pakistan Muslim League-Nawaz (PML-N) and its leader, Mian Mohammad Nawaz Sharif. The PML-N had a record of winning most of the seats of both the National Assembly and Provincial Assembly from the Hazara division. Now, however, the people thought that the party and its parliamentary representatives had not stood up for their interests and had in fact betrayed them. Most of the personalities who now emerged as leaders of the Hazara Movement were opponents of the PML-N and they deliberately tried to use the situation to undermine it in the region. They argued that the PML-N, which emerged as the biggest party of Hazara in the 2008 general elections, had 'failed to protect the rights of the people of Hazara and had no right to speak on behalf of the *Hazarawals* now'.[26]

A future Hazara province is an inviting proposition for many prominent political leaders of the area. There are various political leaders who hope for personal prominence in the new province. Many expected to get high official positions, which they could never achieve in KP. The movement gives rise to conflicting viewpoints in KP. Those supporting a separate Hazara province argue that their demand is reasonable as the Hazara division fulfils most conditions for separate provincial status. Opponents of the idea, primarily the Pashtun-dominated Awami National Party, argue that the proposed province is not viable and will ultimately be harmful to KP.[27] However, exponents of the Hazara province strongly believe that their desired province will remain viable and financially stable due to its rich resources. Talking to the press, the leader of the movement, Sardar Haider Zaman, argued that there are many provinces in different countries which had smaller populations than the Hazara division. Furthermore, a future Hazara province would prove to be a very stable province as it includes two dams, the Tarbela Dam and the Ghazi-Barotha Dam, and boasts natural resources including forestry and minerals, while also remaining a top tourist destination for all of Pakistan and beyond.[28]

The movement has deep historical, cultural, political, and social roots. Additionally, it is driven by administrative incentives. The people of Hazara division always feel uncomfortable travelling towards Peshawar. After coming out of Hazara, they have to cross a vast area of Punjab in order to enter into KP again. But various administrative and official problems compel them to go to Peshawar where most of them also face the problem of language, as they speak Hindko, not Pashto.

This fact is a very strong reason behind the popularity of the Hazara Province movement. Hazara Tehrik leader Sardar Haider Zaman has termed administrative efficiency, and not ethnolinguistic identity, as the fundamental reason behind the demand for a new province. In an interview he clarified that, 'We demand administrative unit because administrative control has become difficult due to increase in population.'[29]

There is a long history of divergence in public opinion between the people of Hazara and the Pashtun region of Peshawar and Mardan. Hindko speakers always supported the separatist Muslim League in pre-Partition politics, while Pashtun-dominated areas supported Congress. According to data on the number of Muslim rural seats in the legislative assembly elections of 1946 in the NWFP, Congress was able to garner only one seat in Hazara district against eight for the Muslim League. In the majority Pashtun areas of Mardan, Peshawar, Kohat, Bannu, and Dera Ismail Khan, however, Congress bagged a combined 17 seats, while the Muslim League received only four seats in these regions. The Muslim League did not gain a single seat in Kohat. Only in Bannu and Dera Ismail Khan did the Muslim League equal the total of Congress.[30]

The people of Hazara also enthusiastically favoured the inclusion of the NWFP in Pakistan during the referendum of 1947, but the people of the Peshawar region were not so enthusiastic in this respect.[31] The overall majority of voters overwhelmingly favoured inclusion within Pakistan in all districts, while only a tiny minority—in Hazara, Kohat, Bannu, and Dera Ismail Khan, less than 1 per cent in Peshawar; 1.5 per cent; and in Mardan, around 3 per cent—voted for India. However, a large proportion of the electorate in the Pashtun areas heeded the call to boycott the elections. In the Hindko-speaking Hazara district, for instance, 83,656 people out of a total of 109,762 voted and of these, 83,269 cast their vote for Pakistan. In comparison, less than 50 per cent of the potential electorate voted in Pashtun-majority Mardan and Peshawar districts, and only around two-thirds of potential voters cast their votes in Kohat, Bannu, and Dera Ismail Khan.[32]

This difference of opinion still exists and is alive in the minds of the people of Hazara. The following verse from a popular Hindko poem during the recent phase of the Hazara Movement reflects this reality:

Asan Surkhay Murkhay Koi Nan Asan Sawa Rang Sajanday
Asan Quaid Di Gal Manni, Tusan Tur Gaay Ghandi Naal [33]

We are not red, we are green
We obeyed the Quaid but you supported Gandhi

Prospects

Despite considerable mobilization for a separate Hazara province in 2010, the present situation seems to suggest, in the words of a newspaper article, 'that the sun is setting on the idea of Hazara province, as many consider it a reactionary movement against the renaming of NWFP as Khyber Pakhtunkhwa'.[34] Explaining the objectives of the Hazara province movement, one of its prominent leaders, Gohar Ayub, stated in an interview:

To achieve the goal of Hazara province, we had four phases of our struggle:

(1) People should realize that the province should be made.
(2) People outside the region should recognize the demand.
(3) Media should start projecting the issue.
(4) Debate at the governmental level.

He claimed that they achieved all of these objectives.[35]

But there is still long way to go to achieve the objective of a Hazara province. We can observe a steady decrease in the level of enthusiasm which had come about as a result of the anger against renaming the province in 2010. Ex-District Nazim Abbottabad, Baba Haider Zaman, who has emerged as the undisputed leader of the movement, has lost his administrative position. Leaders of all major political parties of the region had accepted his leadership in the period between 2010 and 2013. In his aggressive speeches, he openly challenged the incumbent government and demanded the creation of a Hazara province. The following speech reflects his commanding role in the movement:

> Be careful and use your mind. Don't let the people come out, then neither your houses will live nor your parliament. Before this we come out from Kohistan, Batagram, Mansehra, Abbottabad, Haripur … till Charrikas (a small town from where Hazara Division starts) … announce Hazara as a province. Hazara will become the province by the will of Almighty Allah. Whatever you do … and let me tell you that what ANP is losing in this? Taxes are ours, the money is ours … from which ANP is taking the salaries and allowances … using the luxury cars bought with our money … this is not fair.[36]

But he could not properly evaluate the nature and composition of his popularity and the sentiments of the people attending the demonstrations. In fact, it was the support of all political parties which had strengthened the movement. Miscalculating the consequences, he announced the launch of his own political party, Tehreek-e-Sooba Hazara, for the General Elections 2013, and invited the people of Hazara to join it. It was a tactical blunder which significantly decreased the popularity of Sardar Haider Zaman and undermined the demand for a Hazara province. His party could not win even a single seat and the people remained loyal to their party leaders. Other factors have also contributed to the diminishing passion for the movement. The party (ANP) which had hurt the feelings of the people of Hazara by renaming the province is also no longer in power. The ANP's presence in power was a reactionary source of unity in Hazara. However, the province is now being ruled by Pakistan Tehreek-e-Insaf (PTI), which has considerable support in Hazara. There are several parties and groups struggling for the province. The following important groups are presently vocally supporting a separate Hazara province:

(1) Hazara Tehrik with Baba Haider Zaman as its chief coordinator.
(2) Hazara Province Tehrik with Sardar M. Yousuf as Chairman.
(3) Tehreek-i-Huquq-e-Hazara led by Ali Asghar Khan.
(4) Hazara Qaumi Mahaz with Khursheed Ali Hazarvi as its President.[37]

The lack of unity and proper coordination among these groups is a major reason for the weakness of the movement. Although currently the movement does not seem very strong and enthusiastic, it does have the potential to rejuvenate itself. However, a movement based upon ethnic hatred against Pashtuns cannot be durable and successful due to a considerable Pashto-speaking population within Hazara. Out of six districts in Hazara Division, Batgram and Torghar are predominantly Pashto-speaking districts, while there is a sizeable Pashto-speaking population in the districts of Mansehra, Kohistan, and Sirikot Valley of District Haripur. So the demand for Hazara province can attract a greater following in the region if it is based upon administrative convenience and economic prosperity, rather than simply ethnic identity.

Conclusion

The issue of reconfiguring provincial boundaries and creating Hazara province is embedded in various historical, linguistic, socioeconomic, and cultural factors. The district of Hazara was created by the British colonial government for administrative facilitation. However, this decision to define the administrative boundaries laid the foundations for the development of a distinct ethnic identity of 'Hazarawal', located between dominant neighbouring Pashtun and Punjabi identities. This separate identity has provided the foundation for the demand of Hazara province, which gained traction after the decision to rename the province from NWFP to Khyber Pakhtunkhwa. There is no harm in reconfiguring the number of provinces in Pakistan but there are certain complexities involved as far as its implications for national integration are concerned. The division, within the present political structure of Khyber Pakhtunkhwa, will affect not only the economy and sociopolitical setup of the province but would also leave deep-rooted imprints on other provinces, and political demands based on ethnic identity conflict may intensify as a result. So keeping all advantages and disadvantages in mind, political elites should consider carefully before developing a strategy to deal with this delicate issue.

Notes

1. QUOTED IN DR SHER BAHADUR KHAN PANNI, *Tareekh-e-Hazara* [History of Hazara] (Lahore: Maktaba Rehmania, 2001), 33.

2. PUNJAB GOVERNMENT, *Gazetteer of the Hazara District 1883–4* (Lahore: Sang-e-Meel Publications, 2000).

3. Panni, *Tareekh-e-Hazara*.

4. H. D. Watson, *Gazetteer of the Hazara District 1907* (London: Chatto & Windus, 1908), 122.

5. Gulshan Majeed, 'Ethnicity and Conflict: A Theoretical Perspective,' *Journal of Political Studies* 20, no. 1 (2013): 98–9.

6. See *The Oxford Encyclopedic English Dictionary* (New York: Oxford, 1991), 488.

7. Paramanand Khanna and Saroj B. Khanna, 'Ethnicity in Bhutan: Causes and Effects,' *Journal of South Asian and Middle Eastern Studies* 17, no. 1 (1993): 77.

8. Walker Conner, 'Nation-Building or Nation-Destroying?' *World Politics* 24, no. 3 (April 1972), reprinted in *Ethnonationalism: The Quest for Understanding* (Princeton: Princeton University Press, 1994), 29.

9. Frederic Grare, 'Pakistan: The Resurgence of Baluch Nationalism,' *Carnegie Endowment for International Peace* 65 (January 2006): 3.

10. Tahir Amin, *Ethno-National Movements in Pakistan: Domestic and International Factors* (Islamabad: Institute of Policy Studies, 1988).

11. Yasmin Roofi and Khawaja Alqama 'Ethnic Dilemma in Pakistan and Division of Punjab: End or Beginning of the New Era of Conflict,' *Journal of Politics and Law* 6, no. 1 (2013): 156.

12. Government of Pakistan, *Constitution of Islamic Republic of Pakistan* (Islamabad: Manager of Publications, 1973).

13. Moonis Ahmar, 'Conflict Prevention and the New Provincial Map of Pakistan: A Case Study of Hazara Province,' *Journal of Political Studies* 20, no. 2 (2013): 1–19.

14. W. J. Foltz, 'Ethnicity, Status and Conflict,' in *Ethnicity and Nation-Building: Interpretational and Comparative Perspectives*, eds. Wendon Bell and Walter Freeman (Sage Publications, 1974), 8.

15. Akbar S. Ahmed, 'Hazarawal: Formation and Structure of District Ethnicity,' in *Pakistan: The Social Sciences' Perspective*, eds. Akbar S. Ahmed and Zulfikar Ghose (Karachi: Oxford University Press, 1990), 30.

16. Ibid., 29.

17. Ibid.

18. Ibid.

19. Ibid., 32–3.

20. Yasmin Roofi, 'Renaming of NWFP and Hazara Ethnicity: A New Course of Ethnic Conflict in Pakistan,' *European Journal of Social Sciences* 19, no. 4 (2011): 588–93.

21. *The Daily Express*, April 14, 2010.

22. *Daily Mashriq Peshawar*, November 14, 1997.

23. 'Anti-Pakhtunkhwa protest claims seven lives in Abbottabad,' *The News*, April 13, 2010.

24. 'People of Hazara can launch civil disobedience,' *The News International*, May, 17 2010, https://www.thenews.com.pk/archive/print/237286-%E2%80%98people-of-hazara-can-launch-civil-disobedience%E2%80%99.

25. 'Movement for Hazara province refuses to die down,' *The Express Tribune*, June 9, 2010.

26. 'Protests in Hazara against NWFP renaming,' *The News*, April 3, 2010.

27. Ahmar, 'Conflict Prevention.'

28. 'Mansehra. Baba Hadir Zaman tareek Suba Hazara ek din GEO k sath clip 2 (AQEEL AHMED 03135844466),' *News4U*, April 1, 2011, https://www.youtube.com/watch?v=l0CIwG4V5Co.

29. 'Baba Haider Zaman addressing Tehreek-e Sooba Hazara Student Convention 2011,' *HCP Hazara*, December 17, 2011, https://www.youtube.com/watch?v=UTTAUOkX4vI.

30. Government of India, *Returns showing the Results of Elections to the Central Legislative Assembly and the Provincial Legislatures in 1945–46* (Delhi: Manager of Publications, 1948).

31. See Professor Dr M. A. Soofi, *Sooba Sarhad Ki Pakistan Main Shamooliat or Quaid-i-Azam Mohammad Ali Jinnah Kay Sathi* (Lahore: Book Home, 2014), 26–8.

32. Muhammad Shakeel Ahmad, 'Electoral Politics in NWFP, 1988–1999,' PhD Thesis (Islamabad: Quaid-i-Azam University, 2010), 79.

33. 'Suba Hazara Poem Mansehra,' *Muhammad SaqiB*, April 28, 2010, https://www.youtube.com/watch?v=8WJutzd5sUY.

34. Kalbe Ali, 'Hazara movement: divided we fall,' *Dawn*, December 2, 2012.

35. 'Ghustakhi Maaf (Gohar Ayub Khan Hazara Province) 29 April 2012,' *WaqtNews TV*, April 29, 2012, https://www.youtube.com/watch?v=CQb7L7cP2R4.
36. 'A Short Overview of Hazara Province Movement,' *HCP (Hazara.Com.PK)*, https://www.dailymotion.com/video/x1nn77t.
37. Ahmar, 'Conflict Prevention.'

7

Siraiki Nationalism:
Identity Construction and
Politics of Autonomy

Rasul Bakhsh Rais

Introduction

This chapter explores the idea of Siraiki identity construction and whether or not it has been or can be an effective instrument in carving out a separate province or provinces from Punjab. Many strands of theories of ethnic identity formation suggest that identity is essentially a political project for political ends that may employ diverse means from literary traditions to language and cultural symbolism. No less important is the role social and political narratives play in raising the ethnic consciousness of a community. What these narratives are and what traction they have gained within the Siraiki language speaking communities is one of the questions that we intend to address. The Siraiki national issue has a history that needs to be understood and explained with reference to the national and Punjab politics, but more so in the context of ethnic demography, social structures, and social group politics of the Siraiki regions of Punjab and even beyond its boundaries.

The main argument of the chapter is that Siraiki ethnic identity formation is essentially a reflection of ethnic movements of other regions of Pakistan and a reaction to real or perceived appropriation of resources and power by Punjabi elites. A broader sense of Siraiki linguistic identity has emerged, subsuming local linguistic identities such as Multani and Riasti in the districts and regions where the majority of the people speak the Siraiki language. This is perhaps the most remarkable progress of the Siraiki national project—a uniform replacement of regional names.[1] Identity construction in multi-ethnic societies is essentially instrumental in achieving some articulated goals. Keeping the instrumental function of identity in mind, three questions may be raised:

(1) What motives define the Siraiki nationalism?
(2) How coherent and unified is the Siraiki national movement?
(3) What challenges and structural constraints does it face?

The premise and principle proposition of this chapter is that the Siraiki social groups are on the margins of economic and political power and face the grave challenge of creating and promoting ethnic identity. There are many reasons why the Siraiki nationalists are finding it hard to capture the larger social and political space for an ethnic narrative. First, the local political elites have not embraced the idea of Siraiki nationalism, as they see their interests tied to major political parties. Second, the Siraiki communities are spread across four provinces of the country that makes it rather more difficult to develop a coherent leadership or practical vision for the realization of a Siraiki province. Third, the Siraiki regions have witnessed large-scale out-group ethnic migration and takeover of considerable urban spaces, agricultural lands, business, and industry—forcing them to exist on the margins of the power structure of Punjab. The political space for the Siraiki national movement remains narrow and squeezed by the social hegemony of dynastic political families and powerful migrant communities that have changed the demographic character of the Siraiki regions. The creation of a Siraiki province or the two provinces of Multan and Bahawalpur—the articulated political objectives of the movement—may be facilitated by the interplay of politics of federal construction or reconstruction at national level but if and when that happens, it will also be a manifest victory for the Siraiki nationalist movement. The bigger question, and the challenge, is whether or not the sentiment of Siraiki identity and struggle for a separate province or provinces will translate into a significant political movement to force the national political parties—Pakistan Peoples Party (PPP), Pakistan Muslim League (Nawaz) (PML-N), and Pakistan Tehreek-e-Insaf (PTI)—to place this issue on their agenda. To win the support of the Siraiki voters, all the major political parties have pushed vague resolutions without much consistent political commitment to Bahawalpur, Siraiki, or south Punjab provinces. There is nothing on the ground to demonstrate any political commitment to carving up Punjab and creating more provinces out of the largest province. Apart from other structural constraints that will be examined in the chapter, breaking up a province constitutionally rests on the consent of the province concerned. In this case, will Punjab, the most powerful province and with significant Punjabi settler populations in the Siraiki regions, write its own dissolution? In the end, it will be the balance of Punjab politics, the strength and popularity of the Siraiki national movement, and the bandwagoning of the dynastic, feudal political class that will determine the fate of the struggle for provinces in southern Punjab. For some of the reasons we have mentioned here, the struggle for the Siraiki province or provinces remains weak, fragmented, and confined to the narrow bands of local leadership. The crux of the matter is that no major political parties are currently willing to risk alienating central Punjab—the political powerhouse of the country—to adopt the Siraiki issue.

Concept and Theory

Identity construction is a deliberate political act in multi-ethnic societies, both at the regional and national level. In non-homogenous societies, like the Siraiki regions, a complex set of factors have influenced Siraiki identity and nationalism. These are a perception of threat from other ethnic groups that have settled in the Siraiki regions, and a feeling of declining power and influence within their own geographical domains. Therefore, how is this identity constituted in plural communities like the Siraiki regions? According to the interactionist stream of literature, it is language through which an ethnic group constructs, articulates, negotiates, and communicates its identity.[2] What it means is that production of identity and its sustenance rests on the use of language in everyday social interaction within the ethnic group. However, the cultural and emotional affiliation with the linguistic identity may not produce converging visions of a sense of 'nation' or nationalism among speakers of the same language. For this reason, some sociologists like Rogers Brubaker argue that diversity within social groups make it a challenging task to define people as ethnic groups.[3] There are many considerations above and beyond cultural attachment that may push a community or communities toward assimilation with larger groups or reduce the relevance of language and identity for the pursuit of pragmatic economic and political interests. The point is that identity does not translate itself easily or automatically into a political movement for something. It remains, however, a major but dormant source for ethnic politics in plural societies like Pakistan. Its activation and effective use depends on a wide range of factors, issues, and the political and economic environment of the constituent regions.

The concept of identity is problematic for other reasons as well and very difficult to operationalize in any objective fashion. Essentially, identity is subjective—it is about self-identification and out-group recognition.[4] Many other factors impinge on identity selection and its adoption. As an outcome of cultural and emotive issues, identity is not fixed; rather, it is a dynamic process, the way culture both at the national as well as regional level are path dependent. Religion, history, civilization, and, more importantly, modernization and technology are the forces that shape and reshape cultural traditions because of the 'path dependence' of culture, values, and attitudes.[5] In a similar vein, Fredrik Barth regards culture, which is generally understood as a central feature of ethnicity, as 'an implication or result, rather than a primary and definitional characteristic of ethnic group organization'.[6] The reason is that cultures and identities can change across time and space. The formation of Siraiki identity as an emerging uniform marker that has gradually replaced narrow but historical linguistic identities like Multani and Riasti shows progress towards the formation of an imagined cultural identity.[7] The question is that can Siraiki substituting for historically different titles of the language even be a sufficient factor by itself for Siraiki identity? In this respect, Ryan Brasher makes an important point that 'the content of ethnic identification is determined by the economic and social function of a group'.[8] In the case of the Siraiki regions, a sense of deprivation, marginalization, and economic and political domination of Punjab have created a sense of grievance against Punjabis as outsiders, the other. In turn, Siraiki-speakers have developed a greater sense of group cohesion. The language and culture are simply the instrument of expressing internal coherence, which is still in the making, and asserting a claim over political resources—autonomy and creation of a province/provinces.

While debating identity construction, one has to keep in mind that in modern-day complex societies, more so in multi-ethnic communities cohabitating the same spaces, individuals may have more than one identity or, in the words of Henry Hale, multiple dimensions of one wholly integrated identity. Depending on the context and situation in which one finds oneself, an identity dimension, which may have existed a priori, can become thicker or thinner with both personal and political meaning.[9] In the Siraiki regions, where caste, tribe, and location have historically been powerful identifiers, one finds multiple identities quite a common social affair that unfold depending on the place and context of social and political interaction. In the context of Punjab and national politics, Siraiki identity politics has grown and is likely to remain an important cultural and social influence on the political orientations of the peoples of the Siraiki regions.

Politics in its every aspect is the most powerful influence on shaping, reshaping, and shifting of identities. The distribution effects of both economic rewards and political power in a socially uneven place like Pakistan has created a sense of deprivation among certain ethnic groups. Siraiki-speaking populations have increasingly come to believe that they are discriminated against, have been left behind, and denied their legitimate rights. In a way, it appears to be a success of the Siraiki national narrative. Clearly, social incentives are emerging in adopting the Siraiki identity in the hope that Siraiki regions will be able to create their own provinces. The formation of Siraiki political parties and their rallies, slogan, manifestos, and participation in several elections have brought the Siraiki national issue to the attention of the people. Their failure in achieving electoral victories may overshadow other areas of political success. Popularizing the Siraiki issue or even creating this sentiment is a big accomplishment. Siraiki political groups will have to create a more supportive environment for their goal of creating new provinces by coming together and forming alliances with outside groups. While intellectuals and social entrepreneurs play a big role in framing and disseminating identity discourses, political activists play a disproportionately greater role than any other source.[10]

Identity formation is a first essential step that we believe has already occurred in the case of the Siraiki regions. But that is not enough; it might be considered the beginning of a long and equally unsettling historical process. The real challenge for all social groups adopting or focusing on particular identities, like the Siraiki, is how to obtain political recognition.[11] That transformation will be subject to many issues at the regional and national level. The politics of Punjab and national identities being fluid and shifting, it is hard to imagine a single trajectory either for the Siraiki identity or the social and political groups involved in its instrumentalist construction. It is equally difficult to predict how the provincial or national politics would influence ethnic orientations in Punjab.

Means of Identity Construction

Siraiki social entrepreneurs have played a key role in the construction of Siraiki identity from settling on a uniform, standard linguistic brand to its promotion. These are highly motivated individuals committed to the idea of preserving and promoting Siraiki as a mother tongue, as well as Siraiki culture and literary heritage as essential markers of identity. They have come from different backgrounds—from teaching in schools and colleges to other intellectual and worldly pursuits. They have worked through cooperation, made concerted efforts with meagre personal resources, and built coalitions with like-minded intellectuals. The first efforts came purely as individualistic pursuits. Love for the language motivated individuals such as Mohammad Ahmad Fakhruddin Razi who compiled the first Multani *Qaida* (alphabets) in 1933. Similarly, Muhammad Azizur Rehman Aziz formed a committee of experts to report on the Siraiki alphabet in 1942.[12] They retained the Urdu alphabet but added a few to account for unique Siraiki sounds and pronunciations. That was the first essential step that we witnessed, even before the creation of Pakistan, to found a Siraiki literary tradition. The general impression within and outside the Siraiki regions then, and even in some quarters now, is that Siraiki does not meet the standard and criteria of an independent language. Rather, it is mainly a spoken dialect and variant of Punjabi language. These original writers were hardly defensive or conscious of what others wrote or said about the Siraiki language. They worked out of the belief that Siraiki was a language, a heritage in the classical poetry of Sachal Sarmast and Khawaja Fareed, in folklore and popular genre of songs that have been widely popular beyond the Siraiki regions.[13] The first generation of these literary figures considered that their commitment to the 'homeland' was to preserve the Siraiki heritage and propagate it.

The second generation of Siraiki intellectuals, poets, and political activists built on the work of the first generation to construct the

Siraiki identity. They have argued that Siraiki is a common language of people living in southern Punjab and on the periphery of three adjoining provinces, which makes them one linguistic-cultural group. They have created multiple links among themselves through cultural and political means. Among the cultural means are convening of Siraiki *mushaira* (poetic or poetry reciting sessions) and Siraiki festivals in different parts of the regions.[14] The cultural activities in the Siraiki regions have historically been part of the annual festivals of shrines. They are less religious and more of a trade and secular affair, with entertainment-like songs, dance, music, and theatre being some of the essential elements. Social entrepreneurs like Ashiq Buzdar, a celebrated and highly regarded poet and activist, have founded annual Siraiki *mela*s (festivals) which have matured into a gathering of intellectuals, artists, poets and Siraiki nationalist activists.[15]

A third generation of ethnic social entrepreneurs have motives that move beyond ethnolinguistic moralism—a duty toward the mother tongue. They are inspired by ethnic and nationalistic considerations. They place identity at the top of their hierarchy of preferences because of its assumed effectiveness in political empowerment. They believe Siraiki is not only one of the native languages of the Indus but also a culture, a community, and a nationality.[16] It has its own separate linguistic identity and now the same can be used to construct an ethnic identity of the peoples and the regions that constitute their historical homelands.[17] The most important tool, however, remains political mobilization. The demand for a Siraiki province appears to be attractive at the popular level and may gain wider acceptance and support in the future. The narrative of Punjabi dominance resonates in political rhetoric and demand for a Bahawalpur and Multan or Siraiki province. This has proved to be an effective strategy to advance Siraiki national identity. At least educated, young, professional middle class persons, mainly settled in cities outside the Siraiki regions, appear to have embraced the idea of separate provinces.

Politics of New Provinces[18]

Since the passage of the Eighteenth Amendment, we have seen that voices in support of more provinces have become louder. Furthermore, we have also seen that an increasing number of minority ethnic groups and parties seem to be demanding that the existing provinces—if not all, then at least Punjab—should be broken up into small units.[19] Let us first try and understand the reasons behind these demands and then explain how the future of the Pakistani federation is likely to be affected, and whether or not a Siraiki province or provinces may be realized.

There are three reasons that should matter in our consideration of this issue. The first is the devolution of power to the federating units of Pakistan—a dream of the provincialists and a long-standing demand of subnational political forces struggling for their rights.[20] One fault of the previous government has been to hold back on the local government system during its time in office and this has only reinforced the apprehensions of those who seek greater autonomy beyond the provinces down to the level of the districts and regions. One of the single most important issues which is generally ignored is that provincial capitals have become the new centres of power that generate alienation and resentment among the local elites. This resentment, at least in the Siraiki regions, has taken an ethnic form—a resentment directed at Punjab and the *takht-e-Lahore* (seat of power).

The second reason relates to the issue of ethnic majorities and minorities in each province. One may argue that since they have coexisted for centuries, why is there a problem now. The problem is that Pakistan has changed, and the ethnic configuration of its provinces has changed as well. Populations have increased manifold and the struggle over resources and physical spaces has consequently intensified. The Baloch have historically been trickling down to Sindh and Punjab, a process that has been defined by economic opportunities opened up first by the digging of the canals and then by industrial growth and development.[21] The Pashtuns from Afghanistan, borderlands, and Khyber Pakhtunkhwa (KP) have been continuously migrating into all other provinces, generating competition over jobs and business and raising ethnic tensions.[22] The Baloch nationalists resent the presence and flow of the Pashtuns from Afghanistan in the guise of refugees. They fear the demographic balance turning against them.[23]

The historical glue of keeping multiple ethnic groups together in one provincial fold began to loosen with the renaming of North-West Frontier Province (NWFP) to Khyber Pakhtunkhwa. The political desire and some discernible political trends to create more provinces were already there but on a much lower scale and without critical mass. What changed things was the insistence of the majority of Pashtuns on an ethnic name for their province. Perhaps a pragmatic approach might not have generated feelings of alienation among other ethnic groups once the new name was adopted. This was not done and the people of the Hazara division understandably protested when the name was changed.

The third reason is the spillover effect of democracy in Pakistan and a product of the 'law' of unintended consequences. One may always dispute the quality, style, and substance of democracy, but it has been there in Pakistan for a very long time. Even in its damaged and subverted form, it has created a new politics of entitlements, rights, and group consciousness. Furthermore, it has helped people shape and reshape their ethnic identity in a quest to access or retain power. Democracy is about rights, and democratic politics has always created greater space for social groups to demand their rights, and this includes those related to the creation of their own provinces.

What has already happened in India is now being demanded in Pakistan—ethnic mobilization of minority ethnic groups for their own provinces.[24] Democratic politics by necessity forces political parties to adopt popular issues, or popularize new issues where space for them exists. This is exactly what the PPP has done by raising the issue of the Siraiki province. Before this, the Muttahida Quami Movement (MQM) also voiced its support for the Siraiki issue, again because it wanted to expand its influence. Had there been no popular feeling for the Siraiki and Bahawalpur provinces, the PML-N would not have jumped on the bandwagon. After the elections, the political temperature for the movement to create the new provinces has cooled off. It is yet to be seen if and when the federation will be restructured, since new provinces will require a much broader national consensus. Also, when it happens, the change will not be confined to Punjab alone.[25]

Regional disparity at the national level—a wide gap in development and per capita income—and within each province of the country, has given rise to narratives of oppression and discrimination.[26] Ethnic movements and parties are the first to use these to lay the foundations of their politics and to use it against the federation, and against the largest province, Punjab.[27] In the emotional politics of ethnicity, no one looks at the history of the development, the natural endowment of different regions, and the legacies of colonial rule. At the time of Independence, the provinces and regions were at different levels of social and economic development, owing to the economic, political, and security needs of British colonial power in the subcontinent. Punjab was at the top of all of them because of its representation in the state structure, the military, and bureaucracy, as well as its vast size and fertile lands.

The rationale of a nation-state is to end disparities by careful planning and allocation of national and provincial resources. Not that every region of the country and regions within provinces have the same matrix of development and similar disparities that existed during colonial rule, but the fact is that Pakistan has not really succeeded in bringing all parts of the country at an appropriate, respectable level of parity. Maybe that is too ambitious an objective. The minimum elites could do would be to target poverty, lack of educational facilities, poor literacy rates, and the stark economic inequality that exists among the different regions of Pakistan even after 70 years of its independence.[28]

In restructuring the federation under the Eighteenth Amendment, we have taken the first right step—transfer of power, responsibility, and resources to the provinces. Each province is a new centre of power. If power and resources are not devolved further to the regions and districts, the new centres are likely to ignite ethnic identities that have historical roots and that may also transform into demands for new provinces. Punjab is more vulnerable to division than the other provinces. The Siraiki linguistic identity and the history of the two states of Multan and Bahawalpur run deep in the political minds of ordinary people in southern Punjab. In recent decades, the ethnic groups within these regions have developed a political narrative of neglect and discrimination that is supported by facts relating to uneven development among the various geographic regions of Punjab. There is still time to do some path correction in southern Punjab to avert the politicization of linguistic and ethnic identities.

It is true that in recent years the development allocations for the southern regions represent the population size of the districts. But there are also other factors such as landlessness, poverty, a low literacy rate, and an oppressive feudal system that require a more thoughtful intervention to create social and economic space for the marginalized. Even a bigger allocation of resources for development may end up in private pockets without proper accountability and transparency. The problem is that political and social power is in the hands of tribal and feudal families, supported by the federation and the provincial power structure. The levers of justice, governance, law and order, and equity in development have thus left a strong imprint of partisan politics that only works in the interest of patronage politics.

Sensing a sentiment for Siraiki identity, former President Asif Ali Zardari, co-chairperson of the PPP, made one of those clever moves by sending a reference in 2013 to the Speaker of the National Assembly for establishing a commission to create two new provinces—Bahawalpur and Multan.[29] It was the first serious move to get the ball rolling on these two proposed provinces. The objective was point-scoring politics as well as aiming at gathering political support from within the region. Whatever the motives, Zardari brought the issue of a province in southern Punjab to the national discourse. The activists for Bahawalpur and Siraiki provinces found new energy for their old dream with the support of the major political parties. It is one of the positive spin-off effects of competitive democratic politics that the idea of the Bahawalpur and Multan provinces appeared to be gaining bipartisan support in both parties. By not supporting this issue, the PML-N feared loss of popular support in the region. Feeling that President Zardari had struck the right popular chord in southern Punjab, the PML-N made a counter move by supporting the revival of the Bahawalpur province and indicating that it would also help create the south Punjab province. If that was not enough to match the PPP initiative, it moved a resolution in Punjab Assembly in support of its ideas. In yet another counter move, the National Assembly also passed a resolution in support of the southern Punjab province.

Besides the positive gains of competitive democratic politics—which forces political parties to adopt popular issues or popularize issues that they hope will win them public support—is the issue of elite interaction, negotiation, and compromise. This aspect of Pakistani politics was quite remarkably demonstrated in the consensus that developed on the Eighteenth Amendment that has restructured federalism and appears to be a catalyst for the demand for new provinces. It was the same process that appears to be working behind the move for the Bahawalpur and Multan provinces.

Elite competition, as was quite apparent in the Bahawalpur-Multan provinces move, is what may lead to their establishment eventually. The competition is essentially among the three major political parties—the PML-N, PPP, and PTI—as these would be likely to win the support of the Siraiki voter. The regional leaders belonging to these parties understand the Siraiki sentiment better than their national leaders, and they have kept impressing upon their top leaders to adopt the Siraiki province/provinces as a political plank.[30] The leaders of the political parties have been echoing the demands of the Siraiki peoples, often to garner political support.[31] It is likely that the dormant, passive, and so far, ineffective political forces of the region will put their collective strength behind this move that no party will be likely to resist. The leaders of the major political parties are wary of ethnicization of the Siraiki issue because they fear a political backlash from the central Punjab populations. It would make better sense for them to support non-ethnic, administrative provinces to make it politically viable. If Siraiki nationalists change their demand from a Siraiki province to either a southern Punjab province or two provinces of Bahawalpur and Multan, the mainstream political leaders might show better resolve to support the move than they have in the past. Bahawalpur and Multan, as names of the provinces, would reflect the history, heritage, culture, and the traditional identity that both regions, once autonomous political entities, possessed.[32] Heritage names for states and provinces should be inclusive of all ethnicities and send a positive political message to minority language groups of common ownership, as linguistic labels alienate such groups. One important note of caution: the move for the new provinces is not going to end with the carving up of Punjab even with bipartisan support. Khyber Pakhtunkhwa, Balochistan, and Sindh, even with loud vows of 'indivisibility', may not remain unaffected in the face of strong minority ethnic movements.

The Siraiki Card[33]

The report of the parliamentary commission on carving up new provinces came out in 2013.[34] What the commission produced was a piece of shoddy political work that was not going to help the country restructure the present federating units. Rather, it could polarize ethnic communities, regions, provinces, and political parties and make the task of creating new provinces more controversial than the issue had been so far. The PML-N opposed the report, fearing that creation of provinces based on ethnic groups would damage the federation.[35]

First, let us admit that dividing provinces along ethnic, historical, or administrative lines is always a controversial matter and not an easy one to deal with in a polarized and over-politicized society like Pakistan's. Unlike India, we have retained the colonial boundaries of the provinces, except that we created the province of Balochistan with the disbanding of the One Unit system by a martial law regime in 1969. Another anomaly was that Bahawalpur maintained a province-like status until the formation of One Unit in 1954, when it was absorbed into Punjab. It was a questionable move on the part of Punjabi bureaucracy and the dominant political class. Their real interest was in the fertile lands of the Bahawalpur State. The results of that move are obvious to all of us in the changed demographic character of this formerly princely state. Today, Punjabi settlers from other parts of Punjab dominate the political economy of the Bahawalpur division. The people of Bahawalpur resisted the change in their status peacefully and by democratic, political means. They formed the Bahawalpur Suba Mahaz (BSM) and contested the 1970 elections on the Bahawalpur province platform. They won a good number of provincial and national assembly seats. This was the only region that was not entirely swept aside by the Zulfikar Ali Bhutto (ZAB) wave. The PPP government, then with a firm hold over Punjab under Bhutto, gradually extended its sway over Bahawalpur by making political deals and aligning powerful figures in the area with the party. Within a few years, the BSM disintegrated but the sentiment and memory of the Bahawalpur State and the dream of reviving the provincial status have lived on.

One of the moves that the PPP strategists thought would have a lasting effect on the region was the creation and promotion of a Siraiki identity. The party sponsored intellectuals, writers, and activists from Siraiki regions and Sindh to organize the first major three-day Siraiki Adbi (literary) conference in 1975 in Multan, the city that has emerged as the centre of Siraiki consciousness. This included major names of that age among speakers who spoke on how to revive, celebrate, and preserve the Siraiki language and literature. The subtext of the conference was awareness about Siraiki identity.[36] The issue of a common Siraiki identity of various regions that spoke the same language had already been on the agenda of Sindhi and Siraiki intellectuals and activists for almost a decade. The convening of a national Siraiki conference in Multan in 1975 introduced a new discourse on Siraiki identity. However, not much has been written about the first Siraiki convention, including the actors, the motives, and the effects of this movement.

Weaknesses of Siraiki Nationalism

Siraiki nationalism has not been able to make a big political wave either in national politics or in politics of Punjab. It faces quite a few structural problems, which nationalists find themselves powerless to address. The wheel of history has moved too fast for the Siraiki regions. It was perhaps too late when Siraiki nationalists, very limited in number and fragmented among different groups, realized that they had lost much of the demographic and economic space to Punjabi settlers that started coming to this region well before the creation of Pakistan. Interestingly, the Nawab of Bahawalpur, on the pattern of canal colonies in Punjab, made land grants to Punjabi cultivators from districts now in the Indian Punjab to settle in the state. The Muslim migrants from India at the time of Partition have taken up much of the urban spaces in the Siraiki regions.

The biggest shift that may work against the Siraiki dreams is the demography of the region. The Siraiki-speaking population is no longer a majority ethnic community in Multan. The migrants from India dominate trade and business, while Punjabi settlers are in greater numbers in the government and service sectors. Comparatively and proportionately, the middle class among the Siraiki populations appears to be much lower than the immigrants and settlers. Likewise, the incidents of poverty and low levels of skills and education among the Siraiki speakers is far larger than other populations. The Siraiki intellectuals attribute these developments to the power and domination of Punjab. Unfair distribution of resources has been a major issue that has prevented the region from being on a par with the central and northern Punjab regions.

The most important factor retarding the Siraiki national movement, however, is the feudal character of Siraiki society and domination of the dynastic political families. Electoral politics are run as succession in the royal families. They have never realized the need to build broader social alliances with other layers of society. It is only in urban centres, where a decisive demographic shift has occurred, that immigrants and settlers with national party labels have ousted the dynastic feudal families. The feudal Siraiki political families continue to retain their stronghold over the Siraiki populations. In the end, it will be their conversion to the cause of provinces in the Siraiki regions—in their own interest—that may transform the Siraiki national movement. That is not possible as long as they remain within the fold of national parties. No ethnic movement, whatever its goals might be, has succeeded without a broad national front. Siraiki nationalists and ethnic entrepreneurs get only comforting words but no concrete measures from the lords.

Compared to Siraiki nationalists and groups, the rival ethnic communities, immigrants, and Punjabi settlers are better connected, are more resourceful, and exercise greater influence in association with one another and in the forums of national political parties. The

Siraiki groups face a dual challenge. One is confronting the dynastic families, which they do not appear to be doing, hoping that they can bring these families around on the issue of separate provinces. Secondly, they have to compete with more powerful communities with very little social, economic, and political resources. The idiom and symbolism of Siraiki nationalism may drive rival communities to support the opponents of separation from Punjab within the regions and also at national level.

Lastly, the claims of the Siraiki nationalist groups regarding the geographic boundaries of the Siraiki *wasaib* (society or ethnic group) are highly exaggerated. The regions beyond Multan and even Mianwali or Jhang may not wish to identify themselves as Siraiki. The Siraiki-speaking tribes, castes, and groups are spread across the four provinces of the country. A big chunk is obviously in Sindh, from where the word Siraiki comes. Eastern parts of Balochistan and the two southern districts of KP have significant Siraiki-speaking populations. The tragedy of the Siraiki districts of KP is that they have gradually lost their numerical superiority due to Pashtun migration and takeover of business, trade, and even lands. Some say that successive governments in the province have encouraged Pashtun colonization. The refugees from FATA and Afghanistan have further added to the numbers of the Pashtuns. There is a degree of Siraiki national sentiment in KP and activists there maintain links with the Siraikis of Punjab, but they have little hope of separating themselves from the Pashtun stranglehold. The Siraiki national movement remains confined to southern Punjab and is not in a position to develop itself as a trans-provincial Siraiki movement.

Conclusion

Some gains of Siraiki nationalism are quite remarkable. First, the Siraiki ethnic identity that has been politically manufactured has quickly wholesaled itself.[37] Local and regional variants of the language do exist but all have assumed a singular identity of Siraiki. The social conversion of these variants into a single linguistic identification is unprecedented. Another important characteristic of this change has been voluntary, without any resistance or enforcement from above. It seems as if the people of the Siraiki regions found a common symbol that would give them a strong sense of cultural unity within and across provincial boundaries.

Second, there is a pride in the Siraiki identity that is widely shared. A feeling of being culturally homogenous gives the people a sense of having unique social characteristics, similar to the cultural particularism of other ethnic communities. They speak at the same level with members of other ethnic communities within the Siraiki regions and outside. It is a major gain for all, even those that may not be strongly attached to the Siraiki identity, a sense of being equal to others. The Siraiki ethnic identity has over time become widely acknowledged. At least at the political level, it is being considered as a serious political issue that needs to be resolved. But this recognition is far below the threshold of creating an emergency for Punjabi, Siraiki, or national elites to take up the issue of creating one or more provinces in the Siraiki regions.

Its weaknesses are the same that other marginalized communities face. Here is a familiar template of them: lack of commitment of the dominant Siraiki elites as their use of Siraiki identity is situational, opportunistic, and meant to take political advantage at the local levels.[38] So far, there appears to be no strong ideological commitment of political families of the Siraiki regions, except in the case of restoration of the Bahawalpur province. The strongest support for the restoration has come from the former ruler of the State, the Nawab of Bahawalpur.

Political fragmentation is another issue. This is because individual leaders of the factions wish to use the Siraiki turf for economic or political patronage from powerful national political actors or state institutions. Being together and having a larger decision-making group would interfere with their respective pursuit of personal interests. In a way, their narrow politics mirrors the feudal character of the region they come from. They would not like to share power, privilege, and leadership with others. Fragmentation reduces their capacity to mobilize public support for their cause and broaden the support base even among Siraiki-speaking social groups.

Siraiki national symbolism and ethnic identity creates ripple effects among the settler populations that are more powerful, more numerous in the urban centres, and well-connected through caste and ethnicities with the major centres of power in Punjab and at the national level. The settler population with a powerful presence in every district of the Siraiki regions is not comfortable with the development of a Siraiki identity and its use for separating these regions from Punjab. Perhaps their opposition might be reduced by giving historical names to the new provinces in southern Punjab—such as Bahawalpur and Multan.[39] However, Siraiki nationalists may not compromise on administrative or historical names.[40]

In addition to the problem of dependence on feudal, dynastic leaders among the peoples of the Siraiki region, and low socioeconomic development and mobility, Siraiki nationalists suffer from another problem. This is cultural determinism, which denies them the inherent power and faith in their numbers and historical significance as the inhabitants of two former states of Bahawalpur and Multan. These states have glorious histories, a great past, and have evolved an accommodative multiculturalism. The construction of a Siraiki identity is a remarkable achievement in itself but at present appears a grandiose and essentially divisive project not only between the peoples of Bahawalpur and Multan—not cities but states—and the Siraiki populations and settlers that have effected a big and irreversible demographic shift. Finally, the translation of Siraiki sentiments into a political movement has not been achieved.

Notes

1. The first major Siraiki conference was convened on March 14–16, 1975. It was a three-day gathering of prominent writers, intellectual, and political activists from Sindh and southern Punjab. For details, see Christopher Shackle, 'Saraiki: A Language Movement in Pakistan,' *Modern Asian Studies* 11, no. 3 (1977): 379–403.

2. Judith A. Howard, 'Social Psychology of Identities,' *Annual Review of Sociology* 26 (2000): 367–73.

3. Rogers Brubaker, *Ethnicity Without Groups* (Cambridge: Harvard University Press, 2004), 1–4.

4. Jimy M. Sanders, 'Ethnic Boundaries and Identity in Plural Societies,' *Annual Review of Sociology* 28 (2002): 327–57.

5. Samuel P. Huntington, 'Foreword: Cultures Count,' in *Culture Matters: How Values Shape Human Progress*, eds. Lawrence E. Harrison and Samuel P. Huntington (New York: Basic Books, 2000), xv.

6. Fredrik Barth, *Ethnic Groups and Boundaries: The Social Organization of Culture Difference* (Long Grove: Waveland Press, Inc., 1969), 9–38.

7. Writing his book in 1970, Russian linguist U. A. Smirnov uses the word *Lahndi* repeatedly for Siraiki. He makes an observation that Siraiki organizations were demanding recognition of Siraiki and creation of a Siraiki province as far back as 1969. See U. A. Smirnov, *The Lahndi Language*, trans. E. H. Tsipan (Moscow: Nauka Publishing House, 1975). Reprinted as *The Lahndi (Seraiki) Language* (Multan: Saraiki Adbi Board, 2006), 36.

8. Ryan Brasher, 'Ethnic Brother or Artificial Namesake? The Construction of Tajik Identity in Afghanistan and Tajikistan,' *Berkeley Journal of Sociology* 55 (2011): 102.

9. Henry E. Hale, 'Explaining Ethnicity,' *Comparative Political Studies* 37, no. 4 (2004): 458–85.

10. David Rousseau and A. Maurits van der Veen, 'The Emergence of a Shared Identity: An Agent-Based Computer Simulation of Idea Diffusion,' *The Journal of Conflict Resolution* 49, no. 5 (2005): 686–712.

11. David B. Knight, 'Identity and Territory: Geographical Perspectives on Nationalism and Regionalism,' *Annals of the Association of American Geographers* 72, no. 4 (1982): 514–31.

12. For details on these publications, see Akhtar Waheed, *Multani Zaban da Qaida* [Alphabets of Multani language] (Multan: Kashan Adab, 1953), 3.

13. Syed Noor Ali Zamin Husaini, *Maarif-e-Siraiki* [Introduction of Siraiki] (Multan: Saraiki Adbi Board, 2009), 9–34.

14. One of the most noted Siraiki festivals is at Mehraywala, a village in district Rajanpur. It was founded by Ashiq Khan Buzdar, a noted poet, nearly 34 years

ago. The festival has attracted poets, writers, intellectuals, and political activists from all parts of the Siraiki region. There are historic and seasonal festivals around shrines in which Siraiki *mushaira* has been added as a new feature. My conversation with Ashiq Buzdar, Rajanpur, December 26, 2016.

15. My interview with Ashiq Buzdar, Mehraywala, August 22, 2017.

16. Zahoor Ahmad Dhareja, *Seraik Wasib* [The Siraiki Society] (Multan: Jhoke Publishers, 2003).

17. Siraiki nationalists have an extensive scope of Siraiki homelands that includes two districts of KP—Dera Ismail Khan and Tank. They insist that Mianwali, Khushab, and Jhang in western Punjab are also parts of the Siraiki lands. Based on my field work and interviews.

18. The following discussion has been adapted from my opinion piece in *The Express Tribune*, 'Restructuring the Federation,' May 8, 2012.

19. For instance, Muhajir in Sindh, Pashtuns in Balochistan, and Hazara in KP demand the creation of new provinces and by the same logic support the Siraiki groups demanding a Siraiki province.

20. Mohammad Waseem, 'Federalism in Pakistan,' *Forum of Federations* (August 2010).

21. Arif Hasan and Mansoor Raza, *Migration and Small Towns in Pakistan* (London: International Institute for Environment and Development, 2009); and Mahim Maher, 'From Zardaris to Makranis: How the Baloch came to Sindh,' *The Express Tribune*, March 28, 2014.

22. Khalid Ahmed, 'The Pakhtuns in Karachi,' *The Express Tribune*, August 28, 2010.

23. Rafiullah Kakar, 'Understanding the Pakhtun question in Balochistan,' *The Express Tribune*, June 5, 2015; and Umair Jamal, 'Pakistan's Balochs Fear Minority Status in Their Own Province,' *The Diplomat*, February 11, 2016.

24. Carving up new states from the territories of existing states requires a simple majority in the Indian Parliament. In the case of Pakistan, it had been made deliberately difficult. Besides a two-thirds majority in parliament, it may require a two-thirds majority in the legislature of the province from whose territory a new province will be created.

25. The following discussion has been adapted from my opinion piece in *The Express Tribune*, 'Punjab Periphery,' July 15, 2013.

26. Ibid.

27. Sajjad Akhtar, 'The Trends in Regional Inequality in Pakistan: Evidence Since 1998,' *The Lahore Journal of Economics* 13 (Special Edition) (September 2008): 205–20.

28. Ikram Junaidi, 'Economic inequality rising in Pakistan,' *Dawn*, July 30, 2016.

29. The following discussion has been adapted from my opinion piece in *The Express Tribune*, 'Bahawalpur, Multan, and More,' June 10, 2012.

30. See, for instance, 'The Seraiki Suba bandwagon,' *Dawn*, July 4, 2018.

31. 'President directs NA to form commission on south Punjab provinces,' *The Express Tribune*, July 11, 2012.

32. Bahawalpur was a princely state and remained autonomous within Pakistan until formation of the One Unit in 1954. Multan was a state until it was taken over by the expansionist Punjab State of Maharaja Ranjit Singh in 1818.

33. The following discussion has been adapted from my opinion piece in *The Express Tribune*, 'The Seraiki card,' January 29, 2013.

34. *Report of the Commission for the Creation of New Province (s) in the Province of Punjab* (Islamabad: National Assembly Secretariat, 2013), http://www.na.gov. pk/uploads/documents/province-reoprt.pdf.

35. Anwar Abbas, 'PML-N rubbishes parliamentary Committee's report on new provinces,' *Pakistan Today*, February 20, 2013.

36. Pir Hassamudding Rashdi and Ghulam Rabbani Abro were two prominent writers from Sindh. The then Nawab of former Bahawalpur State, and an English linguist and specialist on the Siraiki language, Professor Christopher Shackle, also participated. My interview with Mazhar Arif, who was a student leader and one of the members of the organizing committee of the conference (over the phone on February 27, 2017).

37. Hussain Ahmad Khan, *Re-thinking Punjab: The Construction of Siraiki Identity* (Lahore: Research and Publication Centre, National College of Arts, 2004).

38. Masihullah Jampuri, *Nigarkhana* (Multan: Jhoke Publishers, 2015), 117–20.

39. My interview with Allah Nawaz Khan Durrani, Multan, March 30, 2015.

40. Zahoor Ahmed Dhareja, *Suba Siraikistan Kis Liye* (Multan: Jhoke Publishers, 2013).

8

The Disintegration of Pakistan Oppressed Nations Movement (PONM) and its Impact on the Siraiki Movement

Nukhbah Langah

Introduction

This chapter is written in the context of the socioeconomic grievances of the Siraiki people, their political resistance, and their demand for the creation of a Siraiki province by partitioning the present Punjab and seeking political support from other ethnic minority groups from other provinces. While my previous research used the example of contemporary resistance poetry to discuss the political insecurity resulting from the cultural hegemony of Punjabi-Muhajir ruling elite, this discussion deals primarily with the unanticipated fizzling out of ethnic alliances which has resulted in strengthening the elite hegemony in Pakistan. I trace the history of ethnic alliances and seek to explain the resulting lack of coordination and affinity between various ethnic groups in Pakistan. The failure of the Pakistan Oppressed Nations Movement (PONM) and the targeting of Siraiki labourers in Balochistan are discussed as an example of the failure of cooperation between various ethnic groups in Pakistan, which has damaged the Siraiki ethnolinguistic movement and nationalist question.

On a personal note, this chapter is also stimulated by my engagement with the people creating the first alliance of nationalist groups in Pakistan in the late 1990s. One of the first such alliances was called PONM. The alliance was created by Sindhi, Baloch, Pakhtun, and Siraiki nationalists.[1] The concerns of all these nationalist groups and their stance against the hegemonic control of Punjab created the basis of this alliance. I also identify the creation of this alliance as a watershed moment in the history of Siraiki identity politics as this was the first time when all the nationalist groups recognized Siraikis as a 'nation' which shared political and socioeconomic concerns with Sindhis, the Baloch, and Pakhtuns.

This study is ethnography-based; I am partially relying on the first-hand information gathered through attending various political forums organized by Siraiki nationalists and their meetings with the nationalist groups from other provinces. I have also reviewed their party literature created in this process of planning the political alliance. For information such as the job situation in the area of Rahim Yar Khan and specifically Janpur (discussed later in this chapter), I have relied on personal interaction and communication with people whose children migrate to Balochistan in search of jobs. These people are impacted by the installation of industries set up by the ruling elite in the area of Rahim Yar Khan. However, the main focus of this chapter remains the diminishing association between the ethnic/nationalist groups within Pakistan and the impact of this failure on Siraiki mobilization.

In summary, my primary interest is to discuss ethnic politics in the context of the Siraiki-speaking region. I am also interested in how Siraiki identity is strengthened or weakened through political alliances created with the Baloch, Pakhtuns, and Sindhis. In a previous publication, I have stated that Punjabi-Muhajir economic and sociopolitical domination within the province of Punjab has highlighted the case of Siraiki identity.[2] I traced the overlapping objectives behind preserving ethnic identities in the case of Sindhis and Siraikis against Punjabi and Muhajir ruling elite. For Sindhis, the intervention of Muhajirs in local politics in Sindh to create space as a migrant community became a challenge to their Sindhi identity as sons of the soil. In Punjab, Punjabi-Muhajir ruling elite's strong grip over economic resources deprived the Siraiki-speaking majority residing in south Punjab of progress in every domain of life. In both cases, the focus narrows down to resisting the political control of Punjabi-Muhajir ruling elite over Sindhis and Siraikis in particular, and all the other ethnic groups (e.g. Balochi, Pakhtun, and Hindko-speakers) in Pakistan in general.[3] Building on this argument, this chapter contends that gaining political strength from these ethnic groups became a necessity for Siraiki nationalists as evident through several political alliances, especially PONM.

I begin with a discussion of the primordialist-constructivist approaches to the study of ethnic identity politics in Pakistan. Secondly, I discuss two major ethnonationalist alliances created in the 1990s: the United Nations Alliance (1994), and PONM (1998). Finally, I discuss where the political associations of these ethnic alliances are heading and propose recommendations as a way forward.

Various scholars have examined ethnic identities within the context of Pakistan and their impact on internal and external conflicts. Corsi has argued that sectarian clashes, jihad, Islamization, Talibanization, and military domination are a major part of the internal conflicts within Pakistan, also indicating that Islam is not a binding force. However, he does not address the problem of ethnic conflict in Pakistan in sufficient depth, making only oblique references to the topic. My chapter develops this discussion further by presenting an example of interprovincial ethnic affiliation created through PONM and the complications that resulted in the breaking of this alliance.[4]

One of the most interesting academic debates regarding ethnic identities is about the primordial or non-primordial nature of ethnic identities and the concept of 'nationalism' as a 'political principle'.[5] Ernest Gellner argues that processes inherent in industrialization have led to the modern concept of the nation as a bounded group with a common ethnicity, culture, and history. Nationalism, in his view, is the demand that every ethnic group should have its own state, and that states should be ethnically homogenous either through assimilation of non-nationals or the expulsion or even elimination of non-nationals.[6]

Brubaker rejects the understanding of 'ethnicity' through 'groupism' because ethnicity does not work 'through bounded groups, but in and through categories, schemas, encounters, identifications, languages, stories, institutions, organizations, networks, and events'.[7] He regards 'groupness as a contextually fluctuating conceptual variable'[8] and understands ethnicity and nationalisms through relational, dynamic, eventful, and disaggregated terms. This means thinking of ethnicity, race, and nation not in terms of substantial groups or entities but in terms of 'practical categories, situated actions, cultural idioms, cognitive schemas, discursive frames, organizational routines, institutional forms, political projects, and contingent events'.[9]

Following Gellner and Brubaker, Christophe Jaffrelot has also argued against the primordial nature of ethnic identities.[10] Giving the example of the Sindhi ethnic movement, he argues that it has mobilized in reaction to socioeconomic and political marginalization. He therefore argues, 'The identity movements affecting the unity of Pakistan do not stem from primordial collective bonds: their ideologies have been constructed in order to promote specific interests, political as well as socio-economic.'[11] In his view, the issue of ethnic identity depends on institutional factors such as ethnic groups having quotas, their representation in the military, achieving government jobs, and having a reasonable share in the country's budget.

Feroz Ahmed presents a counterargument to the constructivist understanding of ethnic identity in Pakistan in his discussion of Sindhi nationalism. He argues that ethnic identification among Sindhis began to grow after the interference of Muhajir identity through their representative party, MQM or Mohajir Qaumi Movement (which later became the Muttahida Quami Movement) in Sindh. He further suggests that Sindhis based in urban centres and the diaspora became more politically conscious of their primordial identity due to the Muhajir presence in their province. This became evident when they started teaching Sindhi to their children in order to preserve their cultural ties and ethnic identity. The leading political parties, like the Pakistan Peoples Party (PPP), therefore, fell back on the ethnic issue in Sindh in order to maintain their support and following.

The concept of one nation, one language reflects a top-down perspective, whereas the ethnic debate issue is a bottom-up perspective. At one level, both make a primordialist argument because the national perspective is grounded in the primordialist two-nation theory, whereas the regional one is based on local ethnic identity. However, I contend that at a deeper level the ethnic boundaries within the context of Pakistan are certain to create a challenge for national boundaries because they are observed as a threat to Pakistani nationalism based on the ideology of one language, one religion, one nation. The major reason being that ethnicity is perceived to symbolize a diversity of identities and cultures. In order to achieve the holistic understanding of Pakistani identity, all ethnicities must be acknowledged.[12] Even if ethnic groups in Pakistan are regarded as an outcome of political and socioeconomic concerns as argued by Jaffrelot, their claims cannot be rejected in their entirety. This is because ethnic groups, such as Sindhis, adhere to their language, culture, traditions, and geographical territory as a symbol of their personal as well as Pakistani identity. This philosophy might seem shaky in the case of the Baloch involved in the war for independence. However, a majority of ethnic groups assert the primordialist view through their 'son of the soil' agenda while also regarding the non-native presence (read as Punjabi-Muhajir) as an attempt to construct a new nation by wiping out subnational identities. The ruling elite's false assumption that ethnicities damage the founding ideology of Pakistan and threaten its federation adds to this misinterpretation of their ideologies.

While Feroz Ahmed has only discussed the significance of the Urdu language and its role in maturing Sindhi identity, he has vividly elaborated the issue of Sindhi language as one of the strongest identity markers reflecting people's ethnolinguistic and nationalistic aspirations in this province. Thus, in light of Ahmed's arguments, Sindhi identity can be comprehended both through constructivist and primordial approaches. If approached through the primordialist argument of ethnic identity as being organic, biological, and unchanging, Sindhi political consciousness at a deeper level relates back to its deeper association with the Indus Valley Civilization and demand for separating from the Bombay Presidency. No doubt, on the basis of the constructivist argument, Sindhi identity has become overemphasized mainly due to the Muhajir presence in the province. However, the primordialist perspective was always part of the Sindhi ethnic argument even before the politicization of the Muhajir identity after the creation of Pakistan.

United Nations Alliance and Pakistan Oppressed Nations Movement

The discussion above was necessary to understand the significance of ethnic identities within the context of Pakistan. Nonetheless, my aim is to discuss the relationship of the Siraiki movement with other ethnic groups within Pakistan through the creation of political alliances, and the success and failure of such alliances. This chapter discusses two major alliances created jointly by various ethnonationalist groups operating within Pakistan in the late 1990s. The first alliance was called UNA or United Nations Alliance and the second was titled PONM or Pakistan Oppressed Nations Movement.

The nationalist groups involved in creating the UNA included the Mazdur Kisan Party, Jamiat Ulama-e-Sindh, Sindh Sagar Party, Jeay Sindh Tehreek, the Pakistan Siraiki Party, and various Siraiki nationalist groups.[13] The base of this alliance was Sindh (Karachi) and its agenda included the following major concerns:

(i)   Accepting the historical identity of five nations (Sindhi, Pakhtun, Baloch, Siraikis, and Punjabis).
(ii)   Their languages should be the national languages of Pakistan.
(iii) Their fundamental and human rights should be protected within the federation of Pakistan.
(iv)   Each *qaum* (nation) should become part of the ruling system, defence, foreign policy, etc.[14]

The second opposition alliance created by these nationalists in 1998 was the PONM. It specifically debated and critiqued the failing federal structure in Pakistan mainly due to the rejection of the diverse ethnicities existing within the country. The creation of Bangladesh in 1971 emphasized the multi-ethnic identity of Pakistan, given its ethnic diversity with the presence of Pakhtuns, Sindhis, Punjabis, Siraikis, and the Baloch, vis-à-vis the ideology of religious uniformity.[15] Thus, the PONM proposed that the overall political crisis in Pakistan occurred due to the emphasis on brotherhood, unilateral ideology, religious fundamentalism, fascist government, corrupt leadership, and bureaucracy. This alliance acknowledged that Pakistan is a multi-ethnic country where, even after the detachment of Bangladesh, five *qaums* (nations) reside: Sindhi, Punjabi, Pakhtun, Siraiki, and Baloch—the idea of nation within a nation. All the activists who joined the PONM believed that their mother language was a crucial identity marker for them. This included selected political factions from all the provinces joining the PONM, comprising various Baloch, Sindhi, Pashto, and Siraiki political factions.[16] They mutually agreed on their common political objectives based on their historical origins, culture, and literature. Moreover, they regarded themselves as being oppressed because they shared a joint struggle against the neo-colonizers existing within Pakistan and sometimes even belonging to their local domain. In the context of Siraiki nationalism, this struggle meant fighting against feudal lords, the military establishment, bureaucracy, and, most importantly, Punjabi-Muhajir dominated ruling elite.

Based on primordialist assumptions, the PONM contended that these nations have resided in specific regions for thousands of years—an idea somewhat questionable for constructivists. The PONM strengthened the Siraiki movement but was also critiqued for its unrealistic objectives.[17] They agreed that, like all the provinces, a fifth Siraiki province should be added to the federation of Pakistan. The term 'independence' from Punjab is often misinterpreted within the context of the Siraiki issue. For clarification, by 'independence', Siraiki activists joining PONM meant economic independence and having political rights and constitutional recognition as a fifth province created within the federation. For Siraiki nationalists, this also meant the recognition of Siraiki identity within the federation of Pakistan and having constitutional rights by being acknowledged as a province detaching from the present hegemony of Punjabi-Muhajir ruling elite. The PONM asserted that the construction of Siraikistan[18] as a federating unit along the pattern of the other four provinces will ensure the recognition of the Pashto, Sindhi, Siraiki, Punjabi, and Balochi languages; this will ensure that the resources produced within their provinces are utilized by the people residing here, and they will get due representation within the parliament, army, central offices, jobs, and within all the national institutions.[19]

According to one Siraiki activist (Abdul Majeed Kanju) interviewed by Eva Cheng:

> [...] PONM [was] fighting for the reconstitution of Pakistan on the basis of the All-India resolution agreed on March 23, 1940, which spelled out that the five national groupings—the Sindhis, Pashtuns, Balochis, Siraikis, and Punjabis—should constitute Pakistan on an equal basis.[20]

The overlapping aspects of both these alliances included promoting linguistic, ethnic, and cultural diversity; they were also based on mutual reverence and confidence developed among various ethnic and nationalist groups. They were progressive, democratic, and optimistic about achieving the goals of political recognition within the federation of Pakistan. Their objectives were progressive because they rejected fundamentalist elements influencing Pakistan's political scene and resisted dictatorship and feudalism. Broadly, PONM proposed that if all the ethnic groups in Pakistan joined hands, they could counter the domination of Punjabi-Muhajir ruling elite and the process of 'Punjabization' which rejected their primordial origins.[21]

It is important to elaborate why these ethnonationalist groups came together as oppressed 'nations'—the word 'nation' or '*qaum*' signifying both a Muslim 'nation' in the context of Partition and various ethnic groups after the creation of Pakistan. Unlike the idea of 'nationhood' (*qaumiat*) based on Urdu and Islam promoted at the time of Partition and adopted by the ruling elite (mainly Punjabi and Muhajirs)[22] of Pakistan, for these nationalist groups joining the PONM, the concept of a 'nation' or '*qaum*' is clearly based on their primordial origins, historical, ethnic, and/or geographic association with their motherland and mother language.[23]

The close affiliation of Siraiki nationalists with Sindhis reflects through the following statement:

> Sixty per cent of the population of Punjab is Siraiki People. The Siraikis are as oppressed as Sindhis. Their culture and history are equally vulnerable. There is a similarity between Khawaja Ghulam Fareed's poetry and Sachal's philosophy, and we have a historical relation with Bhutto [...] we feel the pain of underprivileged Sindhi nation [...] Siraiki feudals, Chaudhrys of Punjab, Sindhi landlords, feudals of Balochistan, and landlords belonging to Khyber Pakhtunkhwa; Punjab's military and bureaucracy; they are all the same.[24]

The statement above indicates that the proponents of the PONM not only base their case on ethnonationalistic grounds but also on the class difference that flourished mainly due to Punjabi-Muhajir domination which marginalized all the other ethnic identities within Pakistan.

It is significant to spot the absence of the MQM from the PONM.[25] MQM has used both Islam and the Urdu language to establish itself as a political party mainly in Sindh—an issue much debated by various scholars.[26] The promotion of an Urdu-speaking group in Sindh was encouraged in the Ziaul Haq era and some critics blame him for aspiring to create a province for Muhajir in order to empower the Muhajir community in Sindh, routing the Sindhi nationalist struggle along with strengthening military influences in this province. He even encouraged the demand for a separate province for the Muhajir, which unjustifiably legitimized the MQM's political role in Sindh.[27] At one stage, the MQM leadership aspired to ally with Sindhi and Siraiki nationalists in Sindh and Punjab respectively, but this was done primarily for temporary political gain by securing the Sindhi and Siraiki vote bank within these two provinces. However, the MQM has never been acknowledged as Sindhi mainly because it has failed to understand and protect the political and democratic rights and historical and cultural basis of the Sindhi people and has targeted violence against them in this province instead.[28] It remains to be seen whether MQM's interest in allying with Sindhi nationalist is a genuine shift to acknowledging Sindhi identity or simply a temporary strategy for political gain.

The discussion above indicates that if the MQM leadership aspired to join hands with Sindhis or later even with Siraikis as oppressed nations in Sindh and Punjab, they had to somehow become part of the PONM. Nonetheless, the MQM failed to join mainly because there was much opposition against the MQM in the PONM. Secondly, it also wanted to remain in a good bargaining position with the establishment and Punjabi ruling elite.[29] The impact of this strategy is still visible through the party's sweeping political failure in Sindh and the drastic failure of their *Quaid* (founding leader of the party), Altaf Hussain. This resulted in the division of this party into two factions. The PONM claimed that the establishment had imposed a challenge for nationalist alliances by promoting the MQM which had resulted in economic and security crises in Sindh.[30] As indicated earlier, this was done on the pattern of Punjabis dominating Siraikis in Punjab and Muhajir dominating Sindhis in Sindh.

In addition to the fact that most of the nationalists disagreed with the historical basis of the MQM and its participation in the PONM, a few more factors resulted in the failure of this political alliance of the nationalists, especially debate surrounding the leadership of the alliance. There remained differences among factions joining the PONM, such as when the Sindhi nationalist, Palejo, criticized Mengal for erroneously arguing to include the MQM in the PONM which, in his view, made the efforts of the Awami National Party (ANP) and Jeay Sindh Qaumi Mahaz (JSQM) redundant. Despite their common political, cultural, and historical concerns as 'oppressed nations', Sindhi, Baloch, Pakhtun, and Siraiki nationalists carried the burden of their intricate local sociopolitical and cultural realities. While the Siraiki movement and identity was a product of the postcolonial era, the historical contexts of the Baloch, Pakhtuns, and Sindhis were rooted in the pre-Partition era and were based on their varied experiences during the process of colonization and Partition. For this reason, based on their local context, certain political concerns benefited one group more than the other, which prevented their complete understanding to sustain this alliance.[31] While most of these nationalist groups took a stance against the hegemony of Punjab, they also sometimes criticized each other for favouring Punjabi establishment. At times, the ANP, the largest Pakhtun nationalist party in Pakistan, was criticized by the rest of the nationalist groups for joining hands with the government and abandoning their political affiliation with the other nationalist groups who had joined them in the shape of the PONM.[32] The Pashtun lobby was criticized for not allowing certain Sindhi nationalists to join the PONM due to their separatist agendas. A case in point is the JSQM which was excluded from this alliance primarily due to their slogan of 'independent Sindhu *Desh* (native land)'. For this reason, a separate Sindh National Alliance was established under the headship of G. M. Syed because it did not own the slogan of an 'independent Sindhu *Desh*'.[33] The members of the Sindh National Alliance actively joined all PONM meetings. Due to all these differences, Sindhi nationalists like Imdad Shah joined the alliance independently whereas Palejo joined with his party, the Awami Tehreek. As a result of these complications, the PONM gradually fizzled out after the elections in 2008.[34]

Siraiki Grievances

The discussion above indicates how nationalist groups and their collective efforts towards breaking Punjabi-Muhajir hegemony by creating political alliances such as the PONM failed due to various external and internal pressures. The present section contemplates on how this failure resulted in ongoing differences between Siraikis and the Baloch against the spirit of PONM. I have discussed Siraiki grievances against the hegemony of Punjab elsewhere at length.[35] Their major cause is achieving political recognition within the federation of Pakistan and the demand for a separate Siraiki province on the basis of their history and culture. They argue that this province comprises the divisions of Multan, Bahawalpur, Dera Ghazi Khan, and District Jhang in Punjab, and Dera Ismail Khan in KP. Siraiki nationalists claim Dera Ismail Khan Division (comprising the areas of Dera Ismail Khan and the Tank districts), which were historically part of the Siraiki-speaking area before the creation of the North-West Frontier Province (NWFP) in 1901.[36] The province claimed by Siraiki nationalists comprises all these areas on the basis of historical, linguistic, and cultural ties. I have indicated in my earlier work that the coinage of the term 'Siraiki' and the concept of a unified Siraiki identity emerged in the postcolonial era. One of the factors behind this was the failure of colonial researchers in identifying various dialects spoken in this region, such as Bahawalpuri, Derawali, and Riasti, to create a connection between them and give them the status of a language.[37] Like Sindhis, Baloch, and Pakhtuns, their language, Siraiki, remains a strong identity marker for them. The preservation of their local culture and literature and their recognition as the fifth federating unit of the country, as also recognized by other nations joining the PONM (Sindhi, Baloch, Pakhtun), remains their strongest argument. They resist the hegemony of central Punjab over the Siraiki region (termed as South Punjab generally) and demand constitutional recognition as a fifth province. In order to contextualize how the PONM supported the Siraiki national question, I briefly discuss the grievances of the Siraiki people, based on socioeconomic issues, cultural discrimination, and constitutional rights, below.

Despite the agricultural richness of this region, most industrial activity is in upper Punjab. In recent years, even if an industry is set up, jobs are not given to the local people. Academic institutions are backward and neglected and, since the creation of the Bahauddin Zakariya University (BZU) in Multan and Islamia University in Bahawalpur by Bhutto in the 1970s, no new universities and colleges have been established. Nishtar Hospital was built in 1951 using local funds and it is serving people from as far away as Quetta, Dera Ismail Khan, Bahawalnagar, and Sukkur. The disparity of development funds between upper Punjab and the Siraiki region is 20 to 1.[38] The lack of law and order and human rights abuses by the police and the bureaucracy is shameful. This area is erroneously identified strongly with terrorist activities due to the establishment of a madrasa culture. However, the fact that is normally disregarded is that various political regimes in general and the Zia regime in particular promoted such activity and established such organizations in this region to entice local people aggravated by their economic deprivations.[39]

The second major grievance is that no cultural and official recognition is given to Siraiki as one of the ancient languages of the region. The Siraiki language and its literature has only recently been introduced as a medium of instruction, whereas Sindhi, Balochi, and Pashto have gained official recognition through language planning.[40] The Siraiki department at Bahauddin Zakariya University, despite securing funds, lacks student interest and competent and qualified staff. No corpus planning[41] for Siraiki language is done at state level; most of the time Siraiki literature is included as part of Punjabi syllabi in higher education institutions. Siraiki creative writers and artists lack jobs and opportunities for their work to be acknowledged and gain recognition at state level. Siraiki activists therefore demand the same cultural acknowledgement, representation, and rights which are given to all the languages spoken in the rest of the provinces of Pakistan.

The former provincial government of Punjab was opposed to maps that depicted Siraiki-speaking regions of Pakistan. Paradoxically, the boundary of the Siraiki province had already been discussed in parliament until the general elections held in 2013.[42] While such political acknowledgement has paved the way for cultural acknowledgement, the response from the ruling elite has shifted from time to time, depending on political demands made by Siraiki activists and cultural proponents. Part of the problem remains a gap between political activists and cultural supporters (writers, poets, singers, intellectuals) as they have never formally joined hands to strengthen their mutually held political cause.

The most important demand of Siraiki nationalists is the creation of a fifth federating unit by the name of 'Siraiki' or 'Siraikistan':

- As also indicated through their association with PONM, the Siraiki nationalists claim that this is their historical right just like that of Sindh and Balochistan, Khyber Pakhtunkhwa and Punjab.
- Their socioeconomic and political deprivations cannot be addressed without the creation of a province.

- The present Punjab province has more seats in the National Assembly than all the other provinces put together. The National Assembly in fact is a Punjab House. The federation is unbalanced and thus not viable. All the Chief Ministers of Punjab since 1970 have regarded the division of Punjab as a threat to their hegemonic control over the Siraiki region.
- The Siraiki people have no due representation in the Supreme Court, other federal, judicial, and administrative forums, such as army, navy, air force, PIA, Wapda, Railway, Information Ministry, Foreign Mission, and even in national agencies which run the country. The reason is that in all these institutions, representation is on a provincial basis and the quota of Punjab is used up by Lahorites and four to five other big cities of upper Punjab.
- The Siraiki region is thus prevented from receiving its due quota of water, electricity, gas, and its share in the NFC Award, as these are distributed on a provincial basis.

These grievances generally include all the causes of 'ethnic fragmentation' identified by Feroz Ahmed. This includes the concern for autonomy, allocation of resources, interprovince migration, and language and culture. In the context of the present discussion, I primarily want to highlight two related concerns. First is the lack of resources resulting in socioeconomic grievances. Second, local and government imposed economic crises within the Siraiki area lead to forced interprovince migrations.[43]

So far my argument has indicated that the social, economic, and political grievances discussed above necessitated an alliance between Siraiki nationalists and other ethnonationalists as evident through the creation of the PONM. For the first time since the emergence of Siraiki nationalism in the postcolonial era in the 1970s, this alliance recognized Siraikis as one of the oppressed nations but also strengthened their cause through this support. I have also indicated that, despite this political consciousness, the PONM fizzled out due to multiple differences among those activists who initially joined this alliance.

Long-term Impacts of PONM's Failure on Siraiki Politics

In this section, I indicate that the political consciousness of all the ethnonationalist groups that formed the PONM has further weakened due to their contextual disparities. This can be observed through the recent targeting of Siraiki labourers by Baloch extremists. These Siraiki labourers migrate to Balochistan due to poor work opportunities available to them within their hometowns, as these are flood areas where the local populations face frequent natural disasters which have a long-term impact on their lives. The government has failed to prevent these calamities through disaster management and protecting the local population. Secondly, industrial capitalism and power politics, as well as uneven economic development, has closed opportunities for local people. Several factories and sugar mills and nearly a hundred flour mills in this area are owned by well-established Siraiki or Punjabi feudal lords and parliamentarians. However, the people hired in these local industries are Punjabis, not Siraikis. The Siraikis belonging to this area have been working in Balochistan for the past 30–40 years for two generations because there are no job opportunities in their hometowns and villages.

My focus in this discussion is on the area of Janpur in Rahim Yar Khan adjoining the Balochistan border from where deprived and illiterate Siraiki men move to Balochistan in search of minor labour jobs. Recently, several incidents have highlighted the targeting of these Siraiki labourers by Baloch extremists. As their domicile was in Punjab, they were brutally murdered and their bodies sent to the families. No support was provided to their families by Punjab government. The media has been reporting such incidents actively without any details of why such brutality is not addressed at government level:

> Bodies of seven out of the eight labourers gunned down after being kidnapped two days ago in Sakran area of Lasbela district reached

Taranda Muhammad Pannah, their native area, some 100 km from here, on Monday. On Sunday, [...] were working in a poultry farm in Lasbela when gunmen forced their way in, checked their identities and shot eight of them dead.[44]

This incident reflects the discrimination against local Siraiki people who are clearly not being accommodated by industrialists operating within this region. It is a fact that if job opportunities are created for the local people, they will be able to make a decent living within their own region. However, in the present circumstances, they face dual neo-colonization: firstly, by local landed elite and industrialists and the ruling elite; secondly, by becoming victims of ethnic cleansing within their own country by the same nationalist groups who were once willing to ally with them in the forum of the PONM. Finally, this abuse continues to relate to the over-arching Punjabi-Muhajir hegemony and its corrupt administration within Punjab.

On the other hand, this violence is an outcome of the Baloch extremists' fear that they might become marginalized within their own province due to the influx of Punjabi and/or Siraiki people seeking jobs in their province.[45]

Some Baloch nationalists have justified such incidents due to fear of ethnic cleansing and prevention of demographic changes in Balochistan.[46] However, progressive Baloch nationalists like Dr Abdul Haye continue to strongly acknowledge the Siraiki issue, condemn such brutality, and support Siraiki nationalists even after the poignant failure of the PONM.[47] Different Baloch nationalists respond differently to this issue mainly because Baloch nationalists are divided into two factions: those who aim towards achieving independence and those who want to achieve their political rights within the federation of Pakistan if they are given royalties for the natural resources and other provincial rights. The majority belongs to the latter group which advocates the rights of all the oppressed nations within Pakistan, including Siraiki.

The 'capitalist development' in the Siraiki region driven by the Sharif government mainly served to establish projects from which the government will benefit.[48] In her Punjab budget speech, former Punjab Finance Minister, Dr Ayesha Ghaus Pasha, said that the focus of the budget would be on eliminating poverty, empowering youth, overcoming energy crises, and strengthening agriculture. Education, health, and the law and order situation would be given top priority.[49] However, it meant more money for upper Punjab and not underdeveloped areas of Punjab, which primarily comprise the Siraiki-speaking region. While PKR 258 billion were dedicated to energy projects, this did not include overcoming the energy crises in this region. People in urban cities like Multan, Bahawalpur, and surrounding vicinities still face long hours of load-shedding daily. No budget for a new women's university had been announced. The 27 per cent of budget for education and 14 per cent for health included no specific budget for a medical college or engineering university. No development projects were announced for providing basic education, sanitation, low cost housing, community health centres, scholarship funds for youth, adult literacy, or youth training programmes. While the area produces excellent handicrafts and has a thriving cotton industry, microfinance projects are not considered important for the empowerment of poor women who have no security for the upbringing and education of their children. Something along the lines of the 'Khud Rozgar Scheme' introduced by the former Chief Minister Punjab could have helped people belonging to various rural areas within the Siraiki region.[50] The incentive of the Metro bus service given by the former Punjab government to the people of Multan has done nothing to resolve the poverty concerns of the local people. Punjab government planned to spend PKR 30 billion for an 18-kilometre-long bus project in southern Punjab, which constitutes a major part of Punjab province (23 districts). But the common people struggle to secure petty jobs in both the public and private sector or have no choice other than to migrate to other provinces in order to provide basic facilities for their families.

Plans for a thermal plant in Muzaffargarh (around Mahmood Kot and Gujrat, Verar Sipra, Rao Bela Sharqi, and Budh, Mouza Jaat) and surrounding villages, followed a pattern of heavy investment with little benefits for locals. The Kot Addu Power Company (KAPCO) and China Machinery Engineering Corporation (CMEC) Pakgen power plants are being installed near Mahmood Kot in the Muzaffargarh district. While the local population understood the significance of the need to generate energy, they are also protested against the ways in which these plans jeopardized their daily lives. The government's policy, since the Land Acquisition Act of 1984, is to grab land from local people on a colonial pattern and leave them helpless. Due to the already operational power plants in this area, these new plans will add to ecological destruction and a significant rise in diseases (skin diseases, asthma, liver, eye diseases, and cancer). Most importantly, the local population will not be allowed to work in these plants and people from central Punjab will be hired instead.[51]

These development projects are also driving a gradual change in the demography of this region, as non-Siraiki people come to work in the region, are then allotted land, and end up settling and taking over the socioeconomic and, eventually, political benefits that should be utilized by the local population. The incident of Siraikis being killed by Baloch separatists referred to earlier relates to all these complex socioeconomic issues which have political implications, especially the relations between ethnic minorities in Pakistan.

Conclusion

While Siraiki nationalists have constantly condemned these killings, critics have argued that, 'There is no evidence to prove […] all killings of non–\-Baloch are the work of Baloch nationalists.'[52] Paradoxically, there is no answer to the problem of why the identities of poor labourers are checked before they are shot. Some media reports suggest that the Siraiki labourers have Punjab domicile and the Baloch extremists have a grudge against Punjab. This argument boils down to the constitutional rights of Siraiki people, which is the only way of giving them the domicile and recognition associated with their own province and reminding Baloch nationalists of the ethnic and nationalistic affiliations that Siraiki nationalists once tried to create with them through the PONM.

The creation of the PONM reflected a collective effort of Siraikis, Sindhis, Pakhtuns, and the Baloch towards uniting against the established hegemonic authority of Punjab. The example of Baloch extremists killing Siraiki labourers indicates that, unlike the alliances discussed earlier (UNA and PONM), there is an internal conflict between ethnic groups which has further established the hegemony of Punjab.[53] I argue that one major reason is the lack of a federal unit for Siraikis who are now being 'passed' as Punjabis and also being marginalized by other ethnic groups. In light of my earlier discussion about the association created between Siraiki, Sindhi, Baloch, and Pakhtun nationalists, such acts seem to contradict their shared political aspirations against Punjabi-Muhajir domination as reflected through the creation of the ONM.[54]

The state has been successful in this power play by breaking alliances like PONM, suppressing the internal issues arising within the provinces, as in the case of Balochistan, and also complicating the relationship between these nationalist groups as discussed through the example of the strained relationship between the Baloch and Siraiki people.[55] There is no understanding of ethnic movements as playing a role in strengthening the federation; instead, they are observed as a challenge to the one nation, one language, one religion theory. However, no serious efforts are being made in terms of improving interprovincial relations. Rather, tension between various ethnic groups will widen the gap between these groups and make the creation of such alliances unachievable. This, of course, goes in favour of Punjab's hegemony but will damage interprovincial relations and affiliations between various nationalist factions.

The dilemma remains that, in order to secure their vote bank, important political parties like the PPP have 'regional pockets' in the Siraiki region, superficially voicing their political demand for a province on a primordialist basis. However, this support from dominating political parties (recently Pakistan Tehreek-e-Insaf) varies from time to time, also depending on state narrative.[56] The purpose of my discussion was to indicate that, due to all these political pressures, the alliances based on indigenous origins and ethnicities such as the PONM are more important for the long-term stability of the federation as compared to the temporary alliances that government parties seek through the support of ethnic and regional parties for electoral gain.

Notes

1. My father, Late Barrister Taj Mohammad Khan Langah (President Pakistan Siraiki Party), being the pioneer of the Siraiki movement, started working with all the nationalists joining the PONM. He prepared several documents of the PONM in 1998 in London. I assisted him in this task and accompanied him to several meetings.

2. Nukhbah Taj Langah, *Poetry as Resistance: Islam and Ethnicity in Postcolonial Pakistan* (New Delhi: Routledge, 2016). I refer to the first section of this book.

3. Ibid.

4. Marco Corsi, 'Internal Conflicts in Pakistan,' *Oriente Moderno* 23, no. 84 (2004): 39–49.

5. Ernest Gellner, *Nations and Nationalism* (Oxford: Basil Blackwell, 1983), 1.

6. Ibid., 1–2.

7. Rogers Brubaker, *Ethnicity Without Groups* (Cambridge: Harvard University Press, 2006), 4.

8. Ibid., 11.

9. Ibid., 1 and 3.

10. Christophe Jaffrelot and Rasul Bakhsh Rais. 'Interpreting Ethnic Movements in Pakistan,' *The Pakistan Development Review* (Part I) 37, no. 4 (1998): 153–79.

11. Ibid., 171.

12. Ayesha Jalal, 'Conjuring Pakistan: History as Official Imagining,' *International Journal of Middle East Studies* 27 (1995): 73–89.

13. I have only mentioned the Pakistan Siraiki Party here as it was the only registered party at that stage.

14. These details are from the Charter of Pakistan Oppressed Nations Movement, published by the alliance in 1998. The concept of 'nationhood' within the context of Siraiki identity is already discussed at length in the first section of my book, *Poetry as Resistance*.

15. For more details, see Jalal, 'Conjuring Pakistan.'

16. Tariq Rahman, *Language and Politics in Pakistan* (Karachi: Oxford University Press, 1998).

17. Thomas C. Muller, *Political Handbook of the World 2012*, eds. Thomas C. Muller and Tom Lansford (SAGE Publications, 2012).

18. Here I use the proposed name used by Siraiki activists.

19. United Nations Alliance (UNA) document published in 1994.

20. 'PAKISTAN: OPPRESSED NATIONAL GROUPS STRUGGLE FOR AUTONOMY,' *Green Left Weekly* no. 493, May 15, 2002.

21. Charter of Pakistan Oppressed Nations Movement (PONM) published by the alliance in 1998. For more information on PONM's stance, see 'APC calls for end to army's role in politics,' *Dawn*, August 20, 2006; 'Ponm refuses to join ARD and MMA agitation,' *Business Recorder*, December 11, 2004; and Amir Wasim, 'Langah wants Tank, D.I. Khan in Seraiki province,' *Dawn*, December 25, 2012.

22. See Hamza Alavi, 'Nationhood and the Nationalities in Pakistan,' *Economic and Political Weekly* 24, no. 27 (1989): 1527–34; and Corsi, 'Internal Conflicts in Pakistan,' 42–3.

23. For understanding identity and language-based ethnicity and the interdependence of language and ethnicity within the context of Pakistan, see Tariq Rahman, 'Language and Ethnicity in Pakistan', *Asian Survey* 37, no. 9 (September 1997): 833–9; and Charles H. Kennedy, 'The Politics of Ethnicity in Sindh,' *Asian Survey* 31, no. 10 (October 1991): 938–55.

24. This was a speech delivered by the Siraiki nationalist, Barrister Taj Mohammad Khan Langah, at the death anniversary of Sindhi nationalist, Fazil Rahu Shaheed, which was sent to me by a Sindhi nationalist whose name is kept anonymous. The excerpt is literally translated from Sindhi to English by a Sindhi student, Saqib Qaisrani, on my request for this paper.

25. Adeel Khan, 'Ethnic nationalism and the state in Pakistan,' PhD Thesis (University of Wollongong Thesis Collection 1954-2016), 247–8.

26. See Farhat Haq, 'Rise of MQM in Pakistan: Politics of Ethnic Mobilization,' *Asian Survey* 35, no. 11 (November 1995): 990–1004; Moonis Ahmar, 'Ethnicity and State Power in Pakistan: The Karachi Crises,' *Asian Survey* 36,

no. 10 (October 1996): 1031–48; and Charles H. Kennedy, 'Policies of Ethnic Preference in Pakistan,' *Asian Survey* 24, no. 6 (June 1984): 688–703.

27. This is discussed at length by Tariq Rahman in *Language and Politics in Pakistan*.

28. Khan, 'Ethnic nationalism,' 247–8.

29. This translation is by a Sindhi student. For more on MQM, also see Jaffrelot and Rais, 'Interpreting Ethnic Movements in Pakistan.'

30. Charter of PONM.

31. This was exemplified through the tussle over the Kalabagh Dam.

32. This was also the time when the name for KP province was being demanded. These thoughts were expressed by some Siraiki and Sindhi nationalists during our informal discussions. Their names are kept anonymous upon their request.

33. My discussions with Sindhi nationalists and political activists on April 6, 2015. The names are kept anonymous upon request.

34. Ibid.

35. Langah, *Poetry as Resistance*.

36. Bahawalpur, Dera Ismail Khan, Dera Ghazi Khan, Rahim Yar Khan, Sargodha, Mianwali, Jhang, Sahiwal, Khanewal, Bahawalnagar, Lodhran, Pakpattan, Muzaffargarh, and Rajanpur. For more details, see Langah, *Poetry as Resistance*.

37. Ibid., Section I.

38. Ghulam Ali, Razia Musarat, and Mohammad Salman Azhar, 'Issue of New Provinces in Pakistan,' *IUB Journal of Social Sciences and Humanities* 9, no. 1 (2011): 31–43. Also see 'Demand for Siraiki Province,' *PILDAT*, Background Paper (March 2011).

39. See Corsi, 'Internal Conflicts in Pakistan,' 42.

40. For instance, see Rahman, *The Politics of Language*.

41. I use the term 'corpus planning' from linguistics here. This involves language planning at state level which I argue is not being done in the case of Siraiki language. Corpus planning involves standardizing language, its grammar, spellings, and publishing dictionaries. For the Siraiki language, only a private effort has been made to publish such works. I have argued elsewhere that this undermines the status of Siraiki as a language and, despite its historical origins, has prompted the controversy of Siriaki being a dialect and not a language. For more on corpus planning, see Heinz Kloss, *Abstandsprachen und Ausbausprachen* [Abstand-languages and Ausbau-languages], in *Zur Theorie des Dialekts: Aufsätze aus 100 Jahren Forschung, Zeitschrift fur Dialektologie and Linguistik*, eds. Joachim Göschel, Norbert Nail, and Gaston van der Elst (Wiesbaden: F. Steiner, 1976), 301–22.

42. Taj Mohammad Langah's and Nukhbah Taj Langah's meeting with Syed Yusuf Raza Gillani in February 2013.

43. Feroz Ahmed, *Ethnicity and Politics in Pakistan* (Karachi: Oxford University Press, 1998), 399.

44. 'Lasbela victims buried in hometowns,' *Dawn*, October 21, 2014.

45. The discussion starting in the above paragraph is adapted from my opinion piece in the *Nation*, 'Where is the budget for the Saraiki belt?' February 4, 2016.

46. Ahmed, *Ethnicity and Politics in Pakistan*, 634.

47. My discussion with Baloch nationalist Dr Abdul Haye on April 7, 2015 in Multan.

48. Ahmed, *Ethnicity and Politics in Pakistan*, 634.

49. 'PROVINCIAL MINISTER FOR FINANCE DR. AYESHA GHAUS PASHA HAS SAID THAT INCENTIVES ARE BEING PROVIDED TO INVESTORS FOR INCREASING RESOURCES IN THE PROVINCE,' *Finance Department, Government of Punjab*, November 17, 2016.

50. Muhammad Saleem, '"Khud Rozgar" Scheme in 4 Districts: Punjab Government to Provide Rs. 4.8 Billion interest-free loans,' *Business Recorder*, February 13, 2014.

51. This information is based on a report prepared by Rana Mehboob Akhtar and sent electronically on September 5, 2015 as part of our discussion about the local issues of the Siraiki people. The installation of two 660 MW Coal Fired Power Plants in Verar Sipra, Rao Bela Sharqi, Gujrat, and Budh, Mouza Jaat by KAPCO and CMEC Pakgen near Mahmood Kot in District Muzaffargarh, Punjab, Pakistan.

52. 'Seraiki party protests labourers' killing,' *Dawn*, April 13, 2015. Such incidents were also reported in 2011, see Abdul Nishapuri, 'Let's mourn five Saraiki labourers killed by Baloch militants,' *LUBP*, July 24, 2011, https://lubpak.net/archives/54076.

53. Mir Ghaus Bakhsh Bizenjo, *In Search of Solutions: An Autobiography of Mir Ghaus Bakhsh Bizenjo*, ed. B. M. Kutty, (Karachi: Pakistan Study Centre, University of Karachi, 2009).

54. The complexity of Baloch nationalism also has a role here. For more on this topic, see Taj Mohammad Breseeg, *Baloch Nationalism: Its Origin and Development Up to 1980* (London: University of London, 2001), also Breseeg, *Baloch Nationalism: Its Origin and Development* (Karachi: Royal Book Company, 2004); Martin Axmann, *Back to the Future: The Khanate of Kalat and the Genesis of Baloch Nationalism 1915–1955* (New York: Oxford University Press, 2008).

55. 'Status of "national language" sought for all regional languages,' *Dawn*, February 21, 2017. The second bill proposed by the PPP Senator, Sassui Paleijo, excluded the Siraiki language and has therefore become controversial in the view of the Siraiki nationalists who aim to protest against her proposal, thus challenging PPP political positioning in the Siraiki region. The differences between ethnic groups also need to be addressed again in the light of rapidly changing policies of the ruling elite. In the case of Balochistan, this depends on military operations in the region affected by a separatist insurgency which is part of the problem.

In the case of the Siraiki region, these policies vary from the debate for a Siraiki province in the parliament initiated by the PPP in 2013, to all regional languages being regarded as national languages of Pakistan. This discussion needs to be addressed separately in a different academic research.

56. Ahmed, *Ethnicity and Politics in Pakistan*, 635–6.

Bibliography

India Office Library Archives:

I.O.R. L/P&S/18/D169.

I.O.R. P/L&S/18 A.83.

I.O.R. 'Gilgit Agency,' 1927. File No. 97-C, 1927, Letter No. 1800-F, dated July 24, 1901, Appendix I.

Published Primary and Secondary Sources

Abbas, Anwar. 'PML-N rubbishes parliamentary Committee's report on new provinces.' *Pakistan Today*, February 20, 2013.

Abbasi, Zubair Faisal. 'Federalism, Provincial Autonomy and Conflicts.' Islamabad: Centre for Peace and Development Initiatives, 2010.

Adeney, Katharine. 'A Step Towards Inclusive Federalism in Pakistan? The Politics of the Eighteenth Amendment.' *Publius The Journal of Federalism* 42, no. 4 (2012): 539–65.

―――. 'Between Federalism and Separatism.' In *Managing and Settling Ethnic Conflicts: Perspectives on Successes and Failures in Europe, Africa, and Asia*, edited by Ulrich Schneckener and Stefan Wolff. London: Hurst, 2003.

―――. 'Constitutional Centring: Nation Formation and Consociational Federalism in India and Pakistan.' *Commonwealth & Comparative Politics* 40, no. 3 (November 2002): 8–33.

Ahmad, Iqbal. *Balochistan: Its Strategic Importance*. Lahore: Royal Book Company, 1992.

Ahmar, Moonis. 'Conflict Prevention and the New Provincial Map of Pakistan: A Case Study of Hazara Province.' *Journal of Political Studies* 20, no. 2 (2013): 1–19.

―――. 'Ethnicity and State Power in Pakistan: The Karachi Crises.' *Asian Survey* 36, no. 10 (1996): 1031–48.

Ahmed, Akbar S. 'Hazarawal: Formation and Structure of District Ethnicity.' In *Pakistan: The Social Sciences' Perspective*, edited by Akbar S. Ahmed and Zulfikar Ghose, 30. Karachi: Oxford University Press, 1990.

Ahmed, Feroz. *Ethnicity and Politics in Pakistan*. Karachi: Oxford University Press, 1998.

Ahmed, Syed Jaffar. *Historical Evolution of Federalism in Pakistan*. Islamabad: PILDAT, 2014.

Akhtar, Sajjad. 'The Trends in Regional Inequality in Pakistan: Evidence Since 1998.' *The Lahore Journal of Economics* 13 (special edn.) (September 2008): 205–20.

Alavi, Hamza. 'Nationhood and the Nationalities in Pakistan.' *Economic and Political Weekly* 24, no. 27 (1989): 1527–34.

———. 'The State in Post-colonial Societies: Pakistan and Bangladesh.' *New Left Review* 74 (1972).

Ali, Ghulam, Razia Musarat, and Mohammad Salman Azhar. 'Issue of New Provinces in Pakistan.' *IUB Journal of Social Sciences and Humanities* 9, no. 1 (2011): 31–43.

Ali, Zulfiqar, 'In Fata: Structural subjugation.' *Dawn*. July 6, 2014.

Amin, Tahir. *Ethno-National Movements in Pakistan: Domestic and International Factors*. Islamabad: Institute of Policy Studies, 1988.

Amnesty International. '"The Hands of Cruelty": Abuses by Armed Forces and Taliban in Pakistan's Tribal Areas.' December 2012. https://www.amnesty.org/en/documents/asa33/019/2012/en/.

Amnesty International (2012). 'Amnesty International Report 2012: The State OF The World's Human Rights.' https://www.amnestyusa.org/files/air12-report-english.pdf.

Anderson, Benedict. *Imagined Communities: Reflections on the Origin and Spread of Nationalism*. London: Verso, 1983.

Anderson, Liam. 'Ethnofederalism: The Worst Form of Institutional Arrangement…?' *International Security* 39, no. 1 (2014): 165–204.

Asad, Malik. 'Senate Approves National Languages Bill.' *Dawn*. May 11, 2017.

Awan, Ayub B. *Baluchistan: Historical and Political Processes*. London: New Century Publishers, 1985.

Axmann, Martin. *Back to the Future: The Khanate of Kalat and the Genesis of Baloch Nationalism 1915–1955*. New York: Oxford University Press, 2008.

Azhar, M., and Ayaz Muhammad. 'Ethnic Fragmentation and Dynamics of Politics in Pakistan.' *Journal of Political Studies* 24, no. 1 (2017).

Aziz, Khalid. 'The Frontier Crimes Regulation and Administration of the Tribal Areas.' In *Tribal areas of Pakistan: challenges and responses*, edited by Pervaiz Iqbal Cheema and Maqsudul Hasan Nuri, 125. Islamabad: Islamabad Policy Research Institute, 2005.

Bahadur, Rai, Anant Ram, and Hira Nand Raina. *1931 Census of Jammu and Kashmir State*. Part I, Volume XXIV. Jammu: Ranbir Government Press, 1933.

Baloch, Inayatullah. 'Resistance and National Liberation in Baluchi Poetry.' Sweden: University of Uppsala, 2000.

———. *The Problem of 'Greater Baluchistan': A Study of Baloch Nationalism.* Stuttgart: Steiner Verlag GMBH, 1987.

Baloch, Mir Ahmad Yar Khan. *Inside Baluchistan: A Political Autobiography of His Highness Baiglar Baigi: Khan-e-Azam-XIII*. Karachi: Royal Book Company, 1975.

Bangash, Yaqoob Khan. *A Princely Affair: The Accession and Integration of the Princely States of Pakistan 1947–1955*. Karachi: Oxford University Press, 2015.

Bank for International Settlements (2011). '81st Annual Report,1 April 2010–31 March 2011.'

Bansal, Alok. 'Factors leading to insurgency in Balochistan.' *Small Wars & Insurgencies* 19, no. 2 (2008): 182–200.

Barth, Fredrik. *Ethnic Groups and Boundaries: The Social Organization of Culture Difference*. Long Grove: Waveland Press, Inc., 1969.

Bizenjo, Mir Ghaus Bakhsh. *In Search of Solutions: An Autobiography of Mir Ghaus Bakhsh Bizenjo*, edited by B. M. Kutty. Karachi: Pakistan Study Centre, University of Karachi, 2009.

Bizenjo, Tahir. *Baba-e-Balochistan: Statements, Speeches and Interviews of Mir Ghaus Bux Bizenjo*. Quetta: Sales and Services, 1999.

———. *Balochistan: Kia Huwa, kia hoga*. Karachi: Pakistani Adab Publisher, 1989.

Brasher, Ryan. 'Ethnic Brother or Artificial Namesake? The Construction of Tajik Identity in Afghanistan and Tajikistan.' *Berkeley Journal of Sociology* 55 (2011): 102.

Brass, Paul. *Theft of an Idol: Text and Context in the Representation of Collective Violence*. Princeton: Princeton University Press, 1997.

Breseeg, Taj Mohammad. *Baloch Nationalism: Its Origin and Development.* Karachi: Royal Book Company, 2004.

_____. *Baloch Nationalism: Its Origin and Development Up to 1980.* London: University of London, 2001.

Brubaker, Rogers. 'Ethnicity without groups.' *European Journal of Sociology/ Archives européennes de sociologie* 43, no. 2 (2002): 163–89.

_____. *Ethnicity Without Groups.* Cambridge: Harvard University Press, 2004.

Bunce, Valerie, and Stephen Watts. 'Managing Diversity and Sustaining Democracy: Ethnofederal versus Unitary States in the Postcommmunist World.' In *Sustainable Peace: Power and Democracy after Civil Wars*, edited by Philip G. Roeder and Donald Rothchild, 133–58. Ithaca: Cornell University Press, 2005.

Bureau of Investigative Journalism (2013). 'Where the Drones Strike Data.' https://docs.google.com/spreadsheet/ccc?key=0AogpD5TbyQnvdEdQQ kIyNE9qSnZ5WFFqZjJSZ0VHdEE#gid=9.

Business Recorder. 'PONM refuses to join ARD and MMA agitation.' December 11, 2004, http://fp.brecorder.com/2004/12/2004121186592/.

Chalk, Peter. 'The Pakistani-Afghan Border Region.' *Ungoverned Territories: Understanding and Reducing Terrorism Risks.* Santa Monica: RAND Corporation, 2008.

Chandio, Jami (December 2013). 'Features on Federalism.' *Strengthening Participatory Federalism and Decentralization: Centre for Civic Education in Pakistan.* http://www.pk.undp.org/content/dam/pakistan/docs/ Democratic%20Governance/Federalism/Features%20on%20Federalism. pdf.

Chandra, Kanchan. 'Ethnic Parties and Democratic Stability.' *Perspectives on Politics* 3, no. 2 (2005): 235–52.

Cheema, Pervaiz Iqbal, and Maqsudul Hassan Nuri, eds. *Tribal areas of Pakistan: challenges and responses.* Islamabad: Islamabad Policy Research Institute, 2005.

Conner, Walker. 'Nation-Building or Nation-Destroying?' *World Politics* 24, no. 3 (April 1972). Reprinted in *Ethnonationalism: The Quest for Understanding.* Princeton: Princeton University Press, 1994.

National Assembly of Pakistan. *Constitution of the Islamic Republic of Pakistan.* http://www.na.gov.pk/publications/constitution.pdf.

Cooley, Alexander. *Base Politics.* Ithaca: Cornell University Press, 2008.

Corsi, Marco. 'Internal Conflicts in Pakistan.' *Oriente Moderno* 23, no. 84 (2004): 39–49.

Dashti, Naseer. *The Baloch and Balochistan: A Historical Account from the Beginning to the Fall of the Baloch State*. Bloomington: Trafford Publishing, 2012.

Dawn. 'APC calls for end to army's role in Politics.' August 20, 2006.

Dawn. 'Lasbela Victims buried in hometown.' October 21, 2014.

Dawn. 'Seraiki party protests labourers' killing.' April 13, 2015.

Dawn. 'Status of "national language" sought for all regional languages.' February 21, 2017.

Dawn. 'The Seraiki Suba bandwagon.' July 4, 2018.

Dawn. 'Win for Ex-Fata.' July 23, 2019.

Dhareja, Zahoor Ahmad. *Seraik Wasib* [The Siraiki Society]. Multan: Jhoke Publishers, 2003.

———. *Suba Siraikistan Kis Liye*. Multan: Jhoke Publishers, 2013.

Dobell, W. M. 'Ramifications of the China-Pakistan Border Treaty.' *Pacific Affairs* 37, no. 3 (Autumn 1964): 283–95.

Eriksen, Thomas Hylland. *Ethnicity and Nationalism*. London: Pluto Press, 1993.

EU Election Observation Mission Final Report (October 2002). 'National and Provincial Assembly Elections.' http://eeas.europa.eu/archives/eueom/pdf/missions/finalreport-pakistan-2002.pdf.

Feyyaz, Muhammad. 'Constructing Baloch militancy in Pakistan.' *South Asian Journal* (2013): 114–35.

Finance Department, Government of Punjab. 'Provincial Minister for Finance Dr. Ayesha Ghaus Pasha has said that incentives are being provided to investors for increasing resources in the province.' November 17, 2016, https://finance.punjab.gov.pk/incentives-provided.

Fishman, Brian. 'The Battle for Pakistan: Militancy and Conflict Across the FATA and NWFP.' *Counterterrorism Strategy Initiative Policy Paper*. Vancouver: New America Foundation, 2010.

Flowerday, Julie. 'Identity matters: Hunza and the hidden text of Britain and China.' *South Asian History and Culture* 10, no. 1 (2019): 46–63.

Foltz, W. J. 'Ethnicity, Status and Conflict.' In *Ethnicity and Nation-Building: Interpretational and Comparative Perspectives*, edited by Wendon Bell and Walter Freeman, 8. SAGE Publications, 1974.

Foot, Michael (October 2009). 'Final report of the independent Review of British offshore financial centres.' https://www.gov.im/media/624053/footreport.pdf.

Foucault, Michel. *Power: The Essential Work of Michel Foucault 1954–1984*. Volume 2. London: Allen Lane, 2000.

Gankovsky, Yu. V. *The Peoples of Pakistan: An Ethnic History*. Moscow: Nauka Publishing House, 1971.

Geertz, Clifford. 'What Is a State If It Is Not a Sovereign? Reflections on Politics in Complicated Places.' *Current Anthropology* 45, no. 5 (December 2004): 577–93.

Gellner, Ernest. *Nations and Nationalism*. Oxford: Blackwell, 1983.

Global Security Organization. 'Balochistan Insurgency - Fourth conflict 1973–77.' 2011.

Government of India. *Returns Showing the Results of Elections to the Central Legislative Assembly and the Provincial Legislatures in 1945–46*. Delhi: Manager of Publications, 1948.

Grare, Frederic. 'Balochistan: The State Versus the Nation.' *Carnegie Endowment for International Peace* (April 2013).

_____. 'Pakistan: The Resurgence of Baluch Nationalism.' *Carnegie Endowment for International Peace* 65 (January 2006): 1–14.

Green Left Weekly. 'PAKISTAN: Oppressed National Groups Struggle For Autonomy.' May 15, 2002, https://www.greenleft.org.au/node/27517.

Haider, Mehtab. 'Concurrent list spending is Rs190b, are the provinces ready?' *The News*. September 28, 2009.

Hale, Henry E. 'Divided We Stand: Institutional Sources of Ethnofederal State Survival and Collapse.' *World Politics* 56, no. 2 (2004): 165–93.

_____. 'Explaining Ethnicity.' *Comparative Political Studies* 37, no. 4 (2004): 458–85.

Haq, Farhat. 'Rise of MQM in Pakistan: Politics of Ethnic Mobilization.' *Asian Survey* 35, no. 11 (1995): 990–1004.

Haq, N. U. 'Balochistan, Disturbances: Causes and Response.' *IPRI* 6, no. 2 (2006).

Harrison, Selig S. 'The Fault Line Between Pashtuns and Punjabis in Pakistan.' *The Washington Post*. May 11, 2009.

_____. *In Afghanistan's Shadow: Baluch Nationalism and Soviet Temptations*. New York: Carnegie Endowment for International Peace, 1981.

Hasan, Arif, and Mansoor Raza. *Migration and Small Towns in Pakistan.* London: International Institute for Environment and Development, 2009.

Hechter, Michael. *Containing Nationalism.* New York: Oxford University Press, 2000.

Heeg, Jason. *Insurgency in Balochistan.* Fort Leavenworth: The Foreign Military Studies Office, 2013.

Hilali, A. Z. 'Confidence- and Security-Building Measures for India and Pakistan.' *Alternatives: Global, Local, Political* 30 (2005): 191–222.

Howard, Judith A. 'Social Psychology of Identities.' *Annual Review of Sociology* 26 (2000): 367–73.

Human Rights Commission of Pakistan (2006). 'The State of Human Rights in 2005.'

Huntington, Samuel P. 'Foreword: Cultures Count.' In *Culture Matters: How Values Shape Human Progress*, edited by Lawrence E. Harrison and Samuel P. Huntington, 13–16. New York: Basic Books, 2000.

———. *Political Order in Changing Societies.* New Haven: Yale University Press, 1968.

Husaini, Syed Noor Ali Zamin. *Maarif-e-Siraiki* [Introduction of Siraiki]. Multan: Saraiki Adbi Board, 2009.

Hussain, Altaf. 'Azad Kashmir is not the Islamic Republic of Pakistan.' *Gilgit-Baltistan Empowerment and Self-governance Order 2009.* December 2009. www.civiceducation.org/wp-content/uploads/2010/08/Gilgit-Baltistan-Reforms.doc.

Hussain, Ijaz. 'Is the Durand Line Dead?' In *Tribal areas of Pakistan: challenges and responses*, edited by Pervaiz Iqbal Cheema and Maqsudul Hasan Nuri, 159. Islamabad: Islamabad Policy Research Institute, 2005.

Hussain, Rafaqat. 'Gwadar in Historical Perspective.' *MUSLIM Institute* (2016), https://www.muslim-institute.org/newsletter-op-gwadar.pdf.

Inden, Ronald B. *Imagining India.* Oxford: Blackwell Publishers, 1990.

Internal Displacement Monitoring Centre (2015). http://www.internal-displacement.org/south-and-south-east–asia/pakistan/figures-analysis.

Internal Displacement Monitoring Centre. 'Pakistan: The worsening conflict in Balochistan.' South Asia Report 119 (2006).

International Crisis Group. 'Pakistan: The Forgotten Conflict in Balochistan.' Briefing No. 69 (October 2007).

International Settlements (2011). http://www.bis.org/statistics/bankstats.

Jabeen, Mussarat. 'Developments in Pak-China Strategic Alliances.' *Berkeley Journal of Social Sciences* 2, no. 2 (2012): 1–16.

Jaffrelot, Christophe, and Rasul Bakhsh Rais. 'Interpreting Ethnic Movements in Pakistan.' *The Pakistan Development Review* (Part I) 37, no. 4 (1998): 153–79.

Jalal, Ayesha. 'Conjuring Pakistan: History as Official Imagining.' *International Journal of Middle East Studies* 27 (1995): 73–89.

————. *Democracy and Authoritarianism in South Asia: A Comparative and Historical Perspective.* Cambridge: Cambridge University Press, 1995.

Jampuri, Masihullah. *Nigarkhana.* Multan: Jhoke Publishers, 2015.

Janmahmad. *Essays on Baloch National Struggle in Pakistan: Emergence, Dimension and Representation.* Quetta: Gosh-a-Adab, 1989.

————. *The Baloch Cultural Heritage.* Karachi: Royal Book Company, 1982.

Johnson, Thomas H., and M. Chris Mason. 'No Sign until the Burst of Fire: Understanding the Pakistan-Afghanistan Frontier.' *International Security* 32, no. 4 (Spring 2008): 41–77.

Kaplan, Robert D. 'Pakistan's Fatal Shore.' *The* Atlantic, May 2009.

Kaufmann, Daniel, Aart Kraay, and Massimo Mastruzzi. *The Worldwide Governance Indicators: Methodology and Analytical Issues.* Washington D. C.: World Bank Group, 2010, http://info.worldbank.org/governance/wgi/pdf/WGI.pdf.

Kennedy, Charles H. 'Policies of Ethnic Preference in Pakistan.' *Asian Survey* 24, no. 6 (1984): 688–703.

————. 'The Politics of Ethnicity in Sindh.' *Asian Survey* 31, no. 10 (1991): 938–55.

Khan, Adeel. 'Baloch Ethnic Nationalism in Pakistan: From Guerrilla War to Nowhere?' *Asian Ethnicity* 4, no. 2 (2003).

Khan, Adeel. 'Pukhtun Ethnic Nationalism: From Separatism and Integrationism.' *Asian Ethnicity* 4, no. 1 (2003): 67–83.

————. 'Renewed Ethnonationalist Insurgency in Balochistan, Pakistan: The Militarized State and Continuing Economic Deprivation.' *Asian Survey* 49, no. 6 (November/December 2009): 1071–91.

Khan, Azmat Hayat. 'Federally Administered Tribal Areas of Pakistan'. In *Tribal areas of Pakistan: challenges and responses,* edited by Pervaiz Iqbal Cheema and Maqsudul Hasan Nuri, 88. Islamabad: Islamabad Policy Research Institute, 2005.

Khan, D. L. 'Federalism and the Eighteenth Amendment: Challenges and Opportunities for Transition Management in Pakistan.' *Forum of Federations* 1 (2012).

Khan, Humayun. 'The Role of Federal Government and the Political Agent.' In *Tribal areas of Pakistan: challenges and responses*, edited by Pervaiz Iqbal Cheema and Maqsudul Hasan Nuri, 104. Islamabad: Islamabad Policy Research Institute, 2005.

Khan, Hussain Ahmad. *Re-Thinking Punjab: The Construction of Siraiki Identity*. Lahore: Research and Publication Centre, National College of the Arts, 2004.

Khan, Mahrukh. 'Balochistan: The Forgotten Frontier.' *Institute of Strategic Studies* (2013).

Khan, Rashid Ahmad. 'Political Developments in FATA: a critical assessment.' In *Tribal areas of Pakistan: challenges and responses*, edited by Pervaiz Iqbal Cheema and Maqsudul Hasan Nuri, 44. Islamabad: Islamabad Policy Research Institute, 2005.

Khanna, Paramanand, and Saroj B. Khanna. 'Ethnicity in Bhutan: Causes and Effects.' *Journal of South Asian and Middle Eastern Studies* 17, no. 1 (1993).

Kloss, Heinz. *Abstandsprachen und Ausbausprachen* [Abstand-languages and Ausbau languages]. In *Zur Theorie des Dialekts: Aufsätze aus 100 Jahren Forschung. Zeitschrift fur Dialektologie and Linguistik*, edited by Joachim Göschel, Norbert Nail, and Gaston van der Elst, 301–22. Wiesbaden: F. Steiner, 1976.

Knight, David B. 'Identity and Territory: Geographical Perspectives on Nationalism and Regionalism.' *Annals of the Association of American Geographers* 72, no. 4 (1982): 514–31.

Kreutzmann, Hermann. 'Kashmir and the Northern Areas of Pakistan: Boundary-Making along Contested Frontiers.' *Erdkunde* 62, no. 3 (2008): 201–19.

Kundi, Mansoor Akbar. 'Insurgency Factors in Balochistan.' *Central Asia Journal* 64 (2009).

Langah, Nukhbah Taj. *Poetry as Resistance: Islam and Ethnicity in Postcolonial Pakistan*. New Delhi: Routledge, 2016.

Latif, Muhammad Ijaz, and Muhammad Amir Hamza. 'Ethnic Nationalism in Pakistan: A Case Study of Baloch Nationalism during Musharraf Regime.' *Pakistan Vision* 10, no. 1 (2009).

Lebowitz, Daniel J. 'Why has the Ethno-Nationalist Insurgency in Balochistan Endured for 66 Years?' *Geostrategic Forecasting Corporation*, 2015.

Leibowitz, Arnold H. *Defining Status: A Comprehensive Analysis of United States Territorial Relations*. Boston: Martinus Nijhoff Publishers, 1989.

Lijphart, Arend. *Democracy in Plural Societies: A Comparative Exploration*. New Haven: Yale University Press, 1977.

Lustick, Ian S., Dan Miodownik, and Roy J. Eidelson. 'Secessionism in Multicultural States: Does Sharing Power Prevent or Encourage It?' *The American Political Science Review* 98, no. 2 (May 2004): 209–29.

Mahmud, Ershad. 'Status of AJK in Political Milieu.' *Policy Perspectives* 3, no. 2 (2006): 105–23. http://www.jstor.org/stable/42922642.

Majeed, Gulshan. 'Ethnicity and Conflict: A Theoretical Perspective.' *Journal of Political Studies* 20, no. 1 (2013).

Manan, Abdul. 'Murree agreement: PM urged to let Malik continue as CM Balochistan.' *The Express Tribune*, December 5, 2015.

Mansoor, Hasan. 'Khair Bakhsh Marri: a fighter all the way.' *Dawn*. June 14, 2014.

Marri, Shah Muhammad. *Baloch Qaum Aed-e-Qadeem say Asre Hazir Tak*. Lahore: Takhliqat, 2000.

Marshall, Geoffrey. *Constitutional Conventions: The Rules and Forms of Political Accountability*. Oxford: Oxford University Press, 1984.

Marten, Kimberley, Thomas H. Johnson, and M. Chris Mason. 'Misunderstanding Pakistan's Federally Administered Tribal Area?' *International Security* 33, no. 3 (Winter 2008/2009): 180–89.

Masood, Wajahat. 'The Murder of Akbar Bugti.' *Monthly Nawa-e-Insan* 279, no. 7 (2006).

McGarry, John, and Brendan O'Leary. 'Must Pluri-national Federations Fail?' *Ethnopolitics* 8, no. 1 (2009): 5–25.

Millward, J. A., and N. Tursun. 'Political History and Strategies of Control, 1884–1978.' In *Xinjiang: China's Muslim* borderland, edited by S. Frederick Starr, 63–98. New York: Routledge, 2004.

Moj, Muhammad. *The Deoband Madrassah Movement: Countercultural Trends and Tendencies*. London; New York: Anthem Press, 2015.

Muller, C. Thomas. *Political Handbook of the World 2012*. Edited by Thomas C. Muller and Tom Lansford. SAGE Publications, 2012.

Musharraf, Pervez. 'Understanding Baluchistan.' *AML US*. 2011.

Naseemullah, Adnan. 'Shades of Sovereignty: Explaining Political Order and Disorder in Pakistan's Northwest.' *Studies in Comparative International Development* 49, no. 4 (2014): 501–22.

Naseer, Mir Gul Khan. *Tareekh-e-Balochistan*. Quetta: Rubi Publisher, 1986.

Naseer, S. *Federalism and Constitutional Development in Pakistan*. Kathmandu: Centre for Nepal and Asian Studies, 2007.

Nawaz, Shuja. 'FATA—A Most Dangerous Place.' *Centre for Strategic & International Studies*. Washington, D. C.: New American Century Foundation, 2009.

Newby, Laura. *The Empire and the Khanate: A Political History of Qing Relations with Khoqand c. 1760–1860*. Leiden; Boston: Brill, 2005.

Nigar, Mohammad Anwar. 'Merge FATA with Khyber Pakhtunkhwa.' *FATA Reforms*. https://fatareforms.wordpress.com/2014/10/29/merge-fata-with-khyber-pakhtunkhwa-muhammad-anwar-nigar/.

Nishapuri, Abdul. 'Let's mourn five Seraiki labourers killed by Baloch militants.' *LUBP*, 24 July 2011, https://lubpak.net/archives/54076.

Nishtar, Sania. 'The federation and provincial autonomy.' *The News International*, December 12, 2009.

Palan, Ronen. 'Tax Havens and the Commercialization of State Sovereignty.' *International Organization* 56, no. 1 (2002): 151–76.

Panni, Dr Sher Bahadur Khan. *Tareekh-e-Hazara* [History of Hazara]. Lahore: Maktaba Rehmania, 2001.

PILDAT Background Paper. 'Demand for Siraiki Province.' (March 2011).

PILDAT Issue Paper. 'Balochistan: Civil-Military Relations.' (March 2012).

PILDAT. 'The Aghaz-e-Haqooq-e-Balochistan Package: An Analysis.' (December 2009).

PILDAT Briefing Paper. 'Balochistan: Case and Demand.' (April 2007).

Press Trust of India. 'Pakistan Army admits to Kargil martyrs.' *NDTV*, November 18, 2010.

Punjab Government. *Gazetteer of the Hazara District 1883–4*. Lahore: Sang-e-Meel Publications, 2000.

Rahman, Sheikh Asad. *Lack of Democracy and Socio-Economic Development of Balochistan*. Islamabad: Sungi Development Foundation, 2009.

Rahman, Tariq. 'Language and Ethnicity in Pakistan.' *Asian Survey* 37, no. 9 (2007): 833–9.

———. *Language and Politics in Pakistan*. Karachi: Oxford University Press, 1998.

Rais, Rasul Bakhsh. 'The Balochistan Package: Redefining Federalism in Pakistan.' *Center for Civic Education Pakistan.* December 2009.

Rawlings, Gregory. 'Taxes and transnational treaties: responsive regulation and the reassertion of offshore sovereignty.' *Law & Policy* 29, no. 1(2007): 51–66.

Razi, G. Hossein. 'Legitimacy, Religion, and Nationalism in the Middle East.' *American Political Science Review* 84, no. 1 (March 1990): 69–91.

Rector, Chad. *Federations: The Political Dynamics of Cooperation.* Ithaca: Cornell University Press, 2009.

Report of the Commission for the Creation of New Province (s) in the Province of Punjab. Islamabad: National Assembly Secretariat, 2013. http://www.na.gov.pk/uploads/documents/province–reoprt.pdf.

Rezvani, David A. 'Dead Autonomy, a Thousand Cuts, or Partial Independence? The Autonomous Status of Hong Kong.' *Journal of Contemporary Asia* 42, no. 1 (2012): 93–122.

———. 'Partial independence beats full independence'. *Territory, Politics, Governance* 4, no. 3 (2016): 269–96.

———. *Surpassing the Sovereign State: The Wealth, Self-Rule, and Security Advantages of Partially Independent Territories.* Oxford: Oxford University Press, 2014.

Roeder, Philip G. 'Ethnofederalism and the Mismanagement of Conflicting Nationalisms.' *Regional & Federal Studies* 19, no. 2 (2009): 203–19.

Roofi, Yasmin, and Khawaja Alqama. 'Ethnic Dilemma in Pakistan and Division of Punjab: End or Beginning of the New Era of Conflict.' *Journal of Politics and Law* 6, no. 1 (2013).

———. 'Renaming of NWFP and Hazara Ethnicity: A New Course of Ethnic Conflict in Pakistan.' *European Journal of Social Sciences* 19, no. 4 (2011): 588–93.

Rousseau, David, and A. Maurits van der Veen. 'The Emergence of a Shared Identity: An Agent-Based Computer Simulation of Idea Diffusion.' *The Journal of Conflict Resolution* 49, no. 5 (2005): 686–712.

Roy, Olivier. *The New Central Asia: The Creation of Nations.* New York: New York University Press, 2000.

Saleem, Muhammad. '"Khud Rozgar" Scheme in 4 Districts: Punjab Government to Provide Rs. 4.8 Billion interest–free loans.' *Business Recorder.* February 13, 2014, http://fp.brecorder.com/2014/02/201402131152988/.

Samad, Y. *A Nation in Turmoil: Nationalism and Ethnicity in Pakistan, 1937–1958.* New Delhi: SAGE Publications, 1995.

Sanders, Jimy M. 'Ethnic Boundaries and Identity in Plural Societies.' *Annual Review of Sociology* 28 (2002): 327–57.

Sayeed, K. B. *Pakistan: The Formative Phase, 1857–1948.* Oxford University Press, 1968.

Shackle, Christopher. 'Saraiki: A Language Movement in Pakistan.' *Modern Asian Studies* 11, no. 3 (1977): 379–403.

Sial, Safdar, and Abdul Basit. 'Conflict and Insecurity in Balochistan: Assessing Strategic Policy Options for Peace and Security.' *Conflict and Peace Studies* 3, no. 4 (2010).

Siddiqi, Farhan Hanif. 'Security Dynamics in Pakistani Balochistan: Religious Activism and Ethnic Conflict in the War on Terror.' *Asian Affairs: An American Review* 39, no. 3 (2012): 157–75.

_____. *The Politics of Ethnicity in Pakistan: The Baloch, Sindhi, and Mohajir Ethnic Movements.* Oxon: Routledge, 2012.

_____. *The State and Politics of Ethnicity in Post-1971 Pakistan: An Analysis of Baloch, Sindhi, and Mohajir Ethnic Movements.* Karachi: University of Karachi, 2009.

Smirnov, U. A. *The Lahndi Language.* Translated by E. H. Tsipan. Moscow: Nauka Publishing House, 1975. Reprinted as *The Lahndi (Siraiki) Language.* Multan: Saraiki Adbi Board, 2006.

Sökefeld, Martin. 'From Colonialism to Postcolonial Colonialism: Changing Modes of Domination in the Northern Areas of Pakistan.' *The Journal of Asian Studies* 64, no.4 (2005): 939–73.

Soofi, Dr M. A. *Sooba Sarhad Ki Pakistan Main Shamooliat or Quaid-i-Azam Mohammad Ali Jinnah Kay Sathi.* Lahore: Book Home, 2014.

Spruyt, Hendrik. *The Sovereign State and its Competitors.* Princeton: Princeton University Press, 1994.

Subbiah, Sumathi. 'Security Council Mediation and the Kashmir Dispute: Reflections on Its Failures and Possibilities for Renewal.' *Boston College International and Comparative Law Review* 27, no. 1 (2004): 173–85.

Talbot, Ian. *Pakistan: A Modern History.* New Delhi: Foundation Books, 2005.

The Charter of Pakistan Oppressed Nations Movement. 'Pakistan Oppressed Nations Movement. Thinking Pakistan's History.' 1998. http://humshehri.org/civics/gilgit–baltistan/.

The Imperial Gazetteer of India. 'Volume VI: Argaon to Bardwan.' 1908.

The People's Republic of China-Pakistan. Agreement on the Boundary Between China's Sinkiang and the Contiguous Areas, Peking, March 2, 1963. *The American Journal of International Law* 57, no. 3 (July 1963): 713–16.

The Researchers. 'Post and Update: Balochistan Package.' 2009.

Tripathy, Sasmita, and Saeed Ahmed Rid. *Democracy as conflict-resolution model for terrorism: A case study of India and Pakistan.* Colombo: The Regional Centre for Strategic Studies, 2009.

UN Statistics Division. (2009). https://data.un.org.

Van Evera, Stephen. 'Primed for Peace: Europe After the Cold War.' *International Security* 15, no. 3 (1990/1991): 7–57.

Waheed, Akhtar. *Multani Zaban da Qaida* [Alphabets of Multani language]. Multan: Kashan Adab, 1953.

Waseem, Mohammad. 'Federalism in Pakistan.' *Forum of Federations.* August 2010. http://www.forumfed.org/pubs/Waseem-Fed-Overview.pdf.

———. *Democratization in Pakistan: A Study of the 2002 Elections.* Karachi: Oxford University Press, 2006.

———. *Politics and the state in Pakistan.* Lahore: Progressive Publishers, 1989.

Wasim, Amir, 'Langah wants Tank, D.I. Khan in Siraiki province.' *Dawn.* December 25, 2012.

Watson, H. D. *Gazetteer of the Hazara District 1907.* London: Chatto & Windus, 1908.

Watts, Ronald. *Comparing Federal Systems in the 1990s.* Kingston: Institute of Intergovernmental Relations, Queen's University, 1996.

Webb, Michael. 'Defining the boundaries of legitimate state practice: norms, transnational actors and the OECD's project on harmful tax competition.' *Review of International Political Economy* 11, no. 4 (2004): 787–827.

Weber, Max. 'The Origin of Ethnic Groups.' In *Ethnicity*, edited by John Hutchinson and Anthony D. Smith, 35–40. Oxford: Oxford University Press, 1996.

Wittfogel, K. A. 'The Marxist view of China (Part 2).' *The China Quarterly* 12, no. 1 (October–December 1962): 154–69.

Xiaomin, Zhang, and Xu Chunfeng. 'The Late Qing Dynasty Diplomatic Transformation: Analysis from an Ideational Perspective.' *Chinese Journal of International Politics* 1, no. 3 (2007): 405–45.

Zahab, Mariam Abou. 'Kashars against Mashars: Jihad and Social Change in the FATA.' In *Beyond Swat: History, Society and Economy along the Afghanistan-Pakistan Frontier*, edited by Benjamin D. Hopkins and Magnus Marsden, 51–60. New York: Columbia University Press, 2013.

Zaman, Haider. 'Problems of education, health and infrastructure in FATA.' In *Tribal areas of Pakistan: challenges and responses*, edited by Pervaiz Iqbal Cheema and Maqsudul Hasan Nuri, 73–80. Islamabad: Islamabad Policy Research Institute, 2005.

Zulfqar, Saman, 'An Overview of Pakistan's Security Situation after Operation Zarb-e-Azb,' *Journal of Current Affairs* 2, no. 1 (2017): 116–36.

Index